OFFICIALLY
DISCARDED

FOREIGN AND DOMESTIC POLICY
IN EASTERN EUROPE IN THE 1980s

The decade of the 1980s may well prove to be a turning-point in the post-war history of Eastern Europe. The enduring crisis in Poland, the need for greater economic austerity in the light of mounting energy prices and foreign debts, and renewed tensions in East–West relations are among the most important sign-posts of change to come as the decade begins. How have these problems affected the communist states of Eastern Europe thus far, and how are they likely to develop in the immediate future? It is questions such as these that the essays in this volume explore.

The nine experts assembled here examine a variety of political, economic and social issues that are not only of critical importance to Eastern Europe's recent past and future prospects, but are also of theoretical relevance to social scientists interested in studying the region systematically. The contributions provide both a comparative overview of problems common to Eastern Europe as a whole and in-depth treatment of specific issues in six of the region's largest states.

Part I deals with the linkage between foreign and domestic policy in three countries where this connection is especially significant. William Zimmerman's study of Yugoslavia sheds new light on that nation's domestic policy processes as it grapples with the problem of disbursing development funds obtained from outside sources. The essay offers a timely analysis of the kinds of decision-making procedures available to Yugoslav leaders in the post-Tito era. Ronald H. Linden's investigation of the domestic bases of Romanian foreign policy is an enlightening example of how internal factors affect a nation's international activities, while Michael J. Sodaro's essay on the German Democratic Republic demonstrates how forces originating in the international environment can affect the domestic system.

Part II focuses on a topic of growing concern in all the communist states of Eastern Europe: the role of specialists and professionals in the policy-making process. Sharon L. Wolchik looks at the impact of demographers on the formation of social policy in Czechoslovakia. Jane L. Curry uses the current unrest in Poland as a backdrop for her study of Polish journalists, not only before and during the period of national "renewal" inaugurated in the summer of 1980, but also after the imposition of martial law in December 1981. Rudolf L. Tőkés examines the status of the intelligentsia in Hungary. Each of these essays raises questions that extend far beyond the scope of the countries examined, as they touch on the sensitive relationship between pragmatically oriented specialists and politically minded party elites, an issue that exists in all communist systems.

Part III addresses a series of problems confronting Eastern Europe as a region. Economic integration within Comecon is analyzed in Stanislaw Wasowski's penetrating analysis of the divergence between plans and realities in Eastern Europe's principal trading organization. Thomas Cason's survey of the Warsaw Pact after twenty-five years highlights the scope and limits of Eastern Europe's military cooperation with the Soviet Union. Finally, Roger E. Kanet provides a comprehensive overview of Eastern Europe's growing relations with the Third World.

All of the essays conclude with a section on the outlook for the 1980s, spelling out possible courses of development in Eastern Europe as the present decade progresses. The result is a timely and provocative contribution to our understanding of where Eastern Europe may be going at this critical juncture in its political evolution.

Foreign and Domestic Policy in Eastern Europe in the 1980s

Trends and Prospects

Edited by
Michael J. Sodaro
and
Sharon L. Wolchik

St. Martin's Press   New York

© Michael J. Sodaro and Sharon L. Wolchik 1983

All rights reserved. For information, write:
St. Martin's Press, Inc., 175 Fifth Avenue, New York, NY 10010
Printed in Hong Kong
First published in the United States of America in 1983

ISBN 0–312–29843–9

Library of Congress Cataloging in Publication Data

Main entry under title:

Foreign and domestic policy in Eastern Europe in the
 1980s.

 1. Europe, Eastern — Politics and government.
2. Europe, Eastern — Foreign relations. I. Sodaro,
Michael J.   II. Wolchik, Sharon L.
DJK50.F67   1983   327.47   82–3265
ISBN 0–312–29843–9   AACR2

DJK
50
.F67
1983

APR 17 1984

Contents

Acknowledgements

Like many books of scholarly interest these days, the present volume grew out of a conference. Under the auspices of the Institute for Sino-Soviet Studies, a group of some thirty specialists gathered at the George Washington University on 4 and 5 April 1980 to participate in discussions on the theme of "Eastern Europe in the 1980s: Trends and Prospects." Although the conference participants, particularly those who presented the papers which formed the basis of the chapters in this book, were for the most part professional scholars, the audience was by no means limited to academicians. A considerable part of the funding for the conference was provided by the US Department of State, and representatives of that institution as well as of other US government agencies also participated actively in the conference sessions.

Unfortunately, space does not permit us to mention by name all those who helped make the conference a success and who, in one way or another, contributed to the preparation of this volume. We owe special thanks, however, to three individuals without whose encouragement and generosity neither the conference itself nor this book would ever have seen the light of day: Gaston J. Sigur, Director of the Institute for Sino-Soviet Studies at George Washington; Andrew Gyorgy, our respected colleague and fellow member of the Institute; and Eric Willenz of the Division of Intelligence and Research of the State Department. Our editor at Macmillan, Mr T. M. Farmiloe, deserves particularly warm thanks for his enormous patience and skill in piloting this project to publication. We would also like to express our gratitude to Dorothy Wedge and Sheila Murphy for their enormous help in organizing the conference and typing the final drafts of the manuscripts, and to Suzanne Stephenson, Nathaniel Richmond and Kelly Eaton for invaluable editorial assistance. We wish also to thank Brevis Press for helping us to prepare this volume for publication.

No list of debts accumulated by the editors of a book of this kind would be complete without a word of gratitude for our authors. All of them graciously responded to our request that the original conference papers be revised in 1981 and 1982; in some cases, the papers were completely rewritten for this volume to reflect rapidly changing events in Eastern Europe (particularly in Poland). We consider ourselves fortunate to have worked with such a distinguished and personable group of scholars.

In closing, we wish to single out the following conference participants for their valued contribution: R. V. Burks, Walter D. Connor, Richard T. Davies, Charles Gati, John Hardt, James Kuhlman, Jaroslaw Piekalkiewicz, Robin Remington, Carl W. Schmidt, Paul Shapiro and Robert Sharlet. The editors also wish to note that we shared our editorial burdens equally, and that the order in which our names appear on the cover was determined at random.

M. J. S.

S. L. W.

February 1983

Notes on the Editors and Contributors

Michael J. Sodaro is Assistant Professor of International Affairs and Political Science and a member of the Institute for Sino-Soviet Studies at the George Washington University. His articles on the domestic and foreign policies of the GDR, French and Italian communism, and Soviet foreign policy have appeared in several books and in such journals as *Problems of Communism* and *Studies in Comparative Communism.* He is presently at work on a study of recent Soviet relations with the two Germanies.

Sharon L. Wolchik is Assistant Professor of International Affairs and Political Science and a member of the Institute for Sino-Soviet Studies at the George Washington University. She has written numerous articles on the status of women in Eastern Europe and on women in politics. Her other research includes studies of the West European communist parties. At the present time she is working on a book on policy-making in socialist states, with an emphasis on the role of specialists.

Thomas Cason is a Major in the United States Air Force and a doctoral candidate in political science at the George Washington University, where he is completing a dissertation on the political and military reliability of the East European members of the Warsaw Treaty Organization. He served as Assistant Professor of Aerospace Studies at the University of Maryland, and has contributed to publications and conferences dealing with the Warsaw Pact and NATO.

Jane L. Curry is an Assistant Professor at Manhattanville College and a Senior Research Associate at the Institute on East–Central Europe at Columbia University. She is also a Senior Consultant to the RAND Corporation, which has published a series of her monographs on the media and inter-elite communications in Poland. She is the co-editor of *All the News Not Fit to Print,* editor of *Dissent in Eastern Europe,* and author of *The Black Book of Polish Censorship.*

Roger E. Kanet is Professor of Political Science and a member of the Russian and East European Center of the University of Illinois at Urbana–Champaign. He has published widely on the subject of Soviet and East European foreign policy. His most recent publications include *Background to Crisis: Policy and Politics in Gierek's Poland* (co-edited with Maurice D. Simon), and two edited volumes entitled *Soviet Foreign Policy in the 1980s* and *Soviet Foreign Policy and East–West Relations.*

Ronald H. Linden is Assistant Professor in the Department of Political Science at the University of Pittsburgh. He is the author of *Bear and Foxes: the International Relations of the East European States, 1965–1969* and the editor of *The Foreign Policies of East Europe: New Approaches.* He is currently researching the effects of international change on Yugoslavia and Romania under a grant from the National Council on Soviet and East European Research.

Rudolf L. Tőkés is Professor of Political Science and Associate Dean of the Graduate School at the University of Connecticut. He has been a Senior Fellow at the Research Institute on Communist Affairs, Columbia University, and a Senior Associate Member of St Antony's College, Oxford, and has taught at Wesleyan University and Yale University. He is the author of *Bela Kun and the Hungarian Soviet Republic,* co-editor (with H. H. Morton) of *Soviet Society and Politics in the 1970s,* and editor of *Dissent in the USSR, Eurocommunism and Detente,* and *Opposition in Eastern Europe.* Between 1972 and 1976, and since May 1981, he has served as Associate Editor of *Studies in Comparative Communism.* He is currently working on a history of the Communist Party of Hungary.

Stanislaw Wasowski is Professor of International Economics at the School of Foreign Service, Georgetown University. He has written extensively on Soviet energy problems, economic integration, and the economic aspects of East–West relations. He is presently conducting research and writing on the questions of economic reform and the role of self-governing enterprises in Poland.

William Zimmerman is Professor of Political Science and Associate Dean of the College of Literature, Science, and the Arts at the University of Michigan. He is also associated with its Institute of Public Policy Studies, and the Center for Russian and East European Studies. His work has focused on Soviet–American relations, the political economy of Soviet–East European relations, and Yugoslavia. His recent articles have appeared in *World Politics, International Journal,* and the *British Journal of Political Science.* His most recent book (with Morris Bernstein and Zvi Gitelman) is *East–West Relations and the Future of Eastern Europe.*

1 Introduction

MICHAEL J. SODARO and
SHARON L. WOLCHIK

The projection of political trends into the future is always a risky enterprise, and the countries of Eastern Europe offer no exception to the rule. As Charles Gati has pointed out,[1] many of the critical events in the region's post-war history could scarcely have been anticipated at the start of the decades in which they occurred. The upheavals that rocked Poland and Hungary in 1956, for instance, would have been unthinkable to most observers of Stalinist Eastern Europe in 1950. Romania's foreign policy challenge to the Soviet Union starting in 1963, and the reform movement in Czechoslovakia that culminated in the Soviet invasion of 1968, were barely visible on the political horizon in 1960. Such developments as the fall of Gomulka in 1970 and the subsequent outbursts of working class discontent in Poland later in the decade, or Ulbricht's fall from power in the GDR in 1971 and the rather smooth normalization of inter-German relations that subsequently developed under his successor, were simply not clearly predictable in the opening months of 1970. Nor have the authors of this book been spared the frustrations of the volatile nature of East European politics. When the initial drafts of the chapters that follow were prepared in the early spring of 1980, none of us had the omniscience required to foresee the unprecedented strike movement that would spread across Poland only a few months later, let alone the establishment of a labor union independent of the ruling communist party. By the same token, many of us were taken by surprise by the imposition of martial law which occurred in Poland on 13 December 1981. As these very lines are being written, the situation in Poland still swings precariously from day to day, with such questions as whether martial law will soon be entirely lifted, or whether the Soviets may yet intervene directly, the object of spirited controversy but of no safe bets.*

*Certain features of martial law were "suspended" by the Polish authorities on December 30, 1982.

Inspired to modesty by this instructive record, the authors of the present volume have no illusions about our ability to foresee with any assurance what may, or may not, transpire in Eastern Europe in the 1980s. Such is not the purpose of our effort. Our aim is analytical rather than predictive. The chief purpose of the following essays is to investigate some of the major trends that have arisen in Eastern Europe over the past ten to fifteen years, and to sketch several alternative courses of development for the remainder of the present decade on the basis of our examination of these tendencies. The emphasis is therefore on the recent past, and on the question of how the tendencies observable in the 1970s may help condition political life in Eastern Europe over the course of the 1980s.

The nine chapters which follow the present one survey various topics and employ a variety of approaches, with each author concentrating on the events and using the research methods most appropriate to the task at hand. All the essays, however, are held together by the recognition that the past decade has included elements of both substantial change and broad continuity in the circumstances surrounding the political development of Eastern Europe, and that these contrasting tendencies have manifested themselves in both the international and domestic milieux of the East European states. In particular, these trends have taken two specific directions. Internationally, the 1970s witnessed a remarkable increase in Eastern Europe's interactions with the outside world. This was true both for the region as a whole and for most of the individual states within it. No longer was the Soviet Union the only relevant actor in the foreign affairs of the nations of Eastern Europe, even if it continued to be the major factor in the political and economic relations of most of the members of the Warsaw Treaty Organization. Over the course of the 1970s, the nations of Eastern Europe expanded their ties with the non-communist world on a scale unmatched in previous decades, and were accordingly penetrated by influences originating in the international environment to an unprecedented degree. In addition to expanding their political and economic ties with the West as a result of detente, the East European states recorded significant increases in their dealings with the international economic system, the Third World, and one another.

East European countries also have witnessed numerous changes domestically in the past decade. To a large extent, these changes pose additional constraints which political leaders must take into account as they enter the 1980s. Among the most important of these from the perspective of mass-elite relations and political stability are the impact of continued modernization and slow economic growth.

Although the situation varies somewhat from country to country, political leaders in most East European states have had to face the increasingly difficult task of satisfying popular demands for improvements in the living standard and less widespread, but important, demands of intellectuals for greater autonomy and professional leeway in a time of dwindling economic resources. Stressing the material advantages of socialism, political leaders in most countries sought throughout the 1970s to secure popular support by raising the standard of living.[2] This strategy, which was facilitated by increased contacts with Western countries, was relatively successful through the mid-1970s. After that time, however, external events coupled with chronic economic difficulties have made elite efforts to modernize while simultaneously satisfying consumer demands increasingly problematic. Faced with problems in energy and raw material supplies as well as difficulty in selling exports for hard currency, political leaders in many of these countries were forced by the end of the 1970s to enact a number of measures designed to come to terms with an economic slowdown. Thus, East Europeans, who at the beginning of the 1970s had expected to enter a period which communist theorists described under the rubric of "developed socialism" as an era of increased material well-being, found themselves facing at the beginning of the 1980s a period of increasing economic constraints. For the populations in question, this period brings the likelihood of stagnating or declining real wages and slowed social mobility. For East European leaders, efforts to impose economic austerity also bring political risks.

The political implications of such measures were most clearly illustrated by events in Poland, where a series of economic crises and open displays of popular discontent led to the removal of three party First Secretaries within eleven years. As the 1980s began, Poland's communist party faced the extraordinary situation of having to share power with two trade unions, a host of dissident intellectuals, a politically assertive population, and a Catholic Church fully conscious of its institutional responsibilities. While the imposition of martial law and the banning of the leading trade union, Solidarity, together with the arrest of prominent union leaders and dissidents, demonstrated that the regime would no longer tolerate strikes and other open manifestations of discontent, sporadic protests and work stoppages occurring subsequently indicate that dissatisfaction continues to be widespread. Moreover, the repressive measures adopted by the martial law leadership do not address the underlying economic roots of popular discontent. Poland's new leaders, like their predecessors, discuss the need for economic reform, but thus far have not taken any serious steps in this direction.

The Polish situation is clearly an extreme case, and events in Poland have had few echoes in the other countries in the region. However, the strikes and their aftermath demonstrate the threat which austerity measures pose in Eastern Europe, particularly in those countries in which corruption and inefficiency have eroded public confidence in the ruling elite. They also illustrate the important political role which mass publics can play in Eastern Europe under particular circumstances.

The responses of other East European leaders to developments in Poland reflect an awareness of this potential. In an effort to prevent possible repercussions in their own countries, leaders in Hungary, Yugoslavia, and the GDR took steps starting in 1980 to moderate some of the effects of recently enacted price increases. East German leaders, as well as the Czechoslovak leadership, also increased surveillance of dissidents and attempted to insulate their populations from Polish influences. The Romanians, as well as several other ruling elites, at least gave lip service to the need to improve the functioning of unions in their countries.

The crackdown in Poland at the end of 1981 has allowed East European elites to breathe a little easier, as it has signaled to potential dissenters in all these countries that there are sharp limits to official tolerance of open dissent in Eastern Europe. However, it obviously does not eliminate the need for continued efforts on the part of these leaders to prevent persisting economic difficulties from leading to political disturbances in the first place.

These efforts may prevent disruption in the short run, but the ability of leaders in other East European countries to avert a situation similar to that which occurred in Poland in 1980–81 will in the long run depend on their ability to devise a new strategy for ensuring popular compliance and producing more effective public policies. The success of East European leaders in meeting this challenge, along with others emanating from the international environment, will depend in turn on a number of other domestic factors. Among the most important of these is the nature of the elite's relationship with specialists, professionals, and intellectuals in each country. As these societies become more developed and as political leaders face problems which cannot be solved by reference to ideology, these groups become increasingly important in determining the success or failure of policy measures. In the 1980s the ability to coopt members of these groups so as to benefit from their expertise while at the same time preventing them from challenging the prevailing political order will be a crucial determinant of how successful political leaders throughout the region will be in maintaining political stability while coming to terms with increasing economic constraints and slowed economic growth.

It is these unmistakable tendencies towards change in Eastern Europe, together with the persistence of certain pre-existent patterns of behavior, that constitute the principal themes of this book. More specifically, we have attempted to isolate three areas which, in our view, have come to represent the most dynamic sources of change in the region over the past decade, and which most probably will continue to be among the most important determinants of political life in Eastern Europe in the 1980s and beyond. They are also areas which raise important theoretical questions for the study of communist states.

The first of these areas centers on the linkage between the international environment and the domestic political system in individual countries in Eastern Europe. The second concerns itself with the role of specialists and intellectuals in policy-making in East European states. The third area looks at the interactions of the region as a whole, both among the various states of Eastern Europe themselves and between Eastern Europe and the rest of the world. The remainder of the book is consequently divided into three parts, corresponding to these three separate areas of analysis.

Parts I and II consist of country studies of the six most prominent states of Eastern Europe. In Part I, Yugoslavia, Romania, and the German Democratic Republic are examined in the framework of international–domestic linkages, while Part II examines the growing impact of specialist elites in Poland, Czechoslovakia, and Hungary. The selection of these states as case studies of these particular issues was a deliberate choice on the part of the editors. In approaching the topics of linkages and of specialist elites, we placed primary emphasis on three highly illustrative examples of each topic which exemplified in an especially vivid fashion the tendencies operating in these two key areas of political development. Thus, Yugoslavia, Romania, and East Germany are countries in which the connection between domestic and international politics has assumed a particularly high salience in recent years. Similarly, it was our view that Poland, Czechoslovakia, and Hungary offered the most fruitful opportunities for exploring the changing status of specialist elites and intellectuals.

Of course, the changes discussed in the arena of linkage politics are not confined to the three countries selected for examination in Part I, nor do we feel that only the countries examined in Part II are subject to the rising influence of specialists and professionals. On the contrary, it is our assumption that the processes examined in these two areas are present in all the states of Eastern Europe, albeit in different forms and in different degrees. Furthermore, as will be apparent to our readers, there are some significant differences between the countries studied in Parts I and II. Before we move to the country studies themselves, therefore, it may be worthwhile to make these assumptions about the cross-national relevance of these themes a bit more explicit. At the same time, we wish to pull together some of the main points raised by the writers of these chapters for the purpose of drawing some pertinent generalizations applicable to Eastern Europe as a whole.

INTERNATIONAL–DOMESTIC LINKAGES

As Ronald Linden points out in his study of Romania in Chapter 3, students of linkage politics have traditionally concentrated their research on the impact of international forces on the national political system. This international-to-national focus, moreover, has been the analytical framework most frequently adopted by specialists on Eastern Europe who have utilized the linkage approach.[3] Linden rightly indicates, however, that linkage patterns also flow in the opposite direction. Analysts of linkage politics must therefore not only be attentive to the inputs streaming into a domestic system from the international environment, but must also be aware of the domestic factors which impinge on a nation's orientations to the outside world.

Recent studies of communist countries tend to support Linden's contention that the national-to-international angle of vision may be just as revealing as the more traditional international-to-national approach in explaining the linkage patterns of the states of Eastern Europe.[4] In addition to enhancing opportunities for analyzing national-to-international linkage flows in Eastern Europe, however, the events of the past ten to fifteen years have also changed the way we look at international-to-national linkages in the region. William Zimmerman observes in Chapter 2 that the earlier tendency of linkage analysts to regard communist states as subject to the impact of a single external source – the Soviet Union – is no longer valid. His study of Yugoslavia begins with the proposition that, under conditions of growing global interdependence, states are increasingly penetrated by a plurality of outside influences. Moreover, these multiple sources of penetration can have a pronounced effect on domestic political processes, as Zimmerman's analysis of the impact of funds obtained from international lending institutions on Yugoslavia's delicately balanced federal structure indicates.

Yugoslavia is not the only country in Eastern Europe to be penetrated by plural sources. In Chapter 4, Michael J. Sodaro suggests that the GDR, a state traditionally dominated by the Soviet Union, must also confront external influences stemming from a variety of other sources. More importantly, both the quantity and the intensity of these linkages have increased significantly in recent years, a development which may have serious repercussions on East Germany's domestic political and economic systems.

How do these three studies relate to one another, and what are their implications for the linkage patterns of the other leading states of Eastern Europe? To begin with, whereas Linden's study of the domestic setting of Romanian foreign policy views the linkage patterns primarily "from the inside looking out," Zimmerman and Sodaro approach their analyses "from the outside looking in." Both of these directional approaches are relevant not only to the three cases of Yugoslavia, Romania, and the GDR, but to the other East European states as well. National-to-international linkages, for example, are gaining an increasing importance throughout Eastern Europe. Over the past decade virtually all of the states of the region have experienced mounting domestic pressures of one kind or another which have seriously conditioned the ruling elites' approach to international politics. This has been the case not only for countries pursuing a relatively independent foreign policy, such as Yugoslavia or Romania, but also for regimes which more closely toe the Soviet line. As Linden states in Chapter 3, the factors that explain why a state "stays in line" need to be explored just as much as those that contribute to foreign policy deviance.

The cross-regional relevance of this domestic-to-international focus in Eastern Europe also extends to international-to-domestic linkages. The penetration of Yugoslavia and the GDR by a plurality of outside sources represents a phenomenon that has swept across the region in the 1970s and early 1980s. As a result of such developments as detente, global economic interdependence, and rising energy prices transmitted to Eastern Europe largely by the Soviet Union, nearly all the states within our purview are now increasingly exposed to a variety of external influences.

The three studies on linkage politics presented here are quite specific about the nature of the domestic and international factors which combine to form linkage patterns in the countries they examine. On the domestic side, all three deal in varying degrees with such perennial topics of East European politics as nationalism, the domestic economy and regime stability. While none of our authors contends that these are the only elements of the internal system which may impinge on a regime's foreign policy, certainly they are among the most important. Moreover, their salience in countries as diverse as Yugoslavia, Romania, and the GDR suggests that the same factors may also exert a strong conditioning impact on the international orientations of the other leading states of Eastern Europe as well, although the form these linkages may actually take will vary from one country to the next.

Thus, to cite just a few examples, nationalism in countries like Yugoslavia, Romania, or Albania is a powerful stimulant to the independent (and at times overtly anti-Soviet) foreign policies pursued by these communist regimes, whereas in the GDR, where the ruling elite has only a very tenuous base in popular nationalism owing to the bifurcation of Germany into two states, the absence of a separate East German national identity compels the regime to draw closer to the Soviet Union as the ultimate protector of the GDR's internal and external security. In Poland and Hungary, on the other hand, the prevalence of anti-Russian nationalism in the population has induced the local communist elites to recognize that they cannot advertise the Soviet connection too demonstrably at home for fear of arousing popular indignation. While these proclivities have been present in the countries just mentioned throughout the post-war period, the past decade has witnessed an intensification of nationalist pressures on at least some of them. The issue of a single Yugoslav national identity, for instance, has lately assumed greater urgency in this ethnically divided state now that Tito is gone; the tremendous upsurge in contacts between citizens of the two German states since the onset of inter-German detente in 1972 has greatly complicated the GDR's efforts to build a separate national identity; and the current labor unrest in Poland unquestionably contains a strong national component recently reinforced by the election of Cracow's Cardinal Wojtyla as Pope John-Paul II.

The domestic economies of the East European states also offer a variety of imputs into the international politics of the communist regimes. As the countries with the most flexible and decentralized planning systems in the region, Yugoslavia and Hungary have been able to extend their economic dealings with the West to a greater degree than most of the other countries of the region in recent years. Romania's rather unique economic strategy, which combines continuing industrialization with the notion that Romania is a "socialist developing country," opens the way to expanded economic ties with the West, the Third World, and international financial institutions. The GDR's heavily trade-dependent economy is especially (and increasingly) dependent on wider economic contacts with the West, and particularly with West Germany. Poland, for its part, opted in the early 1970s to rely on massive Western imports and credits to reinvigorate its chronically ailing economy, but its failure to utilize these acquisitions effectively has only aggravated domestic tensions and severely hampered its ability to obtain further assistance from its Western creditors. Czechoslovak leaders, on the other hand, have deliberately reversed most of the economic reforms which were launched during the reform period of 1968 for the purpose of facilitating economic cooperation with the West; this policy and other economic difficulties have had an inhibiting effect on its trade outside of Comecon.[5] Finally, Bulgaria's predominantly agricultural economy and Albania's strategy of economic "self-reliance" have continued to make these countries the least active world traders in Eastern Europe.

Maintaining the stability of communist party rule remains the highest priority of all the elites of Eastern Europe. In the 1970s and early 1980s this factor has continued to play a major role in conditioning Eastern Europe's international environment and the foreign policies of several of the region's leading states. Zimmerman notes in Chapter 2, for example, that the desire to reinforce regime cohesion is a principal motivation behind Yugoslavia's quest for funding from international lending agencies to help finance domestic economic development projects. Linden stresses that the Ceauşescu regime's tight grip on the domestic political system is one of the chief reasons for Moscow's forebearance in the face of Romania's autonomous foreign policy initiatives. Similarly, the stability of the Kádár regime's position in Hungary helps explain the USSR's acceptance of the far-reaching reforms that the Hungarians have implemented since 1968. In other countries where the stability of the regime is subject to persisting pressures, such as the GDR or post-Dubcek Czechoslovakia, political leaders have discovered that "it pays to advertise" their dependence on Soviet power for the maintenance of party rule, a conclusion Polish leaders themselves may reach even after the establishment of the martial law regime should further popular disruptions create new dangers for party and state authority.

The domestic context of Eastern Europe's orientations to the outside world thus appears to have acquired heightened significance in the course of the 1970s for most of the states in the area, and this significance is likely to increase in the years ahead. The same case can be made for linkages viewed from the opposite side of the lens. As noted earlier, international-to-national linkages are the principal subject of Zimmerman's and Sodaro's analyses, and their importance is explicitly acknowledged by Linden in his chapter on Romania. Once again, all three authors agree on several of the main external influences that in recent years have penetrated the countries they investigate. In different ways, they discuss such elements of the international constellation as the USSR, the West, and the international economic system; they also refer to the special implications which the recent developments in Poland have for each country. While other outside sources of penetration also make their presence known in various countries in the region, the impact of these four factors is felt in nearly all the leading states of Eastern Europe, albeit in different ways and in different degrees.

Among the external influences on Eastern Europe, the Soviet Union unquestionably occupies the top position. For all the states belonging to the Warsaw Treaty Organization, the USSR remains the final guarantor of the maintenance of the local party's leading role in the domestic political system. In these respects, nothing has changed in the Soviet Union's predominance over its East European allies since the 1950s. Although the Soviets have demonstrated their willingness to allow a measure of domestic or foreign policy deviation from Soviet preferences in most of these states, all the leaders of the Warsaw Pact countries are aware that there are limits to Soviet tolerance which cannot be transgressed without provoking some kind of reaction from Moscow. What has changed in more recent years has been the impact of Soviet economic policies towards these regimes. As a result of the steep price increases for petroleum and other energy supplies which the Soviets have imposed on the European members of Comecon since 1975, all of these regimes have experienced a rapid deterioration in their terms of trade with the USSR and have had to make major adjustments in their domestic economic priorities. These adjustments have involved such measures as cutbacks in the rate of growth of consumer goods production, costly efforts to improve energy conservation, and, in most cases, price increases for food or other consumer necessities. As noted earlier, both in the short and the long run these econonomic constraints are fraught with serious political implications for the ruling elites. Moscow's decision to proceed with further energy price hikes in the future and to freeze the amount of its oil exports to Eastern Europe at 1980 levels makes a gloomy economic prognosis almost unavoidable for the rest of the decade in just about all the states of the region. It therefore appears that Soviet influence in Eastern Europe will not decline in the near future, but will quite probably increase. This may also be true in Yugoslavia, whose trade with the Soviet Union increased in recent years due to difficulties the Yugoslavs experienced in selling their products to the West.

Moreover, these influences will not be predominantly supportive of regime stability in the area, as they had been between the mid-1960s and the mid-1970s, when Eastern Europe came to constitute more of a drain on Soviet resources than a positive economic asset for the Soviets.[6] Rather they will most likely involve a combination of positive and negative effects on regime stability. Thus, while the Soviets may yet intervene directly in Poland in the event of serious challenges to General Jaruzelski's martial law regime, they will most probably continue to undermine the domestic bases of party support elsewhere by exacerbating the economic problems faced by the communist party leaders. It is this latter phenomenon which constitutes the principal change in Soviet–East European relations since the middle of the last decade, and chances are great that these unfavorable influences will increase in the decade of the 1980s.

The West comprises another major source of external influence on Eastern Europe, and few would dispute the contention that the level of Western penetration of the area increased dramatically in the 1970s. As in the case of Soviet relations with Eastern Europe in the past decade, the West's ties with the region have also involved a mixture of positive and negative influences on the economic underpinnings of regime stability in most of the area's major states. The great irony in all this is that, while the influences stemming from the

USSR of late have been increasingly negative in this respect, those emanating from the West have been characterized by a greater infusion of positive elements than at any time since the beginning of the post-war period. Most of these regime-supportive tendencies have come from West Germany. The detente policies of the Federal Republic of Germany during the period since the end of 1969, including such radical departures from past policies as the recognition of the GDR and acceptance of the current boundaries of Poland and Czechoslovakia, have had a legitimizing effect on the regimes affected by these moves. The extension of technology transfers, loans and other commodities and financial resources to Eastern Europe which accompanied these policies, together with the expansion of similar assistance by other Western countries, have helped prop up the economic bases of regime stability in a number of the region's principal states.[7] Over the course of the past decade, West Germany and other Western states have acquired a large political and economic stake in detente with Eastern Europe, and they would be seriously concerned if political instability in a country like Poland were to jeopardize the benefits of detente by provoking Soviet intervention. These interests in detente, in short, lead to an increasing interest in political stability in Eastern Europe. At the same time, however, detente also has several negative aspects that carry at least a potential for destabilizing political life in the area. The most obvious examples are the enormous increase in direct citizen-to-citizen contacts between the two Germanies since 1972, and the human rights provisions of the Final Act of the Helsinki Conference on Security and Cooperation in Europe, signed in 1975.

The international economic order is a third major source of external influence on Eastern Europe whose importance may be briefly signaled here. Although it includes the Soviet Union and the West, whose economic policies towards the region have already been mentioned, the world economy can be looked upon as a separate variable consisting of the whole global set of interconnected economic relations which tie together the nations of the world. As a consequence of the intensified interdependence of national economies that developed in the 1970s, Eastern Europe finds itself enmeshed in a web of worldwide interactions that exercises a profound effect on its economic, and at times, political, conditions. Rising OPEC oil prices, recession and inflation in the West, contractions in international assistance funds and other economic disturbances eventually tend to make their mark on the states of Eastern Europe.[8] To the extent that these interdependencies proliferate in the 1980s, as is likely, Eastern Europe will continue to be penetrated by a host of external economic impulses that are largely beyond its control. Here again, however, the precise impact of these outside forces will vary from country to country, as they are filtered through the mediating conditions specific to the internal order of each individual state.[9]

The fourth and final source of external influences on Eastern Europe to be highlighted here centers on the communist world itself. Recently the two most prominent of these influences have emerged from what used to be called Eurocommunism in Western Europe, and from the extraordinary events that have transpired in Poland since the summer of 1980. Although the impact of the revisionist West European communist parties (particularly the Italian, Spanish, and French parties) on Eastern Europe was at best questionable even during the heyday of Eurocommunism in the mid-1970s,[10] the effects of the Polish events on the other states of the region may prove to be considerably more serious. Even prior to the declaration of martial law in December 1981, the spillover effects of the Polish workers' movement were not especially strong. Moreover, the observable ramifications of the Polish trade union movement have varied from one state to another. The GDR, Hungary and Czechoslovakia have thus far managed to keep their workers relatively appeased, despite a brief flash of miners' strikes in the latter country in the fall of 1980.[11] Romanian leaders, however, clearly had reason to worry about a repetition of the miners' strikes that took place there in 1977. For now, all that can be said with any assurance is that the Polish regime's (and Moscow's) temporary acquiescence in independent trade unions armed with the right to strike created a new political phenomenon in Eastern Europe, one with which all the region's ruling elites must still come to terms. Despite the rigors of the martial law regime, popular support for Solidarity has not been eradicated inside Poland; nor has the power of Solidarity's example been completely eliminated in other East European countries. While the actions taken by the martial law leaders have clearly dealt a severe blow to independent trade unionism in Poland, the issue is by no means fully resolved. Solidarity's leaders may yet figure, although in a greatly reduced way, in whatever political arrangements follow the martial law government in Poland. It is also possible that workers' unrest may indeed surface again in Poland or elsewhere.

SPECIALISTS, PROFESSIONALS AND INTELLECTUALS

The linkages discussed above also influence the domestic context which conditions the role of specialists and intellectuals in policy-making in Eastern Europe. Controversy over the proper place of intellectuals and specialists in communist societies is not new. Since the time of Lenin, communist leaders have puzzled over the issue of how to use the specialized knowledge of experts and professionals and yet prevent them from challenging the existing order. As developments in the 1970s illustrated, the issue is still an important one. Relying on improved living standards to maintain a certain degree of popular support or at least acquiescence, and leading increasingly developed societies, communist political leaders have become more dependent on specialists' contributions to public policy-making. This dependence may be expected to increase in the 1980s, as political leaders seek to minimize the negative effects of economic slowdowns and maintain political stability. The issues posed by this need to use available expertise are particularly acute in the more developed East European countries, such as East Germany, Czechoslovakia, and Hungary, where sophisticated economies and more differentiated populations have led political leaders to attempt to reach compromises with important intellectual groups. As recent economic projections illustrate, economic difficulties and the need to come to terms with reduced possibilities will also be evident in the less developed East European countries in the 1980s. Together with the spread of higher education, which has led to the creation of an educated cadre of specialists and generational change, these factors may be expected to increase the importance of specialists and other intellectuals in other countries of the region as well.

The three papers in this section examine the role of different types of intellectuals in Poland, Czechoslovakia, and Hungary. Curry focuses on the role of journalists in policy-making in the Polish context. Discussing members of a professional group which plays a special role in communist societies, she illustrates the impact which growing professionalization of an occupation has on the desire of its members to influence policy. Her discussion also illustrates the role which journalists may play in determining public events in communist states by virtue of the opportunities their professional duties provide for contact with broader groups of the public as well as members of the political elite. Although it is difficult to generalize from the Polish situation, the role of journalists in Poland in 1980–2 suggests that they may play at times a crucial role in furthering links between other professionals or intellectuals and mass publics in communist states. Her analysis also highlights the role which certain professionals play in supplying information needed by top political leaders. At the same time, Curry's study clearly indicates the limits on professionals' activities and ability to influence policy.

Wolchik examines the role of a somewhat less institutionalized group of specialists in the making of policy in a less sensitive policy area in Czechoslovakia. Tracing the development of demographic policy in that country, her essay highlights the function which specialists serve in bringing problems to the attention of political leaders; it also illustrates the way in which specialists formulate and argue for policy alternatives that eventually become the basis for choice by political leaders. Noting that specialist influence appears to be exerted not so much through particular organized groups as through informal coalitions of specialists and officials in different institutions who share similar policy preferences, she argues that the process by which specialists intervene in policy-making has become more institutionalized and routinized over time, at least in this policy area. Her study indicates that the political elites in Czechoslovakia have been relatively successful in the post-reform period in utilizing specialized expertise in policy-making while at the same time avoiding any overt challenge to the current political order.

Tőkés reaches much the same conclusion in his study of the relationship of political leaders and different types of intellectuals in Hungary. Drawing on the work of the Hungarian writer Konrád and the sociologist Szelényi, Tőkés focuses on the compromise which political leaders in Hungary have reached with members of both the humanist and technical intelligentsia. He also considers another issue which is of importance throughout the region, namely the relationship between the intellectuals and broader groups of the population. Detailing the potential for conflict which continues to underlie the largely cooperative relationship between political elites and the major part of both intellectual groups at present, Tőkés discusses the continued difficulties which political leaders have in maintaining this relationship, due to the different functions of the intelligentsia and the political elite. At the same time, his essay demonstrates that, except in special circumstances, there is little reason to expect intellectuals to serve as the catalysts for major political change in communist states. It also suggests that, despite the recent Polish exception, we should not necessarily expect intellectuals in communist states to support mass movements for change, particularly if those movements threaten to reduce or eliminate the advantages they have received for keeping their side of the bargain with the political leadership.

Although it is difficult to generalize from the three studies included in Part II to other societies, the questions they examine are relevant for the other countries of the region as well. Of these, four appear to be of greatest importance for present purposes. First, how efficiently is expert knowledge utilized in policy-making in East European states and under what conditions? The essays in this volume suggest that the answer to this question depends on a number of factors, including the policy area being discussed, the links of specialists and professionals to political decision-makers, and the resources, institutional and professional, of particular specialists and intellectuals. All three studies indicate that the way in which specialists influence policy-making and the extent of their input vary as well according to the general political climate. Despite fluctuations in elite willingness to solicit or entertain the opinions of specialists, elite reliance on intellectuals' input in policy-making appears to have increased over time in two of the countries examined. Tőkés' observation that members of the technocratic intelligentsia have become indispensable to the Hungarian leadership may well be true in other countries as well. Curry's study, however, reminds us that the ability of professionals to take part in policy-making ultimately depends on the willingness of the political elites to allow them to play this role.

Despite the often close relationship between members of the intelligentsia and the political elite, the role of specialists, professionals, and intellectuals also raises issues in regard to political control in all East European countries. As political leaders seek to make more effective use of expertise, they must balance the demands of specialists and professionals for a certain degree of occupational autonomy with the need to prevent members of these groups from using this autonomy as a base for challenging the foundations of the existing political system. How much autonomy or privilege is necessary to promote the efficient production and use of specialized knowledge, and how can political leaders best ensure continued loyalty on the part of those who possess such knowledge? As the essays in this section indicate, the nature of the "compromise," or the terms by which intellectuals of various types have been coopted, varies from country to country in Eastern Europe and depends to some degree on a nation's previous traditions in this regard. These terms have also changed somewhat over time within particular countries. Tőkés and Wolchik demonstrate the varying mixtures of material advantage, professional autonomy, and political surveillance which political leaders have used to ensure participation and compliance on the part of intellectuals in Hungary and Czechoslovakia. While these tactics have been relatively successful in those countries, Curry discusses the continuing problems which Polish leaders have had in maintaining control over journalists during various periods in Poland. During the 1980–1 period it appeared that Polish leaders would take the unusual step of attempting to gain the support of intellectuals and professionals by fostering a sense of genuine participation in national renewal and common responsibility for public policy in that country. This option, also used by the reform leadership in Czechoslovakia in the late 1960s, promises the best results in terms of regime–intellectual cooperation, but it also carries the greatest risks to party control. The internment of intellectuals and reimposition of strict controls on their activities by the martial law government clearly signal the end of this effort in Poland for the time being, but the martial law government or those who follow it eventually will have to find some way of gaining the co-operation of intellectuals and professionals to deal with Poland's problems.

A related question concerns the relationship of specialists, professionals, and other intellectuals to broader groups of the population. As noted earlier, members of these groups are often identified in the West as the primary force working for political change in Eastern Europe. Among the more articulate and educated segments of the population, and most subject to Western influences, intellectuals have traditionally served as catalysts for political change in this region. At the same time, due to their contacts with political decision-makers, many professionals and intellectuals have the opportunity to translate mass demands to the political leadership. To what extent and under what conditions do they serve these functions in Eastern Europe? The three essays in Part II reach different conclusions in this area. All three illustrate the role which intellectuals serve in linking mass publics to the political leadership at various times, but they differ in regard to the extent to which intellectuals serve as agents of political change. Taken together, they suggest that, despite the growth of dissidence in Eastern Europe in the past decade, there is little reason to expect large numbers of intellectuals or specialists to advocate radical political change under present circumstances. Curry's essay demonstrates, however, the facilitating role which members of certain professions can play once political change begins, as well as the limits of professionals' power. In the 1980s, then, we can expect political leaders in all East European countries to seek to channel intellectuals' and specialists' inputs into acceptable directions; we can also expect leaders in other East European states to be wary of the potential political consequences of allowing members of these groups greater autonomy and influence.

A final question which arises in connection with the role of specialists and intellectuals in all East European countries concerns the policy impact of their roles. Does greater participation by specialists, professionals, and intellectuals necessarily lead to better policy in these countries? East European leaders appear to share the belief of certain Western observers that such participation will lead to more appropriate or successful answers to vexing social and economic problems, but it is not clear that this is so. Wolchik's study of demographic policy-making supports the view that increased expert participation in policy-making leads to more effective policy, but it is difficult to generalize from this area to other issues without further empirical investigation. As Tőkés notes in his essay, the routine consultation of experts in the making of policy in Hungary, particularly in the economic sphere, may be one of the factors which account for that country's better than average record of economic performance and stable political system. It is difficult to judge, however, whether greater attention to the advice of specialists would have saved the Polish leadership from the crisis of 1980; it is similarly difficult to know whether the commissions of experts set up in that country to re-examine economic policy, to the extent that they are utilized at all by the martial law leadership, will be any more successful than the previous leadership in resolving the country's myriad economic and political problems. This question, which remains at this time an open one, will be of particular importance in all the countries of the region in the 1980s as political leaders attempt to come to grips with the numerous domestic and international constraints facing them and at the same time maintain some degree of popular support and political stability.

EASTERN EUROPE AND THE WORLD

The last three chapters deal with problems relating to Eastern Europe as a whole. Two of them are concerned with the largest supranational organizations in the region – the Council on Mutual Economic Assistance (CMEA, or Comecon) and the Warsaw Treaty Organization – while the third looks at Eastern Europe's budding relationships with the Third World. All three of them reflect a common interest in certain critical questions which have traditionally captured the attention of students of these subjects, and which almost certainly will continue to be of paramount interest throughout the 1980s. The first of these questions centers on the general patterns of Eastern Europe's interactions with the outside world: how have Comecon, the Warsaw Pact, and Eastern Europe's relations with the Third World developed in recent years under the impact of international economic trends and the evolution of East–West relations? The second question is more directly focused on the states of Eastern Europe themselves: how much coordination or fragmentation has there been among the East European nations in their activities in these areas? That is, have the East Europeans managed to achieve greater integration in their approach to the region's economic and military problems and to their ties with the Third World, or have diverse political or economic interests had an inhibiting effect on the development of cooperative efforts in these fields? A final set of questions which the essays in Part III examine concerns the outlook for the future development of these tendencies in the 1980s.

In his examination of recent trends in the Comecon trading bloc, Stanislaw Wasowski notes that, in the past decade, the East European members of this organization vastly expanded their economic interactions with one another as well as with the rest of the world. At the same time, virtually all of these Comecon countries confronted similar economic problems at home as they moved from extensive to more intensive patterns of growth. These included such difficulties as insufficient economic modernization and efficiency, declining growth rates, and skyrocketing energy costs. In dealing with these and related worries, most of the states in the region decided in the 1970s to follow the Soviet practice of seeking to overcome the domestic obstacles to renewed growth by trading heavily with the West, an option regarded by many communist elites as preferable to instituting politically controversial economic reforms. Meanwhile, measures designed to upgrade the quality of economic integration within Comecon received new emphasis. In 1971 a "Comprehensive Program" was adopted which outlined a series of steps aimed at promoting greater coordination among the planned economies of the region, and in the second half of the decade a series of so-called "target programs" was initiated for the purpose of facilitating joint long-term planning between the USSR and its East European partners in a number of key sectors. However, the actual measures taken by the Comecon states to implement these guidelines generally fell short of expectations. The most critical factor accounting for this gap between plans and outcomes, in Wasowski's view, centered on the reluctance of Comecon leaders to make the decisive changes in established intellectual, managerial, and political procedures that were vital to the effective realization of the new programs. Unless the Soviets and their East European counterparts muster the political will necessary to effect these changes, Wasowski doubts that the prospects for greater integration in Comecon will outweigh the prevailing inhibitions to a more coordinated approach to economic cooperation in the 1980s.

The Warsaw Treaty Organization (WTO) has also been subject to contending pressures towards coordination and fragmentation. Thomas Cason's study in Chapter 9 shows that the USSR in recent years has acted to reinforce earlier efforts directed at ensuring a high level of cooperation among Warsaw Pact military elites. Organizational changes in Warsaw Pact structure since 1969 have helped promote these tendencies. Nevertheless, Cason points out that the Warsaw Pact still falls short of providing the Soviets with a forum for obtaining unequivocal support for Soviet policies on the part of the East European member states. Romania, for example, continues to elude Moscow's search for a common Warsaw Pact position on critical defense and foreign policy issues. The turbulent situation in Poland makes that country an alliance partner of dubious military reliability to the Soviets, while a Soviet-led invasion of Poland might encounter the opposition of Romania and, quite possibly, Hungary. Meanwhile, the Warsaw Pact's role in East–West relations over the past decade has been characterized by yet another set of contradictory developments. On the one hand, the WTO's modernization program and the concomitant Soviet troop build-up in Eastern Europe since 1967 have definitely fortified the Pact's credibility as a formidable military machine in the eyes of Western strategists. On the other hand, the continuing economic debility of several leading Pact members, together with the political instability of Poland, exposes these states to economic and political inroads from the West, particularly from the Federal Republic of Germany. On the assumption that these trends will not be reversed in the 1980s, Cason concludes that the outlook for the political cohesion and military reliability of the Warsaw Pact does not appear to be very bright in the near future.

Roger Kanet sees similarly contrasting patterns of coordination and fragmentation at work in Eastern Europe's relations with the Third World. While observing that the region's interactions with the developing nations have expanded considerably over the past decade, in virtually all aspects of inter-state relations, Kanet indicates that there has been a relatively large degree of cooperation among the USSR and most of the states of Eastern Europe in their political and military policies towards the Third World, but considerably less cooperation in their economic ties with Third World countries. He attributes this inconsistency to the simultaneous existence of general support for Soviet ideological, diplomatic, and military approaches to Third World clients on the part of most East European leaders, together with economic rivalries among the East European states as they each attempt to secure raw materials and stable markets in key Third World nations. With the notable exception of Romania, which has frequently followed foreign policies at variance with Soviet preferences in the Third World, the leading states of Eastern Europe have generally been supportive of Soviet political and military overtures to such clients as Angola, Mozambique, and Ethiopia. In the area of economic relations, however, the East Europeans have often approached the Third World in a *sauve qui peut* fashion with each state scrambling to conclude its own agreements on energy imports or commodity exports with selected Third World countries. Looking forward to the 1980s, Kanet foresees at least the possibility of a more concerted East European economic approach to the Third World, as well as a potential conflict between the East Europeans' support for Moscow's efforts to promote political unrest in various parts of the Third World and their need for economic stability in those areas.[12]

In sum, the picture that emerges from this overview of Eastern Europe as it crosses from one decade into the next is, perhaps all too predictably, a mixed one. Common problems stemming from universally experienced economic difficulties contrast with considerable diversity in the way the countries of the region are affected by, and deal with, the resulting adversities. Linkage patterns reveal both an upward surge in the quantity and intensity of linkages in nearly all the states of Eastern Europe as well as an array of policies that vary from one country to the next as they seek either to promote or resist particular linkage trends. Growing pressures for greater modernization and rationalization in policy-making procedures must contend virtually everywhere in the region with the accumulated legacy of the party elite's dominance of decision-making structures. Efforts to promote integration and coordination in critical political, military, and economic questions affecting Eastern Europe as a whole continue to encounter fissiparous tendencies rooted in the national interests of the individual states. Finally, looming over all of these developments in East European politics, the continuing uncertainty over Poland's future may promote pressures for reform throughout the region or, conversely, inaugurate a period of severe repression involving, in the most extreme case, direct Soviet military intervention.

Viewed superficially, none of these contrasting tendencies strikes the seasoned observer of post-war Eastern Europe as entirely new. Their specific features, however, have been shaped by the critical events of the 1970s, while the manner in which they may evolve in the 1980s can only be the subject of infinitely fascinating speculation. The aim of this book is to provide an accurate assessment of what has happened in the past decade, and to help make sure that speculation about the future, whether verified by subsequent developments or not, is at least informed.

NOTES AND REFERENCES

1. In his remarks to the conference on "Eastern Europe in the 1980s: Trends and Prospects," George Washington University, 5 April 1980.
2. Zvi Gitelman, "The World Economy and Elite Political Strategies in Czechoslovakia, Hungary, and Poland," in Morris Bornstein, Zvi Gitelman, and William Zimmerman (eds), *East–West Relations and the Future of Eastern Europe* (London: George Allen and Unwin, 1981).
3. See, for example, R. V. Burks, "The Communist Polities of Eastern Europe," in James N. Rosenau's seminal volume, *Linkage Politics* (New York: The Free Press, 1969); and Andrzej Korbonski, "External Influences on Eastern Europe," in Charles Gati (ed.), *The International Politics of Eastern Europe* (New York: Praeger, 1976).
4. See Seweryn Bialer (ed.), *The Domestic Context of Soviet Foreign Policy* (Boulder, Colo.: Westview Press, 1981); Bogdan Denitch, "The Domestic Roots of Foreign Policy in Eastern Europe," in Gati, *The International Politics of Eastern Europe*; and Harry Harding, "The Domestic Politics of China's Global Posture, 1973–78," in Thomas Fingar *et al.* (eds), *China's Quest for Independence: Policy Evolution in the 1970s* (Boulder, Colo.: Westview Press, 1980).
5. The East European members of the Council on Mutual Economic Assistance (abbreviated as Comecon or CMEA) include Bulgaria,

Czechoslovakia, the GDR, Hungary, Poland, and Romania. Yugoslavia has observer status.

6. See Paul Marer, "Has Eastern Europe Become a Liability to the Soviet Union? (III) The Economic Aspect," in Gati, *The International Politics of Eastern Europe.*

7. Poland, of course, is a notable exception, but one whose political instability cannot be blamed on inadequate economic assistance from the West, considering that Poland's debt to Western creditors totaled over $26 billion by the end of 1982.

8. See Egon Neuberger and Laura D'Andrea Tyson (eds), *The Impact of International Economic Disturbances on the Soviet Union and Eastern Europe* (New York: Pergamon Press, 1980).

9. See Sarah Meiklejohn Terry and Andrzej Korbonski, "The Impact of External Economic Disturbances on the Internal Politics of Eastern Europe: The Polish and Hungarian Cases," and William Zimmerman, "The Energy Crisis, Western 'Stagflation' and the Evolution of Soviet–East European Relations: An Initial Assessment," both in Neuberger and Tyson (eds), *The Impact of International Economic Disturbances.*

10. See Sharon L. Wolchik, "Communism East and West: Eurocommunism's Implications for Eastern Europe," paper presented at the conference on "The Foreign Policy of Eurocommunism," Airlie House, Warrenton, Virginia, 12–14 May 1977.

11. *Le Monde* (International Edition, Weekly Selection), 16–22 October 1980, p. 6.

12. For a comprehensive treatment of these issues, see Michael Radu (ed.), *Eastern Europe and the Third World* (New York: Praeger, 1981).

Part I

Domestic–international Linkages

2 International–national Linkages and Political Processes in Yugoslavia

WILLIAM ZIMMERMAN

I

In comparative politics generally, comparative foreign policy, and communist studies as well, the study of international–national linkages focused traditionally on states that were largely penetrated by a single external source. For these states it was generally assumed the international–national linkage was the key to explaining internal political development. Dependency theorists in their attempts to explain the internal evolution of Latin American states, for instance, adopted such a focus. The basic satellite model which served students of communist systems well for many years was also of this genre. In that model all sources of external influence save one, even those emanating from other satellites, were excluded. One could predict actions within a state by focusing on decisions taken elsewhere, outside the state, in this instance in Moscow. Indeed, taken to its logical conclusion, the satellite imagery was one in which the putative nation-state was merely another instance of a traditional political institution having been transformed into a transmission belt, that is, into a mechanism for the downward communication of commands.

In recent years there has been a growing awareness that it is not just such states where an attention to international–national linkages is warranted. The burgeoning literature on global interdependence testifies to a diminished disposition to conceive of genuinely independent states as ones where, in contradistinction to dependencies or satellites, the political system operates primarily within the framework of a society and largely autonomously of the extra-national environment. Gone, it would appear, are the days when major approaches to political development largely ignored, as did David

Easton's *The Political System* and Gabriel Almond and James Coleman's *The Politics of Developing Areas,* the linkages between a national system and the international environment.

Instead there is a new attention to the impact of international–national linkages on political development especially in the case of states that are highly penetrated by *plural sources.* Samuel Huntington led the way by arguing that such states may actually have greater control over their own destiny than those that are not coupled to the international environment. Thailand, he argued, demonstrates that a government may grant "access to private, government, and international transnational organizations in such a way as to further its own objectives. . . . The widespread penetration of its society by transnational organizations will obviously have significant effects on society. . . . In the process [however] it may greatly strengthen itself as a government."[1]

My own work on Yugoslavia points to the same conclusion. I would argue that in the 1970s the Yugoslav leadership under Tito seemed to have realized that a viable strategy for internal development could involve increasing domestic political cohesion while, simultaneously, cultivating vigorously the economic penetration of the country by plural sources. Yugoslavia may in this respect be viewed as an organization engaged in a massive and impressively successful effort, at least until recently,[2] to extract grants from its external environment, just as local governments in the US devote considerable energy and resources to playing the grant-getting game from various federal agencies or as academic entrepreneurs attempt to finance a program of research, teaching, and service out of a plurality of grants from public funds and private foundation sources. The academic entrepreneur analogy is especially apt. The Yugoslavs have been able to obtain funding for certain items on their developmental shopping list from several global "foundations" with institutional interests in particular dimensions of Yugoslav developmental aims, interests not often shared by some other external source of funds. The USSR is providing credits to build factories in Montenegro to produce goods to export to the USSR, a project the International Bank for Reconstruction and Development would be unlikely to finance, while the IBRD has provided funds, inter alia, for cultivating the Adriatic and improving cattle raising on *private* farms in socialist Yugoslavia.

This paper extends the effort to conceptualize states that are penetrated by plural sources. My attention is again on Yugoslavia, though the focus here differs considerably from other efforts. Here I am not concerned directly with international–national linkages and Yugoslav political development. Rather I am concerned to illustrate how international–national linkages have affected Yugoslav political processes. That in turn does relate indirectly to Yugoslav political development. The Yugoslav political elite has acted as though one central dimension of its strategy for national cohesion entails a conscious effort to preclude the operation of certain kinds of political processes. My conclusion assesses the relevance of these propositions to the post-Tito Yugoslavia of the 1980s.

INTERNATIONAL LINKAGES WITH DOMESTIC POLITICAL PROCESSES: A FRAMEWORK FOR ANALYSIS

In grossest and most obvious terms, international–national linkages affect Yugoslav political processes indirectly. Events in the international environment bear centrally on the structure of the Yugoslav political system – which in turn influence Yugoslav political processes. Thus, while it is obviously difficult to compare what might have been with what is, there is an abundance of evidence that being a part of the Soviet–East European regional system has distinct implications for the nature of the political system of member states. This the Hungarians learned in 1956 and the Czechoslovaks found out in 1968. Nor can there be any doubt that this factor constrained the evolution of Poland at the outset of the 1980s – whether or not the Soviet Union ultimately invades Poland. The fact that in the aftermath of the Stalin–Tito clash in 1948 Yugoslavia found itself operating in an international environment which was not that of an hierarchical regional system – that is, an environment in which more than one superpower exerts considerable influence – has been of great import for the parameters of the Yugoslav political system. Yugoslavia's international systemic environment provides a context in which internal variables can play a greater role than they would in the Soviet–East European regional system.

Simultaneously it is also probable that the bipolar configuration of the dominant system and the emergence of the Third World have served to constrain the evolution of Yugoslavia in the direction of a Western two-party or multi-party system. The evidence in this regard is not overwhelming. We may at least speculate, however, that, had there been greater asymmetry in the bipolar relationship in the 1950s and had de-colonization proceeded at a slower pace, Milovan Djilas' view of Yugoslavia's proper place in the world, a view which meshed exactly with his vision of a desired domestic structure, would have had far better prospects of success than it did in practice. Given such an international environment, one might more plausibly imagine Yugoslavia as a "Switzerland of the Balkans," in which "Yugoslavia would not have been able to play a prominent part in international affairs . . . [settling instead] for a subordinate position among the small Western nations,"[3] as it is reported Djilas espoused. "Had Djilas' views on foreign policy been adopted," Rubinstein reports a "republican Party official" as having observed, Yugoslavia would have developed "into a two-Party system, along the lines of British Parliamentary democracy," resulting, this official believed, in a "much closer association with the Western camp [and] a dangerous splintering of the Party."[4] Similarly, there demonstrably exists some causal relationship between the substantial re-Leninization of the party which took place after 1971 and the fear among the Yugoslav leadership of Soviet reactions, as both Tito's speech at Karadjor-djevo in December 1971 and Kardelj's September 1972 statement (in which he attacked the more technocratic and Western-oriented Slovenes) bore eloquent witness.

A second aspect of the basic structure of the Yugoslav system which has been greatly influenced by linkages to the external environment is an obvious one, especially since it relates so closely to the nationality problem, but one which ought nevertheless to be mentioned – namely, the integrity of Yugoslavia's borders. Border disputes between states – even disputes in which ethnic distribution is not coterminous with the legal boundaries – of course have been a common occurrence historically. They are, nevertheless, an important element in the definition of state structure. Specifically, controversies over Yugoslavia's boundaries have been an important part of the political history of the country, ranging from the efforts of Albanian nationalists – a linkage group – to unite Kosovo with neighboring Albania to the Italian–Yugoslav controversy over Trieste. Indeed with the resolution of the last vestiges of the dispute between Italy and Yugoslavia over Trieste and Zones A and B, the year 1975 marked the first time since the founding of the Socialist Republic that Yugoslavia's borders had achieved full international status.

II

A less obvious but more direct manner in which international–national linkages influence Yugoslav policy processes is that events originating in the international environment set in motion domestic political processes that vary depending on the issue. To illustrate this proposition I shall depict four salient incidents in the political history of Yugoslavia; taken together the four episodes suggest that, in analyzing the political evolution of Yugoslavia, international–national linkages are ignored only at great cost. Each of the cases corresponds roughly to one of the cells of a paradigm for analyzing the policy process which I have developed. Since that paradigm has been described in detail elsewhere[5] it may be briefly summarized here.

What bears emphasis, however, is that two factors serve to limit the paradigm's relevance. First, the paradigm is applicable only to states that have a minimal social and political consensus such that a direct threat to the existence of the state will be perceived as a challenge to core values. This is generally but not universally characteristic for most modern states. Second, the paradigm assumes non-totalitarian, although not necessarily democratic, regime–society relations. I have argued elsewhere that the paradigm is probably relevant to the post-Stalinist, post-totalitarian, albeit authoritarian USSR.[6] I certainly would argue that it is relevant to the more articulated and relatively pluralist communist states of Eastern Europe such as Poland and Hungary at the outset of the 1980s.

The paradigm represents an effort to combine two seminal articles by Theodore Lowi[7] on the linkage between issue area and the policy process, one dealing with American domestic political processes, the other with American foreign policy. On this basis it is possible to identify two questions whose answers serve as criteria for categorizing a specific policy with reference to one of four issue areas which Lowi identified in one of, or both of, the two articles. The paradigm and the characteristics of the four issue areas ("arenas of power" in Lowi's terms) are summarized in Table 2.1 and Figure 2.1. Each issue area, it was hypothesized, is characterized by different actors, different patterns of interaction and a different power structure. The distributive arena (arena I) is one where the political goods are highly subject to disaggregation and is best exemplified by what in American politics has been called pork-barrel items. Individuals and firms are the actors in the political game: since the political goods are readily subject to being parcelled out, nearly everyone (read: every-one who counts politically) gets his share. (The current argot "a piece of the action" captures this notion nicely.) Log-rolling constitutes the name of the game. Typically, "unprincipled" alliances of uncommon interests are constructed. Needless to add, such politics are relatively consensual, taking place within a largely nonconflicting elite.

TABLE 2.1   *Issue areas and policy processes: a summary*

Arena	Primary political units	Patterns of interaction	Power structure	Foreign policy Domestic policy
I. Distribution	Individual, firm	Log-rolling; "unprincipled" alliances of uncommon interests	Non-conflicting elite with support groups	Both
II. Regulation	Group	"The coalition"; shared subject matter, interest aggregation	Pluralistic, multi-centered	Both
III. (a) Protection (b) Interaction	Individuals "without their institutions"	"Team norms"	Highly elitist	Foreign policy
IV. Redistribution	Classes, movements generations	"Peak associations"	Conflictual elite; elite and counter elite	Domestic

Lowi's arena of regulation (arena II) has groups as its primary actors. In this arena, the patterns of interaction involve groups of the likeminded. Who gets what is decided as a result of the fact that the goods are not as subject to disaggregation as they are in distributive politics. Conflict is consequently greater. Where it is often difficult in the distributive arena to identify specific losers, there are always losers in regulative politics. In the short run, the regulatory decision involves a direct choice as to who will be indulged and who deprived. Some will not obtain a liquor license in Ann Arbor, just as some will not obtain an overseas air route.

The third arena is the one that is traditionally most associated with foreign policy. For twentieth century multi-purpose states it is in fact merely one foreign policy issue area – what I called the protective and interactive arena. The actors are individuals, though, as Lowi

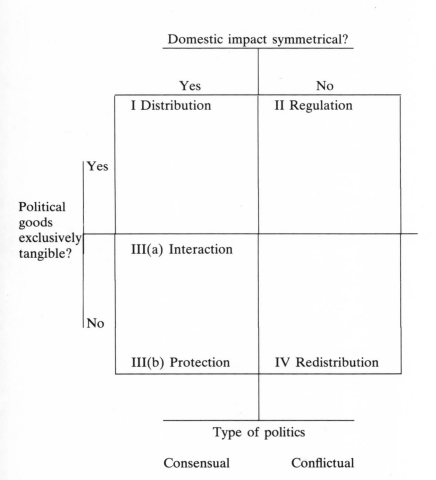

FIGURE 2.1

puts it, largely those individuals who, stripped of their institutions, have a highly legitimate, role-engendered claim to participation in the policy process. Hence, the power structure is highly elitist. Team norms prevail as decisions are made which, it is perceived, are such that the impact of the decisions will be symmetrical for all citizens of the state: in a crisis (protection) the external event or actor is thought to be uniformly threatening; in non-crisis circumstances no internal resources are involved and there are no short-run political consequences. Occurrences of the latter type are obviously likely to be rare. When they do occur, they will occur most often when states are attempting to facilitate the exchange of information and diplomats, to regularize the exchange of mail, and so on, or otherwise enhance state interaction. Like distributive politics, the politics of protection and interaction are more consensual than conflictual. Unlike distributive politics, protective–interactive politics involve values which are non-tangible. Interaction issues do not raise domestic resource allocation questions. Events properly classed in the arena of protection by their very nature pertain to the core values of the society.

Finally, there is the fourth arena, termed by Lowi redistributive. Like the regulative arena, politics are conflictual. Indeed, they are highly conflictual. In this political game, the power structure includes both elite and counter-elite. The primary political units either are, or are potentially, classes, movements, generations, nationalities or other large social aggregates. (The phrase "are potentially" is not intended to beg the question but merely to indicate that counter-elites will speak in the name of, or otherwise attempt to represent themselves as the defenders of the interests of, large social aggregates. In practice they may not succeed in mobilizing these social aggregates – often because the conflict is vigorously suppressed by the elite.) The political goods at issue are both tangible and non-tangible/symbolic. Consequently, disaggregation is exceedingly limited and difficult. The values at stake are less central to the core values of a well-integrated society than those at stake in "protective" questions. The cleavage is often, to paraphrase Wallace Sayre, between those who provide the money and those who demand the services; some kinds of redistributive issues – limited wars for instance – can be even more acutely conflictual because the focal division is between those who demand the money and those who provide the services.

THREE CASE STUDIES

With this scheme in mind let us now see how the notion of issue-area based partitions of the policy process can be coupled with that of international–national linkages to facilitate our understanding of "internal" politics, and transferred from the American pluralist context to Yugoslavia. Only briefest mention will be made of the protective–interactive arena (arena III) since it is the policy process we most associate with reactions to external events – though I think it fair to ask whether the existence of the political system is properly classified as a foreign policy matter. For completeness, however, let it be said that in 1948, when Stalin attempted to bring down the Tito regime, the Yugoslav decisional process, as far as I know, reaffirmed the general notion that crisis politics is the same the world around. The decision was taken by a highly legitimate elite acting as individuals, not as institutional representatives, and team norms obtained. (The major exception to this statement of course is that a few Yugoslav communist leaders – Andrija Hebrang being the most well known – opted for Stalin and the Cominform rather than for Tito and Yugoslavia.)

Let us focus instead on three less well known incidents which correspond to the cells in the paradigm we normally associate with domestic politics. The second incident was prompted by forces originating from outside Yugoslavia and corresponds quite nicely to the political process we associate with the arena of regulation (arena II). I refer to what in Yugoslavia is known as the road affair. Over the years the IBRD has provided considerable funds to Yugoslavia for infra-structural support. One form this support has taken has been the provision of extensive funds for road construction, generally amounting to 40 per cent of the total cost. "The priority list of roads to be financed by a foreign creditor is usually formulated after a preliminary agreement between the federal government and republics has been reached."[8] On this occasion, in 1969, that procedure was not followed completely. Moreover, the substantive outcome was one in which identifiable actors were indulged and others were denied. Specifically the Slovenians, who, from several newspaper accounts,[9] had evidently thought they were to be among the recipients of funds from the IBRD, were not included. (It should be noted that in 1969 virtually every tourist coming to Yugoslavia by car entered the country through Slovenia.) What appears to have happened was that, viewing the individual road projects as entities to be dispensed, the Federal Executive Council of Yugoslavia concluded that some of the projects could be funded while others could not. Probably because Slovenia was the most developed republic it was decided that, if a project had to be excluded, it was most appropriate that it be the Slovenian one which would not receive IBRD funds. Just as some get liquor licenses in Ann Arbor and some do not, some Yugoslavs were indulged and some were not, and the conflictual politics that implies rapidly became manifest. *Politika* nicely summarizes what happened:

> The decision of the Federal Executive Committee . . . has evoked unbroken waves of protest in all regions of Slovenia. At extraordinary sessions of *opština* assemblies, (in which republic and federal representatives and representatives of social political organizations took part) *opštinas* of Celje, Sentjur and Slovenske Konjice decided to send protest letters to the Republic Assembly, the Republic Executive Committee and the Federal Executive Committee demanding that the decision be changed as soon as possible, in view of the great importance of the road for the economy not only of Slovenia but for the whole country as well. Similar protest meetings [*protestni mitinzi*] are being held in many *kolektivs* along the Slovenian coast . . . and today before noon extraordinary sessions of the *opština* assemblies in Slovenska Bistrica, Maribor, Ajdovščina and Nova Gorica, also led to very sharp protests and even to proposals that the Slovenian federal representatives resign if the FEC's decision is not changed.[10]

An international–national linkage had set off a process resembling in many respects regulatory politics as usually depicted by the pressure group theorists. This result was illustrated vividly by the assessment of the affair given by Edvard Kardelj (a Slovene who was for more than thirty years one of the most influential Yugoslav leaders):

> In recent years we have in fact been witnesses to a growing wave of various pressures. . . . For a time most of the pressures were in the framework of our political system or at least within certain limits of tolerance. . . . In a sense the highway campaign was the straw that broke the camel's back. . . . Now let us answer the assertion that the methods were condemned in a sweeping manner, that pressure supposedly already existed, and that the meetings of the *opština* assemblies in which the highway dispute was taken under consider-

ation constituted a normal form of democratic expression of opinion. . . . It is not merely meetings of *opština* assemblies that are involved but above all what preceded them and followed them.[11]

In the road affair a resource extracted from the outside initiated a process which resulted in a regulatory decision in which groups were deprived. The substantive and procedural dimension of that decision in turn set into motion a process which, while initially almost classically illustrative of pressure group politics, had *incipiently* all the qualities of politics in the arena of redistribution: an ethnically cohesive mass available for mobilization, a counter-elite willing to advocate the dissolution of Yugoslavia, and high conflict.

By contrast, the second episode,[12] the burgeoning of nationalism in Croatia in 1970–1 which culminated in the November 1971 student strike at Zagreb University, was an event in which all those attributes were actually present. While the story warrants being told in far greater detail,[13] it suffices here to recount enough of it to grasp the issues and the nature of political process. For a combination of reasons, a recrudescence of Croatian national awareness took place in the 1970s. The reasons included the impact of reforms adopted in the mid 1960s, the genuine devolution of political power from the Federation to the republics, the low birth rate of the Croatian population, and the increased linkages to the outside world. By 1970–1, the national awareness had begun to be harnessed by potential counter-elites in the Croat cultural organization, Matica Hrvatska, and by those among the more nationalistically inclined leadership in the League of Communists of Croatia, Miko Tripalo and Savka Dapčević-Kucar in particular. A focus of the discontent was the foreign currency regime which provided that only a small fraction (10 per cent) of hard currency earnings could be retained by the enterprise that earned the *valuta,* the remainder being deposited in the federal banks located in Belgrade, the federal capital and the capital of Serbia. Croatians perceived this practice as exceedingly discriminatory. Here was a typical instance of a cleavage between those who demand the money and those who provide the services. People from Croatia, the Croatians generally (many ethnic Croats abroad are from Bosnia), represent a disproportionately large fraction of those working abroad and sending remissions back to the country. A disproportionately large share of Croatian industry is highly export-oriented, and a disproportionately high share of foreign tourist expenditures occurs in Croatia.

This discontent came to a climax in the fall of 1971, while Tito was in the US negotiating to increase the amount of American investment in the Yugoslav economy. In November 1971, students in Zagreb went on strike in protest against the foreign exchange system. There then followed in quick order a major confrontation between Tito and the Croatian leadership, the purge of the Croatian leadership, and the arrest and incarceration of hundreds of Croatian nationalists. Tito was subsequently to declare that if he had not moved vigorously "shooting and civil war would perhaps have started in six months time and you know what that would have meant."[14]

Whether civil war or shooting would have occurred or not we, of course, will never know. What we can say is that this was one of the defining events in the history of communist Yugoslavia, an event which bore all the earmarks of the conflictual politics associated with the redistributive arena (arena IV). If the result was not civil war, the actors in the process nevertheless were clearly the large social aggregates of which great socio-political dramas are made. Indeed, there were many public utterances, most importantly by Savka Dapčević-Kucar and Miko Tripalo of the Croatian party leadership, referring to the emergence of a Croatian national mass *movement* – thus evoking the first South Slav national awakening, the Illyrian movement. There existed a counter elite made up of Croatian nationalists outside the Croatian communist leadership who were sufficiently powerful that they could demand that the Croatian communist leadership join them if it wished to retain their support. In the words of Dražen Budiša, the President of the Zagreb Union of Students, the political leadership of Croatia must "place itself at the head of the emerging movement. Our communist leadership, provided that it desires to be this in the future, must not settle accounts with our movement concerning a different approach to political tactics."[15] There were not merely off-the-record mumblings – as there had been in the road affair – to the effect that Croatia would be better off outside the Federation, but public demands of which the following were representative: "We wish to free Croatia of her colonial position"; "The Socialist Republic of Croatia as a state [should] be admitted to the United Nations"; "Let us form a National Bank and immediately appoint its governor and let us send him to Washington for credits"; "We will no longer give our foreign exchange resources"; "The free utilization of foreign exchange resources . . . would make it possible for Croatia to achieve a growth rate of 12–15 per cent and to catch up with Sweden in many respects in its economic development during the coming ten years."[16] In short, Josip Vrhovec, Secretary of the Executive Committee of the League of Communists of Croatia, was not engaging in hyperbole when he declared that this was "a counter-revolution, . . . founded on the concept of a national movement."[17]

The final incident is a much less portentous one. It illustrates how an event originating in the external environment can set in motion the kind of pork-barrel politics which in the United States we associate with the low conflict, distributive arena (arena I). In 1972, a small $7.5 million grant under the United Nations development plan was given to Yugoslavia for the 1972–6 period. The problem faced by the Yugoslav decision makers was as obvious as it was real: how should the funds be allocated? The kind of politics predicted for the distributive arena envisages a process resulting in a low-conflict, relatively consensual outcome in which all those who matter politically are cut in. I know of nothing to suggest that the decision taken was controversial. It may have been, but I saw nothing in the Yugoslav press to suggest that it was – whereas other cases that were controversial were widely reported in the press. The decision itself can only be described as inspired. To appreciate fully the decision, the reader must bear in mind a few elementary facts about Yugoslavia. First, there is considerable asymmetry in the level of development among the republics and autonomous regions. In 1970, annual gross social product per capita – a concept differing slightly from gross national product per capita – was US $999 for Yugoslavia as a whole and for Serbia proper (Vojvodina and Kosovo are part of the Socialist Republic of Serbia). Among the republics the range extended from 182 per cent of the Yugoslav mean for Slovenia and 123 per cent for Croatia, to 65 per cent, 68 per cent, and 73 per cent for Montenegro, Macedonia, and Bosnia–Hercegovina respectively. Of the two autonomous regions, Vojvodina had an average income per capita of 119 per cent of the Yugoslav mean, while Kosovo was by far the poorest of all the major political units, with only 34 per cent of the national average – a mere $340 per capita (see Table 2.2). The republics also vary considerably in population. There are three relatively large republics: Bosnia–Hercegovina, Croatia, and Serbia proper. According to the 1971 census, Bosnia–Hercegovina had a population of approximately 3,746,000; the population of Croatia was roughly 4,426,000, and that of Serbia, 5,250,000. Macedonia and Slovenia were roughly similar in size: 1,647,000 and 1,712,500 respectively. Montenegro is the smallest republic with only slightly more than half a million population, while the populations of Vojvodina and Kosovo were calculated at 1,953,000 and 1,244,000, respectively.

TABLE 2.2   *Yugoslav gross social product per capita and population by republic*

Republic or autonomous region	1970 national annual gross social product per capita (%)[a]	Population 1971 census (000's)[b]	UN grant allocation (%)[c]
Bosnia–Hercegovina	73	3,746	20
Croatia	123	4,426	18
Macedonia	68	1,647	9
Montenegro	65	530	8.5
Slovenia	182	1,725	8.5
Serbia (proper)	100	5,250	18
Vojvodina SR Serbia	119	1,953	7
Kosovo	34	1,244	11

SOURCES: (a) Ivo Vinski, "Društveni proizvod Jugoslavije i zemalja istoka i zapada" *Ekonomski pregled*, nos. 10–11 (October–November 1971) p. 27.
(b) *Statistički godišnjak, 1972*.
(c) *Borba*, 27 January 1972.

Imagine yourself in a committee composed of representatives of each republic and region. You are presented with the following allocation and are invited quickly to present an alternative which appeals to a larger coalition than does the following. As reported in *Borba*,[18] Bosnia–Hercegovina received 20 per cent; Croatia, 18 per cent; Macedonia, 9 per cent; Montenegro, 8.5 per cent; Slovenia, 8.5 per cent; Serbia proper, 18 per cent; and the autonomous regions, Vojvodina and Kosovo, received 7 per cent and 11 per cent respectively. Slovenia, with two and a half times the per capita income and population of Montenegro, received the same share as Montenegro, thus subsidizing the smaller republic while remaining on a level of hypothetical parity with it. All the republics received more than the autonomous region of Vojvodina. Vojvodina and Kosovo together got as much as did either Serbia proper or Croatia. Croatia and Serbia received the same amount. Greater Serbia (the Socialist Republic of Serbia), on the other hand, obtained twice that of Croatia, which was in turn offset by the fact that Bosnia–Hercegovina – so dear to the heart of the Croatian nationalists – obtained the largest share of all.

Consequently, while relatively speaking there were both winners and losers, no one was totally deprived;[19] rather, everyone who counted politically was cut in. Indeed the distribution was keenly sensitive to what may fairly be said to be the rules of the game in Yugoslavia: symbolic parity for republics; regard for Kosovo as a special case; greater benefits and roles for republics than for autonomous regions, except with regard to development funds for Kosovo; and parity for Croatia and Serbia. As a political good, money has the marvelous quality of being readily disaggregated – and hence the politics of distribution.

OUTLOOK FOR THE 1980S

What are we to make of these tales? What relevance do they have for current Yugoslav politics and for the ties between international–national linkages and Yugoslav policy processes in the 1980s? Let me propose an interpretation of Yugoslav institutional evolution in the 1970s which relates to the issue-based paradigm we have been discussing. Briefly put, the institutional developments of the 1970s entailed, first, what many (myself included) have described as a return to Leninist symbols in the early 1970s. This involved in particular a recentralization of the party through a purge of republic party organizations and the press as well as a blurring of the distinction between the League of Communists of Yugoslavia (LCY) and the state. Second and subsequently, several steps were taken beginning in 1973–4 with the new constitution, the delegate system, and the evolving notion of the State Presidency, to strengthen the ethnically defined consociational basis of Yugoslav decision-making. The constitutional changes of the 1970s need not be detailed here.[20] It suffices instead to stress that virtually all the institutional changes related to the state[21] and the LCY taken in the 1970s and in the period immediately since Tito's death in May 1980 have been infused with the spirit of ethnic consociationalism. Thus, the State Presidency is composed currently of eight members, one from each of the six republics and the two autonomous regions, and it is a good bet that the LCY Presidium, currently made up of two members selected by the republic party organization and apportioned on the basis of the nationality "key," will be composed of eight members after the 1982 XII LCY Congress.

From the perspective of the paradigm articulated here, these steps may be seen as efforts to minimize the occurrence of either of the two conflictual policy processes, namely the redistributive or, what is not so obvious, the regulatory. In particular these steps had two effects of relevance to the paradigm. First, it is an open question whether, had an external threat like Stalin's 1948 attack on Tito occurred in 1970, there existed the national integration which the paradigm requires for crisis behavior to correspond to the process I associate with the arena of protection and interaction. By 1975 such cohesion had been reimposed. The result is that it appears that in the early 1980s a crisis prompted by external events would produce decisions taken by a highly legitimate elite acting as individuals in which team norms obtained. Thanks in part to the Soviet invasion of Afghanistan, the old question, "What will happen to Yugoslavia if it isn't threatened from the outside?" has been rendered at least temporarily moot.

Indeed, during the first year since Tito's death, Moscow seemed to share this perception. Despite Soviet–Yugoslav polemics over Afghanistan and the ominous implications for Yugoslavia of a Soviet invasion of a non-aligned communist country outside Eastern Europe, the USSR has been assiduous in its efforts to assure the Yugoslavs about its good intentions. Brezhnev attended Tito's funeral (former US President Carter did not), and Moscow and Belgrade have signed a major ten-year trade agreement. Moscow evidently calculates that direct threats only serve to unify Yugoslavia.

The consociational strategy implemented in the party and state institutional changes of the 1970s, and of the early post-Tito era as well, may likewise be viewed as an effort to minimize the recurrence of (type IV) redistributive politics which the Croatian events of 1971 exemplified. The effort was successful in the 1970s. It was manifestly more difficult for movements or other large social actors to be mobilized in the mid and late 1970s than it was in the early 1970s. Likewise it appears it will be correspondingly more difficult in the 1980s. Whether external actors will take acts to encourage redistributive political processes within Yugoslavia in the 1980s remains to be seen.

International–national linkage issues sufficient to threaten tangible and symbolic values in Yugoslav society may, however, emerge in the absence of external prodding. For a combination of reasons, Yugoslavia's economic situation at the outset of the 1980s is such as to raise the possibility that hard choices will be forced on the Yugoslav political elites that will bear intimately on important symbolic values in society. Decisions about trade orientation, for instance, often in practice bear intimately on the distribution of important symbolic values in a society. Classes, regions, and ethnic groups benefit differentially from trade orientations not only financially but with respect to the distribution of these values. In Yugoslavia in the late 1960s and early 1970s, for instance, the pressure by Belgrade on Slovenia for its putatively excessive trade orientation to the West stemmed from a calculus shared by elites in Ljubljana and Belgrade that the extent of Yugoslavia's linkages with Western Europe had a bearing on the nature of regime–society relations in Yugoslavia. The quarrel was about values, not empirical projections, with the "technocratic" Slovene leadership viewing a more pluralist Yugoslavia more favorably than did the LCY leadership as a whole.

Yugoslavia also faces the cumulative consequences of an enormous trade deficit in the 1980s. That deficit is still largely with the West but has been exacerbated by a large and growing oil import bill from the Soviet Union (which supplies slightly less than half of Yugoslavia's oil imports) and the Middle East, notably from Iraq. The result is that the Yugoslav external debt at the beginning of the 1980s was in excess of US $15 billion. Measures the leadership takes to ameliorate the situation will affect key groups differentially. By the end of 1980 there were already growing signs that the domestic and external economic situation was providing the grounds for major disputes over tangible goods. These could take on the symbolic dimensions associated with major redistributive conflicts. The choice of means for coping with the economic situation – that is, whether to emphasize "market" or "state socialist" strategies – will bear significantly on the course of Yugoslav regime–society relations in the 1980s. Already there have been nationalist undertones in statements made about alternative economic strategies. Mitja Ribičić, the former Prime Minister, stated bluntly in December 1980 that the "working class is no longer united":

That part of the working class which somehow has an interest in inflation, in not working too much, is in favor of an 'easier policy line.' Another part of the working class, however, is no longer ready to share the burden of those who work badly. This is true of all strata of our society. The policy of economic stabilization has become the salient in the demarcation line at which the class struggle is being waged: Should we accept a statist, centralistic distribution of means or should everybody [rely] . . . instead on what he creates himself.[22]

This is not, I stress, to suggest that Yugoslav elites are prone to take decisions about the economy in general or international–national linkages in particular which are fundamentally redistributive in their consequences. Rather, if the analysis of Yugoslav institutional responses to the Croatian events of 1971 is correct, we should witness mighty efforts by the Yugoslav leadership in the 1980s to avoid changes in international–national linkages having such consequences. I would argue, however, that should redistributive processes of this genre nevertheless occur, we can expect the kind of conflictual movement involved in class and/or ethnic based politics as projected for the redistributive arena and exemplified by the Croatian crisis in 1971.

The consociational strategy may be seen not just as a reaction to the Croatian crisis of 1971 but also to the Slovenian road affair. In 1969–71 there were only two occasions when the Presidium of the LCY discussed matters within a republic: the Slovenian road affair and the Croatian crisis. The movement toward a greater emphasis on consociationalism reflects two things. First, there is a realization that given the nationalist "key," classically pluralist practices – the arena of protection – constantly run the danger of exacerbating what LaPalombara calls the pluralistic (that is, ethnic cleavage) structure of Yugoslav society.[23] Second, the road affair was the exception that proved the rule. The road affair was the most striking instance in the years following the 1966 economic reforms in which the Yugoslav leadership opted for economic rationality – making hard choices where some are winners and some losers – rather than politically attractive but economically irrational solutions, for example, the building of several inefficient sea ports or shipbuilding companies which cannot compete internationally.

Ribičić's remarkable interview in December 1980 suggests strongly that the current setup is designed to thwart the dangerous recurrence of economic rationality. "Recently," he laments, "we have lacked a sufficiently firm, strong federal government . . . ; the republics influence it much more than is natural in the present situation. The federal Executive Council should be quarreling with every republic.

[Question: Just as when you were the premier?] Almost like that. I was quarreling with the Slovenes about the road, . . . with Vojvodina about agricultural produce prices, with Serbia about subsidies to Crvena Zastava [the major producer of Yugoslav automobiles], and with the Croatians about extra budgetary spending."[24] Thus far, however, government in post-Tito Yugoslavia has been government as usual, what Ribičić terms a "policy of compromise" and we have termed the politics of disaggregation. There will be pressures for economic rationality and for linking developmental priorities to allocative rationality. These, however, will come primarily from external actors with significant stakes in Yugoslav development: the US, the USSR, West Germany, and the World Bank – and only rarely by choice from Yugoslav leaders like Ribičić. They will prefer to choose principles for allocating resources from such external actors in a disaggregative and consociational manner – by six or eight shares for instance – in order to minimize conflict, even if grossly uneconomical development decisions result.

Unlike the 1970s, however, the flow of funds may not be abundant. The German government may increase its investments in Yugoslavia in order to encourage the repatriation of some of the hundreds of thousands of Yugoslav workers in West Germany (there are a million Yugoslav workers and their families in Western Europe); otherwise the prospects are not bright for an increase in externally generated development funds. Rather, the global economic situation, Yugoslavia's inability to compete effectively in West European markets, and its burgeoning oil deficit may create the kind of zero-sum economic environment which obligates Yugoslav elites to identify unmistakable economic winners and losers within Yugoslavia. Given the pluralistic, ethnically based cleavages in Yugoslavia, such regulatory decisions may pose prospects for conflict involving the large social groups associated with redistributive politics.

NOTES AND REFERENCES

1. Samuel P. Huntington, "Transnational Organizations in World Politics," *World Politics*, April 1973, pp. 364–5.
2. By 1980, growing external debt rendered it difficult for Yugoslavia to obtain foreign loans.
3. Alvin Z. Rubinstein, *Yugoslavia and the Non-Aligned World* (Princeton University Press, 1970) p. 73.
4. Ibid.
5. William Zimmerman, "Issue Area and Foreign Policy Process: A Research Note in Search of a General Theory," *American Political Science Review*, 67 (December 1973) pp. 1204–12.
6. Ibid.
7. Theodor Lowi, "American Business, Public Policy, Case Studies and Political Theory," *World Politics*, 16 (July 1964) pp. 677–715; Lowi, "Making Democracy Safe for the World: National Politics," in

James N. Rosenau (ed.), *Domestic Sources of Foreign Policy* (New York: Free Press, 1967) pp. 11–51.

8. "Slovenians Oppose Government Decisions on Road Building," *Radio Free Europe, Research,* 1 August 1969, p. 2.

9. See, for instance, *Borba,* 23 May 1969, and the weekly *Ekonomska Politika,* 20 January 1969.

10. *Politika,* 31 July 1969.

11. *Kommunist,* 2, 9, 23, 30 October 1969, as translated by Foreign Broadcast Information Service (FBIS), *Daily Report,* 21 November 1969, no. 226, supplement 16, pp. 2–3.

12. It should be stressed that the dispute over the use of foreign currency earnings stems primarily from internal Croatian developments. I have treated it here as an international linkage since the resources are drawn from outside the country and the primary source of the earnings, Croatian workers abroad in Western Europe, are a linkage group.

13. For greater detail, see Fred Singleton, *Twentieth Century Yugoslavia* (New York: Columbia University Press, 1976) pp. 224–7; and William Zimmerman, "National–International Linkages in Yugoslavia: The Political Consequences of Openness," in Jan F. Triska and Paul M. Cocks (eds), *Political Development in Eastern Europe* (New York: Praeger Publishers, 1977) pp. 356–7.

14. *Borba,* 19 December 1971. See also Edvard Kardelj, *Borba,* 22 December 1971: "We were well on the way to being driven by opportunism and nationalism into that same situation in which certain other socialist countries found themselves at moments of political crises, and then experiencing the same consequences."

15. *Studentski list,* no. 26 (26 November 1971), 1971, p. 3. Italics added.

16. The "colonial position" quotation stems from Budiša. The UN advocacy and National Bank citations are from Hrvoje Šošić (*Politika,* 1 November 1971) while the quotations on the foreign exchange are taken from Vladimir Veselica as reported in *Borba,* 21 November 1971.

17. *Borba,* 11 January 1972.

18. *Borba,* 27 January 1972.

19. The relatively deprived, clearly, were Macedonia and Serbia.

20. Steven L. Burg, "Decision-Making in Yugoslavia," *Problems of Communism,* March–April 1980, pp. 1–20, provides a detailed description of those changes.

21. At the enterprise level, the changes gave greater meaning to the term self-management. These changes are described in Laura D. Tyson, *The Yugoslav Economic System and Its Performance in the 1970s* (Berkeley: Institute of International Studies, 1980) pp. 3–30.

22. *Start,* 10 December 1980, as reported in Slobodan Stankovic, "'Dogmatic' Slovene Leader Gives a 'Liberal' Interview," *Radio Free Europe Research,* 19 December 1980, pp. 2–3.

23. Joseph LaPalombara, "Monoliths or Plural Systems? Through Conceptual Lenses Darkly," *Studies in Comparative Communism,* vol. 8, no. 3 (Autumn 1975) p. 325.

24. *NIN,* 14 December 1980, and translated by FBIS, 29 December 1980, p. 126.

3 Romanian Foreign Policy in the 1980s: Domestic–foreign Policy Linkages

RONALD H. LINDEN

LINKAGE POLITICS IN EASTERN EUROPE

Students of Eastern Europe have always been students of linkage politics. How could they be otherwise? If one accepts James Rosenau's original definition of linkage as "any recurrent sequence of behavior that originates in one system and is reacted to in another," we have a concise description of the Soviet–East European interstate system of relations.[1] Studies of these states have, for the most part, not elaborated theoretical formulations of this relationship, especially as it relates to foreign policies; but they have been highly sensitive nevertheless to the permeability of East European borders.[2] This has typically taken the form of assessments of the impact of one or another externally-based phenomenon on the East European states. The "other system" in which these phenomena originate has usually been the Soviet Union.[3] More recently, studies of the region have begun to assess the impact of various international milieux and changes therein on the East European states.[4]

The linkage concept, as originally described by Rosenau, did not mandate an international-to-national direction for these linkages, that is, that one should only examine the impact of internationally-based happenings on national systems, but it was heavily tilted in that direction. Rosenau's three basic linkage "processes" were all cast as reactions to externally based "outputs" which impinged on the national state as "inputs." This dynamic, in Rosenau's scheme, would produce either a "penetrative" process, in which "members of one

47

polity serve as participants in the political processes of another"; a "reactive" process, characterized by "recurrent and similar boundary-crossing reactions rather than by the sharing of authority"; or an "emulative" process where "the input is not only a response to the output but takes essentially the same form as the output."[5] Though Rosenau sought to put a sharper point on this investigative tool with the notion of foreign policy as "adaptive behavior,"[6] and in later writings both buried and praised the original linkage notion,[7] "the linkage concept," as he says, "did not die."[8] And in terms of direction of causal pathways, both in his own later work and in those studies with a significant debt to either the linkage or adaptation idea, the modal view was international-to-national.[9]

The fact that few researchers have chosen to look through the other end of the telescope may have been due in part to the dim theoretical light cast by the linkage concept or by other methodological problems, such as a dizzying proliferation of categories and possible combinations of categories.[10] But foreign policy studies in recent years have demonstrated a greater concern with the domestic-to-international causal path, even if in investigating it they have not employed a specific linkage framework. Approaches such as bureaucratic politics,[11] perceptual analysis,[12] and the aggregate study of national attributes[13] have attracted a number of adherents. Though the results of these approaches have been mixed, especially for small states,[14] the idea of examining internal–external linkages with both eyes open has seemed to take hold.

The last redoubt of minimizing national-to-international linkages has been East European studies.[15] However regrettable, this should not be terribly surprising. The region has been dominated politically, economically and militarily for thirty-five years by a strong, suspicious major power. It is, in fact, only in the recent past that these states have moved from what could be characterized as a "penetrated" process to one approaching the "reactive" or "emulative" pattern. Nor does it seem likely that the dominant state of the region will be inclined (or forced) in the near future to shed these linkages.

Still, the change in "process" that has occurred – or, in more familiar terms, the erosion, polycentrism or Balkanization (in some ways quite literally) of the Soviet empire – has been great enough and has affected these states' international relations significantly enough to cause some students of Eastern Europe to reexamine the familiar assumptions concerning external-to-internal linkages in this region. While not excluding the impact of internationally-based phenomena, research on the region, it is increasingly evident, now has to be alive to the possibilities of flows in the other direction, that is, from the internal milieu of the East European states to its international environment. For foreign policy analysis the question this suggests is: given demonstrable differences in these states' international behavior, what mixture of international and domestic factors accounts for these differences? This question has been addressed in a few studies in a comparative mode and in occasional case studies.[16] The present work falls in the latter category. It is an effort to explore the range of domestic and international factors which have stimulated and allowed Romanian foreign policy to take the unique course it has. The Romanian case is an especially interesting one because of the range of differences its policies have shown from those of its East European allies and from those of the Soviet Union. This is not to argue that only the Romanian case merits attention among the East European states – or even that only those states whose policies differ from their allies merit such attention. On the contrary, the factors explaining why a state "stays in line" need investigation as much as those underlying foreign policy "deviance." While Romanian foreign policy is certainly distinctive, it is precisely because it has emerged out of a setting both similar and dissimilar to that of its allies that the "linkages" between its national and international behavior need to be examined.

BACKGROUND

Since the mid-1960s, the Romanian Socialist Republic has pursued a foreign policy strikingly at variance with the policies of its socialist allies, including the Soviet Union. In terms of both its international interactions, (that is, trade, visits, agreements) and its positions on key international issues, the Romanian government has executed a foreign policy characterized variously by analysts as "dissident," "partially aligned," "independent," and "deviant."[17] From its early opposition to supranational planning in Comecon through its vigorous condemnation of Soviet-led actions against Czechoslovakia and Soviet-backed Vietnamese actions against Cambodia, to its consistent cultivation and improvement of relations with the People's Republic of China, Romania has been out of step with Moscow and its smaller Warsaw pact allies. Its trade patterns have been consistently more oriented toward noncommunist nations, developed and developing, than any of its allies save, on occasion, Poland. On the party level its outspoken support of national party prerogatives in Western and Eastern Europe and in Asia has also put it conspicuously distant from both the CPSU and the other East European parties. At the beginning of the 1980s, the Romanians seem as fervent as ever in the delineation and affirmation of the conceptual bases of their foreign policy. These include the following:

1. The Romanian national state, as part of the full exercise of its sovereignty, is the sole determiner of the nature, pace and direction of Romanian economic development. Economic sovereignty cannot be separated from national sovereignty, which itself cannot be "limited" in theory or practice.[18] In addition, the modern nation is a fundamental, enduring force in the contemporary world and will continue to have paramount significance in world politics for the foreseeable future.[19]

2. Each communist party has the right and obligation to determine the most appropriate manner of building socialism in accordance with its specific national conditions. There can be no "leading center" or superior and subordinate parties, and no parties can be "expelled" for pursuing distinctive policies.[20]

3. In pursuing their development plans, states need to take full advantage of the "scientific and technological revolution" and therefore must be free to have relations with all states "regardless of social system" without discrimination. "The socialist international division of labor cannot mean isolation."[21]

4. The existing military situation, both conventional and nuclear, is detrimental to the security of all states, especially the small and medium-sized states. Hence genuine nuclear disarmament and conventional arms reduction are crucial. In addition, the bifurcation of the European continent into military blocs must end.[22]

5. The international political and, especially, economic order needs to be restructured in order to improve the situation of the developing countries. Since it is itself a developing socialist state, Romania needs to develop more broadly and more rapidly than the industrialized states. It needs to pursue multiple economic contacts with all states, and it is deserving of special treatment and assistance from other states, including its socialist allies.[23]

The persistence and strength of these principles in Romanian foreign policy has meant a continuation of ardent, if often less spectacular, deviance from Soviet preferences in foreign policy. The most significant deviation in Romanian foreign policy in the last decade, for example, has been the shift in Romania's self-definition from a socialist country to that of a socialist *developing* country. This leads Romania to support more strongly than any of its allies the movement for a New International Economic Order, that is, one in which the needs of the less developed and small and medium-sized states would be more adequately served. This "democratization of international relations" can only take place, of course, at the expense of the superpowers, both of whom have come in for criticism for their lack of support for, or outright resistance to, the idea of a new order.[24] In 1976 Romania secured "guest" status (along with Switzerland, the Philippines and Portugal) at the Conference of the Nonaligned States, joined the Group of 77, and participated in the UN Conference on Trade and Development (UNCTAD) "side by side with other developing countries."[25]

In certain areas Bucharest seems to have recognized that discretion is the better part of valor. In early 1980 the Romanians reacted in a restrained if distinctive manner to the Soviet invasion of Afghanistan. Instead of the emotional rhetoric which followed the invasion of Czechoslovakia, or the explicit condemnation which followed the Vietnamese invasion of Cambodia, Bucharest reaffirmed its standard condemnation of policies of force or "*dictat*," of interference in the internal affairs of other states and of dividing the world into spheres of influence or hegemony. Nicolai Ceauşescu, chief of the Romanian Communist Party (RCP), called for "unflinching respect for the right of each nation to develop itself freely, independently, to choose independently its path of social and economic development, without any kind of interference from outside."[26] When the United Nations General Assembly passed a resolution (by a vote of 104–18–18) "deploring" the intervention and calling for "the immediate, unconditional and total withdrawal of the foreign troops from Afghanistan," the Romanians did not participate in the vote.[27] At the same time, however, and since that time, the Romanians have reiterated the need for "respect by all states for the independence and sovereignty of Afghanistan and for the Afghan people's right to choose their development path themselves, without any outside interference."[28] Thus in this case, the Romanians were conspicuous by their lack of support for the invasion, and by their forceful, if indirect, criticism of it.

LINKAGE: STIMULATING AND ENABLING
FACTORS IN ROMANIAN FOREIGN POLICY

Will the Romanians be able to sustain their deviant foreign policy for a third decade? The answer to this will depend upon a mixture of complex factors, operating both inside and outside Romania. While for analytic purposes we can assess the factors crucial to the persistence of the present course of Romanian foreign policy in terms of their internal and external dimensions, it would be more consistent with the aim of this volume and the philosophy underlying the linkage approach to the comparative study of foreign policy to begin with a distinction between stimulating factors, that is, those which seem to be responsible for producing the foreign policy direction the Romanians have pursued, and enabling factors, those which have allowed it to be pursued. It should of course be recognized that untidy reality often blurs our neat analytic distinctions and we should certainly be alert to factors, internal or external, which may both stimulate and enable Romanian foreign policy to take its unusual course.

ECONOMIC FACTORS

Romanian foreign policy is designed to serve the longstanding and much advertised goal of developing the country "multilaterally."[29] The RCP is committed to achieving industrial development and an urban-based economy by 1990. Since the mid-1960s, Romania has sought in the West much of the technology and "know-how" to make rapid development possible.[30] Romania's pattern of international interactions and trade has been directed at complementing this search and at protecting ideologically its right to do so.[31]

From the strictly economic standpoint the future holds uncertain prospects at best. In order to be able to import high technology industrial goods the Romanian economy must be able consistently to earn hard currency through its exports. But despite a general overhauling of foreign trade operations in the last decade, an improvement in trade opportunities (including the granting of MFN by the United States), substantial Western credits, and relatively high – though fluctuating – domestic growth rates, the Romanians' ability to provide exportables to the West remains limited in both amount and diversity.[32] Expanding the export of foodstuffs and industrial consumer goods is still crucial to the country's ability to continue to run deficits in its importing of machines and, increasingly, raw materials. This need is likely to increase as a growing debt to the West has made both creditors and debtors nervous and further financing of trade deficits uncertain.[33] Thus production will have to continue to grow at a time when indications are that the high growth rates of the past decade will be difficult to sustain.[34]

As the most recent (seventh) five-year plan came to an end – and especially after the 1979 and 1980 results came in – the party began pressing both industrial and agricultural sectors for ever greater responsibility, productivity, efficiency and attention to quality and the needs of customers. Before, during and after the Twelfth RCP Congress in November 1979, Ceauşescu engaged in pointed criticism of various enterprises, and of the party cadres involved with them, for delays, waste and other "shortcomings."[35] Taking their cues, virtually all of the leading speakers at the Congress engaged in both criticism and self-criticism, railing against a variety of "bureaucratic manifestations."[36]

The five-year plan for 1981-5 forecasts ambitious economic targets, including an average annual growth rate of 6.7–7.4 per cent, a growth in net industrial production of 9–10 per cent, in agricultural production of 4.5–5.0 per cent, and in foreign trade of 8.5–9.5 per cent. Investments are scheduled to increase by 5.4–6.2 per cent. This is all to be accomplished, moreover, while achieving a 40 per cent *reduction* in energy consumption by 1990. The driving force in this growth is to be labor productivity, which is projected to increase by 7.0–7.5 per cent annually and to account for 80 per cent of overall production increases.[37]

For the Romanians, as for the other East European states, the effects of the worldwide energy squeeze, though somewhat delayed and somewhat less dramatic, have nevertheless spurred the government to push for greater conservation and efficiency, bigger cuts in consumer use of energy, and more intensive searches for both domestic sources of energy and international sources of petroleum. Coal and hydrocarbons currently supply approximately 40 per cent each of Romanian energy needs (the rest is derived primarily from hydroelectric power). The new five-year plan projects a sharp cut in the latter (to 20 per cent by 1985) and an increase in use of the former (to 55 per cent) with small increases elsewhere, including nuclear power. Domestically this will require not only conservation, improved exploitation of existing reserves and discovery of new ones,[38] but also the willingness and ability of Romania's new proletariat both to improve its productivity and efficiency dramatically, and, even more importantly, to continue to pay for the country's economic growth with sacrifices in gains in their standard of living. If the dissatisfaction of the Jiu Valley miners, demonstrably evident in 1977,[39] is an indication of the future, and if the regime should have to redirect substantial resources to meet new domestic demands, some serious questions relating to Romania's foreign policy would be raised. First, such a reallocation would likely further reduce the country's ability to produce quality exportables in sufficient quantity. Second, and perhaps of greater long-term consequence, the government's capacity to satisfy the demands of the workers for better housing and other consumer goods, higher wages, lower prices, etc. is likely to be limited, even with significant budgetary and investment shifting. Failure to meet these demands hurts the credibility of the regime and, as Ceauşescu himself has observed, economic issues can very quickly become political. In recognition of this, the party relentlessly points to recent improvements in the living standards of the workers and peasants, and toward even greater improvements in the next five years.[40] In addition, in particularly critical sectors such as mining, the regime responds relatively quickly and substantively to the demands of the workers.[41] For the most part, though, the RCP has thus far been able to rely to a remarkable degree on nonmaterial incentives and payoffs. But the histories of the other socialist states and signs within Romania itself indicate that the limits of this ability may be nearing.[42]

Whether or not the domestic capacity for deferred gratification is eroding, it is clear already that Romania's ability to continue expanding its trade with developed capitalist countries has peaked. A chronic negative balance of payments situation, rather inelastic parameters in Western markets for Romanian exports, increasing concern over mounting hard currency debts, and worries in Romania about tying the economy to the boom-and-bust cycles of the capitalist countries, are all factors underlying this leveling off.[43] In an attempt perhaps to make up for its sagging ability to continue purchases in the West, the Romanians have increasingly turned to the use of joint production agreements. As of 1976, for example, there were 54 such agreements with the United States, comprising a total second only to that of Poland.[44]

In terms of its exports, Romania has been able to expand greatly its trade with the developing countries, a process which complements its shift in self-identification. This trade has more than tripled since

1960, and according to the new five-year plan, it is expected to account for 25 per cent of Romanian foreign trade by 1985.[45] Not only does this spur Romanian economic growth, especially in the vital machine and semi-manufactured goods sectors, but trade diversification reduces Romanian vulnerability to pressures that might be exerted by its largest customer, the Soviet Union.

A factor of increasing significance will be the ability of the Romanians to continue to secure diversified and dependable energy supplies. Though as noted they foresee a long-term drop in dependence on oil, their immediate need for imported oil – especially in light of economic growth targets – will continue to be significant: fifteen million tons annually, roughly 20 per cent more than the country currently produces.[46] Romania had not been buying Soviet oil until recently, and thus had a head start on its allies who are searching for other suppliers as Moscow reduces the flow and raises the price for what does flow.[47] While this preference for OPEC suppliers did insulate them to some degree from possible Soviet pressure using this particular lever, the Romanians remain dependent on the USSR for a number of other important raw materials such as coking coal and iron ore.[48] Moreover, as all buyers of OPEC oil have found, they are unpleasantly vulnerable to other kinds of often quite unexpected disruptions. The loss of both Iraq and Iran as key suppliers (the latter of an estimated five million tons a year), due to the war between them, sent Romanian diplomats and traders off in search of new supplies.[49]

Almost as crucial as long term planning in Romania has been short term emergency assistance after natural disasters. The widespread flooding of 1970 and 1975 and the devastating earthquake of 1977 were all body blows to the industrial development of the country. If the Romanians had not been able to recover quickly, or if they had been forced to curtail production severely in major sectors of the economy, the capacity of the country to support its deviant foreign policy economically – either through production of exportables or by producing sufficient domestic material payoffs – would have been greatly reduced.[50]

Viewed from the opposite perspective, Romania is also a giver of aid. Since the period 1966–70, when Romanian foreign aid averaged but $40 million per year, aid commitments jumped to an average of $350 million per year for 1971–5, by far the largest in Eastern Europe.[51] Large donors of foreign aid have found that such aid has not often purchased influence, or even good will, but Romanian aid does stimulate the sale of its exports and may benefit the Romanians politically as a supplement to its own "developing country" orientation.

Thus economic factors are both stimulating and enabling. The drive to develop the economy was crucial to producing the original *Drang nach Westen,* and to keeping Romania interested in a variety of contacts and in preserving the broadest possible options. On the other hand, the receptivity of Western markets to Romanian goods, the availability of alternative and cheap energy supplies, and the willingness of the population to forego improvements in living standards allowed both the drive for industrial development, and the foreign policy which supported it, to continue. While this drive is clearly still a goal, the patient domestic environment and the receptive international milieu no longer seem so patient or so receptive as they did at the beginning of the last decade.

POLITICAL FACTORS

Romanian foreign policy is designed to secure for the RCP a degree of national legitimacy by establishing its autonomy vis-à-vis the Soviet Union, by presenting the state as a highly visible, respected and effective international actor, and by characterizing its actions as being squarely within the finest traditions of Romanian diplomatic history, from the time of the Roman empire to the Second World War. It is the party's intention to move close enough to the stove of nationalism to be warmed by it, while avoiding the dangers of being scorched.

Though of course impossible to measure objectively, the party's efforts seem generally successful. One might occasionally hear the view expressed (*sotto voce,* of course) that international visibility has not produced a better life for the country's people,[52] but the political threats to the RCP on this score are minimal. Though there has existed a small dissident movement in Romania, the regime has moved quickly against it using both the carrot (emigration) and the stick (suppression).[53] Firm evidence of any significant opposition at the elite level, that is, a group or faction willing and capable of replacing Ceauşescu and abandoning his policies, is slim, though not nonexistent.[54]

On the contrary, the position of Ceauşescu has grown consistently stronger. He has replaced virtually all significant political actors from the previous regime with people of his own choosing, whose primary political loyalties are to *Conducǎtorul* (the leader) himself.[55] In addition, he has replaced even some of those long associated with Romania's autonomous foreign policy, such as Alexander Bîrlǎdeanu and I. G. Maurer, and has kept potential political rivals insecure with a policy of "rotating" key positions in the party and government.[56] At the same time Ceaușescu himself has assumed leadership of virtually every significant party and state institution in the country: Secretary-General of the Party; President of the Republic – a new position created for him in 1974; and Commander-in-Chief of the Armed Forces. Some of the organs were themselves reorganized to facilitate his personal control: for example, the establishment of the Political Executive Committee in 1965, and especially a Permanent Bureau of this committee in 1974 to replace and circumvent the party Presidium and Central Committee.[57] Finally, the last decade has seen an exploding campaign of glorification of Ceaușescu personally and of his contributions to the social, economic, political and ideological life of the country.[58]

At the local level, cadre support related to foreign policy seems high for reasons similar to those which make Romania's foreign policy popular to the public at large: namely, its anti-Soviet, nationalistic nature. However, there are indications that the party's overall vitality and the present regime's support is becoming increasingly dependent upon its ability to provide material goods and privileges to members and their families. Local leaders are in any case concerned much more with local "economic" issues, for example, the provision of public goods and services, and these concerns vary depending on their region's needs and on their own perception of their role.[59] This should not prevent effective support upward and transmission downward of Romanian foreign policy goals and activities. However, future threats to party coherence could arise from:

(a) the continued growth of a familial and/or personal reward-oriented party;
(b) an increasing recognition of party cadres of the need to de-control and de-centralize in order to meet the country's ambitious development goals; or
(c) the frustrating of the demands of either (a) or (b) by a leadership increasingly desirous of finding scapegoats for the country's stagnating economy.

Ceaușescu has not spared party cadres from criticism for a number of failings, including too much "unproductive" work and (apparently with a straight face) too much reliance on Bucharest.[60] Recognition of the need to take someone to task was clearly heightened by the turmoil in Poland prior to the imposition of martial law. In September 1980 Ceauşescu said: "Let us see that our leadership bodies, from top to bottom, will also be the genuine representatives of the aspirations of our people, of our working class – the leading class of our socialist society."[61] In October the party issued a decree ordering all cadres to declare the total value of their private assets.[62] Ceauşescu is clearly trying to negotiate the ground between the need to keep the party's loyalty and support, and thus to allow some aspects of a new class to develop, and the danger that excesses in this direction could produce reactions such as those in Poland. Party unity has always been an important part of the Romanian leadership's ability to take and hold foreign policy positions unpopular with its allies.

Other dangers in the political realm lie in the party's obsessive fear and suppression of democratizing reforms, especially as they concern relations between itself and the population. To the degree that party legitimacy pursued through a nationalistic foreign policy needs to be supplemented with the acceptance of greater popular input into the domestic political process, the regime runs the risk of allowing faction-building, even greater pressure for reform, or, quite possibly, public turbulence.[63] The danger therein would stem from the opportunity such a situation would provide for external manipulation and pressure, and/or from the Soviet Union's demonstrated concern over preserving "the leading role of the party" in the states of Eastern Europe. At present, however, the leading role of the RCP is threatened only by the *more* leading role of its General Secretary.

The Romanian government has also successfully capitalized upon the non-Slavic character of the population. Both the Gheorghiu-Dej and Ceauşescu regimes have sought to negotiate the narrow ground between constructive, supportive Romanian nationalism, for example, pride in Romanian culture, history, accomplishments and international role, and destructive, dangerous anti-Russian expressions. The RCP executed a broad de-Slavification campaign in the early sixties and Ceauşescu himself was able to capitalize on post-1968 anti-Soviet sentiment.[64] The 1970s provided no similar crises, but the regime still profits by a strong identification with the past and present Romanian nation.[65]

There are two groups whose response to efforts at Romanianization of the country can be considered skeptical at best, hostile at worst. The Hungarian minority, almost 8 per cent of the population according to the last census,[66] presumably regards the independent aspects of Romanian foreign policy as positively as do the majority Romanians. However, the other edge of this nationalistic sword has been de-Magyarization. Hungarians have found themselves alternatively banned and blessed by the regime and are not above casting public appeals for support to attentive ears in Budapest and elsewhere.[67] If anti-regime political factions based on opposition to international actions or domestic policy are not available for Soviet manipulation, a large resentful ethnic minority represents a major potential source of opposition and a useful potential lever for external pressure.

The German minority, though small (1.6 per cent) and evidently more interested in leaving Romania than in improving its lot within it, represents another potential problem. To the degree that the ethnic Germans' desire to emigrate to West Germany is satisfied by the government, the capacity of the country's economy to perform and grow could be hurt, due to the significant role the German minority plays in Romanian industry.[68] Aware of this and yet relatively free from substantial public pressure from West Germany to allow greater emigration, the regime has been unwilling to tolerate the departure of its German minority in the way that it has allowed emigration of its Jews. Should such pressure be forthcoming, or should the volatile mix of cultural and economic factors significantly raise the level of either Hungarian or German opposition to the regime, the RCP's choices and freedom of action could be significantly constrained.

Thus the internal political situation has acted as a stimulating factor to foreign policy deviance in that the party seeks to increase its national authority through recognition of and pride in its international position and through the explicit identification of the party's policy with the country's historical and cultural tradition. On the other hand, the orthodox domestic political system and the lack of significant public or elite opposition to the regime or to Ceauşescu has enabled the RCP to pursue its international policies with the domestic front secure.

Internationally, the political environment, like the economic one, has been supportive rather than provocative of Romanian foreign policy directions. The Sino-Soviet split, for example, did not cause the Romanians to assert themselves vis-à-vis the Soviets, but early Chinese support for Romanian views on autonomy, development, interparty and interstate relations was helpful, even if limited. Romanian support for similar Chinese views was as instrumental as that which it received; it served to legitimize each party's own way to socialism. However, the beginning of the seventies brought recognition of the clear limits of this mutual support, a substantial increase in Soviet concern over Sino-Romanian interactions, and later, Moscow's formal imprimatur on separate roads to socialism. Romanian-Chinese relations, while remaining cordial, seemed to reach a plateau.[69]

The August 1978 visit of CCP Chairman Hua Guofeng to Romania indicated a return to active Chinese attempts to counter Soviet influence worldwide and, in particular, to keep from losing influence in the Balkans despite Albania's rejection of the policies of the new Chinese Communist Party leadership. From the Romanian perspective the visit was similar to visits from Chinese officials in the past. The Romanians were evidently able to temper Chinese condemnations of the USSR and seemed inclined to let Hua's presence speak for itself as an assertion of national and party sovereignty – that is, until vocal Soviet opposition to the visit provoked explicit restatements of these positions by Bucharest.[70] Though this action, as well as Hua's stop in Romania on his way home from Tito's funeral, were indeed provocative to Moscow, Romania is unlikely to veer far from its course of careful neutrality between the Soviets and the Chinese. Movement in either direction could foreclose the very freedom of action that the Sino-Soviet split has provided the Romanian leadership.[71]

The United States' support for Romanian deviance is similarly limited and, more importantly, of less value to Washington than to Peking. As US priorities in the early seventies shifted toward ensuring the prospering of direct US–Soviet detente, it became clear to the Romanians that American support for Romanian autonomy took second place to the assuring of a low level of tension between the United States and the Soviet Union.[72] Still, it is precisely such a low level of tension which allows the Romanians greater room for independent foreign policy choice. As US–Soviet relations deteriorated at the beginning of this decade, the Romanians have been eagerly trying to mitigate the effect on US–Romanian relations and on overall European detente.[73] In terms of support, the West European states have been quite cautious about incurring Soviet wrath and are unlikely to provide significant support for Romanian challenges to Soviet hegemony. Moreover, full Romanian embrace of either the

United States or China is likely to be deterred by Bucharest's recognition of two other factors. First, each of these powers has had important, though differing, reasons to be critical of Romania's domestic situation: the US, due to erratic, but occasionally quite public, human rights concerns; and China, due to equally erratic but equally public concerns over the purity of the revolution. Although both Washington and Peking now evidence less enthusiasm for their respective causes, these could emerge again and create significant sticking points in their relations with Romania. Second, greatly improved or increasing ties with either of Moscow's major adversaries – but especially China – would likely be a net loss for Romania since such actions would stir active attention and concern in the Kremlin.

As for other communist states, the Romanians exchange expressions of political support with Yugoslavia and, to a lesser extent, North Korea.[74] But in the 1980s, neither the uncertain leadership situation in the former nor the extremely limited nature of support available from the latter can be very reassuring.

On the other hand, as regards non-ruling communist parties, RCP leaders have not retreated from – indeed they have reiterated – their support of Eurocommunism, and they could derive future support from this source in two ways. First, outspoken national communist leaders such as Enrico Berlinguer or Santiago Carrillo are likely to continue to remind the Communist Party of the Soviet Union (CPSU) of its proper international role. Second, if any of these parties should in fact come to power, diplomatic and economic benefits presumably would accrue to steadfast friends such as Ceauşescu. Yet this European sword – more of a dagger, actually –is two-sided. The prominence of a communist-ruled state in Western Europe with open borders, relatively greater democracy and economic freedom, might be too dangerous for Romania to embrace very warmly. On the other hand, the potential "demonstration" effect of such a state should be recognized but not overstated. The Romanian government was quite able in 1968 to both support the Czech party's "renovation" of social and economic life and insulate itself from the infection such reforms might have carried. And its fulsome relationship with Yugoslavia has not been damaged by the two states' radically different domestic systems.

Indeed Romania has played a "Balkan card" from time to time; that is, by emphasizing the country's Balkan identity, history and the possibilities of Balkan cooperation and unity.[75] But given traditional

Soviet antipathy to real inter-Balkan unity, not to mention the enormous difficulties of achieving effective cooperation, much less unity, among the diverse Balkan states, this course is unlikely to provide a solid platform on which to build a distinctive Romanian foreign policy.

It is toward the developing countries of the Third World that Romania has cast its net in search of support. As noted earlier, Bucharest has engaged in a persistent campaign to modify its self-definition from that of a socialist country to that of a socialist *developing* country. As the RCP sees it, this sets it apart not only from the developed capitalist states but also from most of its East European allies who are developed socialist states. Bucharest has sought to buttress this position institutionally (by joining the Group of 77, for example) and politically (through ardent support of the movement for a New International Economic Order). But the returns in terms of political support would seem likely to be even more limited than from the Balkans. The continued enunciation of principles and related activities (such as the endless procession of Third World leaders through Bucharest) certainly give Ceauşescu a degree of visibility, access and credibility to his claim to being an internationally respected and desirable partner. But whether support from this particular "attentive public" can insulate Romania from overt Soviet pressure, much less invasion, must be considered doubtful, especially in light of Afghanistan.

A Soviet or Soviet-led military invasion of Romania does not seem likely, however, as long as the RCP keeps its international and domestic behavior within the rough parameters defined by the Kremlin: (1) alliance with, and at least a minimal level of support for, the Warsaw Pact; and (2) dominance of the communist party over the political process. During the past two decades the Romanians have come much closer to violating the former than the latter.[76]

As for possible military support in the event of such an invasion, the regime clearly knows that neither the United States, the West in general, nor China will risk war with the USSR over Moscow's use of force in Eastern Europe. While Beijing may be willing to attack a Soviet ally on its own borders, it is simply too far away, too weak militarily, too unpredictable internally and too preoccupied with its own Soviet frontier to offer any significant military support to Romania. Romanian defense against a hypothetical Soviet attack, which would probably be augmented by invasions from the west by Hungary and from the south by Bulgaria, would depend almost certainly upon Romania's own capacities, with some assistance possibly from Yugoslavia. This does not mean that Romania's non-Soviet contacts cannot serve concrete military purposes, as the acquisition of Chinese gunboats and attack craft indicates.[77] But in the end, the continuation of Romanian foreign policy deviance depends on the leadership's ability to secure economic and political support where it can and avoid or prevent Soviet military intervention, rather than to try to defeat such an intervention once begun.[78]

In sum, the international political environment can provide or deny an atmosphere supporting Romanian deviance. It is an enabling factor. The interesting questions that now arise are: exactly which aspects of this environment are most crucial, and which, if changed substantially for the worse – from Bucharest's point of view – would force significant shifts in the RCP's international policy? Some speculation along these lines is offered in the concluding section.

Levels of Soviet Tolerance

While the unique course of Romanian foreign policy stems from indigenous causes (for example, economic mobilization, desire for party legitimacy) and depends on political and economic support both at home and abroad, it also requires a degree of Soviet tolerance. No one could seriously doubt Soviet ability to curtail or stop altogether Romania's independent actions should Moscow become concerned or alarmed at the direction of such actions or their implications. Thus to assess the enabling factors underlying the future course of Romanian foreign policy one must discuss to some extent the factors underlying Soviet tolerance.

Romania's military/geographic position, one of extreme vulnerability, is ironically a strength of sorts. A low level of Soviet threat perception due to the country's relative isolation enables the Romanian leadership to engage in foreign policy actions which, if taken in Prague, would provoke a quite different response from the Soviet Union.[79] Since in the absence of a general European war this geopolitical situation is unlikely to change, Soviet perceptions of military threat from Romania are also likely to remain low. What could change this level of threat perception would be a serious Greek–Turkish conflict or, less likely, instability within the Bulgarian regime, either of which would present a Soviet rationale for increasing its pressure on Romania.

The situation could become much more difficult for Romania

should a future crisis in Yugoslavia provoke Soviet involvement. Since the earliest days of Ceauşescu's rule, he and Tito forged a close mutually supportive relationship based almost totally on their similar views of the proper norms of interparty and interstate behavior. The two frequently exchanged visits, often hastily arranged in response to some event or situation, and drew on each other's prestige and position to ensure the widest possible options in party and state affairs and to resist Soviet pressure to conform. The passing of Tito, as noted, removed from the scene one key supporting block in Ceauşescu's international constituency. Moreover, in terms of Soviet interest in the region, Tito's departure raises by some moderate degree the possibility that contingencies could occur in the Balkans which would result in increased Soviet "attention." The immediate post-Tito experience suggests that in fact this is less likely in the short run than many popular accounts have suggested. But in the long run, a Yugoslav failure to deal effectively with its serious economic problems and the resulting pressure this might create on its fragile ethnic, regional and political unity could produce unwanted tension and great power involvement in the region.[80] A Soviet military demonstration, for example, designed to support a pro-Soviet faction in Yugoslavia, or the achievement of power by a group desirous of moving the country closer to the Warsaw Pact, would substantially worsen the overall situation for Romania, even without the actual stationing of Soviet troops in the country. On the other hand, the ascension to power of a group hostile to the Soviet Union, or one eager to press the Macedonian issue with Bulgaria, would be equally troubling to Romania as it might increase Soviet pressure on Romania to become less of a free rider in the alliance.

Most crucial to the Soviet view of its own security is its perception of the *political* threat, that is, the threat of system-changing reforms which might fundamentally alter or undermine the socialist system in an East European state or, more seriously, spread to the Soviet Union itself. The Soviet reactions to events in Hungary in 1956 and Czechoslovakia in 1968 are instructive. While Romania is not, as noted, in as sensitive a geographic position as either Czechoslovakia or Hungary, it does border on the Soviet Ukraine, where political stability and loyalty is a continuing Soviet concern, to say the least.[81] Any widespread or widely publicized internal political or economic turbulence or reform in Romania which the Soviet Union could interpret as having broader ramifications for the future of socialism in the region would very likely call forth as forceful a reaction as those mentioned above. While it is a simplification to say that the Romanians have made an explicit deal with Moscow to keep a tight rein at home in return for tolerance of their deviance in foreign policy, the RCP's ardent desire to maintain stability and control of domestic politics does serve *inter alia* its foreign policy goals by not allowing actions that would arouse Soviet suspicion, alarm or, ultimately, intervention.

The breadth of Soviet tolerance is also affected by the status of Sino-Soviet relations. It should be recalled that the original Romanian deviance took place under extremely favorable conditions in this regard. Khrushchev was preoccupied with keeping peace in his own backyard while dealing with Mao Zedong and, in particular, with frustrating further Chinese encroachment into Eastern Europe.[82] As Soviet concern with Chinese–Romanian relations increased in the early 1970s, Soviet pressure seemed to exercise a significant limiting effect on those relations. To state future contingencies in their extremes, in the unlikely event of a substantial Soviet–Chinese rapprochement, the Romanians would be denied even the limited support they currently receive from Beijing. Conversely, in the event of full-scale hostilities in the Far East, Moscow would be increasingly ill-disposed towards continued Romanian "neutrality."

Soviet economic relations with the rest of the world also affect Romanian deviance indirectly. Reference has already been made to Moscow's weaning of its allies from the Soviet oil supply. Decisions such as this, derived both from Soviet domestic and from international factors, affect the trading policy and capabilities of the East European states, though the Romanians have been in a somewhat better position on this score. In addition there is the position of the Soviet Union as a partner to Western trade and credit, one with much greater attractiveness than Romania due, at the very least, to sheer size. As hard currency debt mounts and Western markets for Eastern goods reach their limits, it may be the smaller Eastern countries who are shut out. This is especially true to the degree that trade is seen as a tool for inducing changes in Soviet domestic or international behavior. In addition, direct Soviet–East European economic relations need to be considered, as the Soviet Union can in a number of ways spur or retard both the trade and internal economic development of its allies. In this respect, however, the Romanian economy, which is less developed, less dependent on the Soviet Union, and endowed with a more diversified import and export structure, seems to be in a somewhat better position than other East European economies.

Finally, internal political developments in the Soviet Union affect the limits of Soviet tolerance of all types of deviance, domestic and international. The weakness of the Khrushchev regime in its final days, and the uncertainty in the initial period of the Brezhnev–Kosygin regime, allowed greater latitude for the Romanian policies of the sixties. During the past decade, Soviet leaders have been willing to live with their maverick ally so long as it has shown continued respect for certain limits; but should the internal dynamics of the Soviet regime bring to power a more conservative group, Romanian foreign policy would very likely come under close scrutiny.

MILIEU–OPPORTUNITY FACTORS

A major subset of factors enabling Romanian foreign policy deviance to continue can be characterized as *milieu* or opportunity factors. Foreign policy actions take place in certain arenas which may or may not provide opportunities for the assertion of a distinctive position. It should be recalled by observers of Romanian foreign policy – especially those interested in charting the country's independent course – that there must be opportunities for the assertion of that independence. More broadly, international events which occasion such assertions may be present or absent, and may or may not be uniquely appropriate to such assertions (for example, Czechoslovakia in 1968, Afghanistan in 1980, Poland in 1980–1). One of the chief differences between the period 1965–70 and 1970–5, for example, was the relative lack of such opportunities in the latter period.

Moreover, many of the initiatives of the Romanian party and state which were dramatic acts demonstrating autonomy in the milieu of 1967, such as the recognition of West Germany, have been ultimately imitated by the other East European states, diluting the present – though not the past – uniqueness of the Romanian position. Similarly, Romania's defense of the right of each communist party to set its own policies and follow its own national line may have appeared pale after the formal acquiescence of the CPSU in the legitimacy of this notion in 1976. But in 1980–1, Soviet pressure on Poland, not to mention the invasion of Afghanistan, indicated that the CPSU still feels that, *in extremis,* it knows best. Thus the Romanian position, while itself not changing, is once again cast into distinctive relief.

We should not overemphasize the milieu aspect, however. Certain "opportunities" persist over time; for example, in institutionalized forums such as Comecon, the Warsaw Pact and the United Nations. Others can be created by, for example, ostentatiously entertaining the leader of one of Moscow's *bêtes noires*. The point of delineating this factor separately in an analysis of the future directions of Romanian foreign policy is to remind ourselves of the need to take account of the *milieu* within which foreign policy takes place. Romanian foreign policy no less than that of any other state needs to be assessed contemporaneously. Assertions of foreign policy autonomy by Bucharest serve certain important purposes and thus can be expected to persist, within limits, as long as they continue to serve such goals and as long as the goals themselves persist. But such assertions will also depend to a degree upon the appearance of appropriate opportunities. The Romanians have demonstrated remarkable skill in both recognizing and exploiting, albeit carefully, such opportunities. It is the task of the analyst to be just as keen in his assessment of the *milieu* in arriving at a judgment of Romanian policy.

OUTLOOK FOR THE 1980s

As never before since Ceauşescu achieved supremacy, Romania and Romanian foreign policy are at a decision point. As the 1980s begin, the world as seen from Bucharest has changed, mostly for the worse. Tito has died, eliminating a prestigious individual supporter of Ceauşescu and leaving behind a weakened, divided, largely impotent nonaligned movement, a movement which itself has been the target of sustained Romanian overtures for nearly ten years. The present decade's other dramatic introductory event, the Soviet invasion of Afghanistan, demonstrated starkly that this particular international constituency cannot protect Ceauşescu or his country from intervention should Soviet fears on questions of vital interest be aroused. Even closer to home, Soviet actions toward Poland, including possible Soviet pressures on the Polish government leading up to the proclamation of martial law at the end of 1981, serve to remind everyone that the use of force is ever a live option for the USSR in areas it considers crucial.

Beyond that, the economic picture is difficult at best, grim at worst. The Romanians cannot, without completely disrupting their economy, substantially reduce their dependence on expensive imported oil for at least the first half of the decade. In addition, they have only limited prospects of being able to sell enough of their own products to an increasingly import-wary West to be able to foot the bill. Further, the RCP cannot be sure it can count on the continued acceptance by its population of lower living standards and deferments in improving their everyday life.

The Polish events of 1980–1 seemed to shock and frighten Ceauşescu in a way that the Prague Spring never did. Because it was workers' grievances based on day-to-day material issues that provided the stimulus and continuing strength of the reforms that had been effected in Poland prior to the establishment of martial law, and because the only thing approaching real upheaval in Romania in recent times came from just such a situation – the Jiu Valley miners' strike – Ceauşescu's first reaction was to condemn what was happening in Poland.[83] Bucharest did, however, continue to stress that there should be no outside interference in Poland and that they had full faith that the Polish party could deal with its troubles by itself. Once General Jaruzelski clamped a martial law regime on Poland in December 1981, the Romanians continued this two-pronged approach, combining criticism of "anti-social forces" in Poland with warnings against interference from the outside. The Ceauşescu regime explicitly approved of General Jaruzelski's measures of 13 December 1981, but insisted that the Polish authorities should be allowed to restore order without external interference.[84]

The possibilities indicated by the Polish events have not been lost on the RCP. The continuing campaign of criticism and self-criticism is designed in part to demonstrate the party's willingness and ability to deal with its problems, something Ceauşescu explicitly criticized the Poles for not doing.[85] Moreover, his "levelling" of party cadres has been more than rhetorical, as the decree forcing disclosures of private holdings indicates. The bonuses to energy and raw material workers serves the double purpose of spurring production and satisfying a crucial worker constituency. In December 1980, farmers also received price increases for their products,[86] while other measures were introduced to ease restrictions and improve production and distribution from private farms.[87] Of course the converse impact of such increases, as successive Polish regimes have learned, is on the workers and farmers as consumers.[88] Here the regime must fall back on its endless reiteration of how much better than ever things are and on its fierce repression of embryonic dissident groups, such as its own short-lived free trade unions.[89] Though the economic base of its difficulties are fundamentally the same as Poland's, the political superstructure does allow for a somewhat more energetic reaction.

Until now Romania's deviating foreign policy has served the goals of: (1) supporting ideologically and materially the country's rapid and broad industrial development by securing needed goods, technology and raw materials; and (2) securing for the regime and its leader a degree of national authority and legitimacy by identifying them with the Romanian nation and by trumpeting their active role on the world stage. These two goals remain operative; the regime still seeks legitimacy and economic development. The stimulating factors are also still there, but the enabling factors may not be.

THREE SCENARIOS

If this is an accurate analysis of the present and immediate future situation, three possible scenarios can be suggested.
(1) The "Come in From the Cold" Scenario.
This line is most strongly suggested by the deteriorating economic situation faced by the Romanians, by the death of Tito and near death of the nonaligned constituency, by a new Soviet truculence shown in Afghanistan and an old one in Poland, and perhaps by the possibilities presented by a Soviet leadership change. Under this scenario, Ceauşescu is increasingly forced to depend on the Soviet Union for his oil, increasingly intimidated by Soviet pressure in and through the alliance, and is perhaps also offered attractive economic terms for moderating his foreign policy stances. He is inclined, in other words, to take the "Bulgarian route" to further economic development and to abandon the course he has followed thus far. The scenario develops piecemeal. That is, the RCP finds itself increasingly in agreement with the CPSU on foreign policy issues, it is fearful of the implications and spread of the Polish events, worried and distrustful of a newly belligerent United States, annoyed and impatient with continued stagnation in the Middle East peace process.

Movement in this direction is made all the more possible by Ceauşescu's Stalinesque assumption of responsibility, and credit, for having brought the country to its present successes and for guiding it into the future. That is, Ceauşescu, as the source of all wisdom, inspiration and truth on all issues, may, when he deems it necessary, be able gradually to abandon his outlier positions on foreign policy without serious challenge.

(2) The "New Tito" Scenario.

Under this scenario, Ceauşescu endeavors to replace Tito as the European nonaligned statesman. He profits by both his association with Tito and his own reputation as one who has stood up to Moscow. He continues to underscore the cardinal principles of progressive international behavior originally adumbrated by Tito and the nonaligned movement (for example, sovereign equality of all states, noninterference in each other's internal affairs, right to independence, and so on), and demonstrates his concern with Third World states and issues. As Tito did, he continues to argue for erosion and elimination of military blocs and for a reduction of tension in Europe, and he does this through continued extensive use of personal diplomacy and "summitry," techniques so dear to Tito.

Such a course might be attractive to Ceauşescu for several reasons, not least because it might protect Romania in dangerous times by developing wide international visibility. Moreover, it serves the longstanding need to build national legitimacy and prestige at home. Assuming the mantle of Tito might also improve Romanian access to Third World raw material and export markets, for example, making the country a more acceptable purchaser of the oil of anticommunist oil sheiks. Ceauşescu's exalted position, of course, also makes this scenario possible. At present, Romania does seem to be continuing, even increasing, its support of Third World countries and causes. The Romanians retain, for example, a muted but still distinctive position on the invasion of Cambodia by Vietnam, a position which is similar to the views on this question adopted by most nonaligned countries.

(3) The "Continued Partial Alignment" Scenario.

This is the "muddling through" scenario which finds Romania trying to maintain the autonomy and visibility of its foreign policy in much the same way as it has so far, that is, by maintaining its opposition on some issues, conforming on some others, and continuing to try to advance the country's economic development and the regime's authority. This scenario assumes that the stimulating factors will remain strong and requires that some enabling factors improve sufficiently to offset the deterioration in others. The Romanians will need to achieve economic advances in the Third World sufficient to enable them to sustain and revive their sluggish trade with the West. Alternatively, continued importation of a high level of Western goods will have to be abandoned, due to their cost and the lessons of Poland, and replaced by increases in worker productivity. This will require not simply the continued acquiescence of the population but its industrial mobilization. The people will have to give even more to receive even less. The latest five-year plan suggests this as the present course, and Romanian positions on various international issues also seem to fit this scenario.

A final projection, then, might envisage not one of these scenarios but the appearance in succession of at least two of them. What we may see is an attempt by Romania to continue its foreign policy independence as long as domestic and international circumstances will allow. Then, if economic conditions and the political climate continue to deteriorate, Romania may come in from the cold. But lest that stand as our final prospectus, it is worth recalling that the Romanians have managed to steer this extraordinary and dangerous course for nearly two decades already, in periods of both tension and detente, growth and recession. As long as the goals underlying the policy remain viable, it is unlikely that it will be lightly relinquished.

NOTES AND REFERENCES

The author is grateful to the Faculty of Arts and Sciences of the University of Pittsburgh for a Faculty Research Grant and to Daniel N. Nelson, Michael J. Sodaro and Sharon L. Wolchik for helpful comments on earlier versions of this work.

1. James N. Rosenau, "Toward the Study of National–International Linkages," in Rosenau (ed.), *Linkage Politics* (New York: Free Press, 1969) p. 45.
2. One study which does draw explicitly on the Rosenau framework is Cal Clark, "Balkan Communist Foreign Policies: A Linkage Perspective," in Ronald H. Linden (ed.), *The Foreign Policies of East Europe: New Approaches* (New York: Praeger, 1980) pp. 17–45.
3. A classic nontheoretical example of this would be H. Gordon Skilling, *Communism, National and International* (University of Toronto Press, 1964).
4. See, for example, Egon Neuberger and Laura D'Andrea Tyson (eds), *The Impact of International Economic Disturbances on the Soviet Union and Eastern Europe* (New York: Pergamon Press, 1980); Sarah M. Terry, "The Implications of Interdependence for Soviet–East European Relations: A Preliminary Analysis of the Polish Case," in Linden, *Foreign Policies of East Europe*, pp. 186–266; Andrzej Korbonski,

"Detente, East–West Trade, and the Future of Economic Integration in Eastern Europe," *World Politics,* xxviii, 4 (July 1976), pp. 568–89.

5. Rosenau, *Linkage Politics,* p. 46.

6. See *inter alia* James N. Rosenau, "Foreign Policy as Adaptive Behavior," *Comparative Politics,* 2, 3 (April 1970) pp. 365–87.

7. James N. Rosenau, "Adaptive Strategies for Research and Practice in Foreign Policy," in Fred W. Riggs (ed.), *International Studies: Present Status and Future Prospects* (Philadelphia: American Academy of Political and Social Sciences, 1971) esp. pp. 231–2; James N. Rosenau, "Theorizing Across Systems: Linkage Politics Revisited," in Jonathan Wilkenfeld (ed.), *Conflict Behavior and Linkage Politics* (New York: David McKay, 1973) pp. 25–56.

8. Rosenau, "Theorizing Across Systems," p. 46.

9. Rosenau lists a number of studies which were stimulated or based on the concept, including two of East European States. See "Theorizing across Systems," pp. 46ff.

10. Rosenau concedes both of these points in "Theorizing Across Systems," pp. 44–6.

11. See Graham T. Allison, *Essence of Decision* (Boston: Little, Brown, 1971).

12. See Richard Cottam, *Foreign Policy Motivation* (University of Pittsburgh Press, 1977).

13. See R. J. Rummel, "Dimensions of Conflict Behavior within and between Nations," and J. Wilkenfeld, "Domestic and Foreign Conflict," both in Wilkenfeld, *Conflict Behavior and Linkage Politics,* pp. 59–123.

14. On bureaucratic politics, see Robert J. Art, "Bureaucratic Politics and American Foreign Policy: A Critique," *Policy Science,* iv, 4 (December 1973) pp. 467–90. On national attributes, see Andrew Mack, "Numbers Are Not Enough," *Comparative Politics,* vii, 4 (July 1975) pp. 597–618; and John Vasquez, "Statistical Findings in International Politics," *International Studies Quarterly,* 20, 2 (June 1976) pp. 171–218. See also the discussion in James G. Kean and Patrick J. McGowan, "National Attributes and Foreign Policy Participation: A Path Analysis," in Patrick J. McGowan (ed.), *Sage International Yearbook of Foreign Policy Studies,* vol. 1 (Beverly Hills, CA: Sage, 1973) pp. 219–51.

15. For a review of foreign policy studies of East European states, see Ronald H. Linden, "Foreign Policy Studies and East Europe," in Linden, *Foreign Policies of East Europe,* pp. 1–16.

16. See Zvi Gitelman, "Toward a Comparative Foreign Policy of Eastern Europe," in Peter J. Potichnyj and Jane P. Shapiro (eds), *From the Cold War to Detente* (New York: Praeger, 1976) pp. 144–165; Ronald H. Linden, *Bear and Foxes: The International Relations of the East European States, 1965–1969* (Boulder: East European Quarterly and Columbia University Press, 1979); William C. Potter, "External Demands and East Europe's Westpolitik," in Linden, *The Foreign Policies,* pp. 96–134. See also the discussion in Linden, "Foreign Policy Studies."

17. These terms are employed, respectively, in David Floyd, *Rumania: Russia's Dissident Ally* (New York: Praeger, 1965); Robert L. Farlow,

"Romanian Foreign Policy: A Case of Partial Alignment," *Problems of Communism* (November–December 1971) pp. 54–63; M. K. Dziewanowski, "The Pattern of Rumanian Independence," *East Europe*, XVIII, 6 (June 1969) pp. 8–12; and R. V. Burks, "The Rumanian National Deviation: An Accounting," in Kurt London (ed.), *Eastern Europe in Transition* (Baltimore: Johns Hopkins University Press, 1966) pp. 93–113. For other relevant studies, see Robert R. King, "Rumania: The Difficulty of Maintaining an Autonomous Foreign Policy," in Robert R. King and Robert W. Dean, *East European Perspectives on European Security and Cooperation* (New York: Praeger, 1974) pp. 168–90; and Ronald H. Linden, "Romanian Foreign Policy in the 1980's," in Daniel L. Nelson (ed.), *Romania in the 1980's* (Boulder: Westview Press, 1981).

18. See the discussion in Nicolai Ecobescu and Sergiu Celac, *Politica externă a României Socialiste* (Bucharest: Editura Politica, 1975).

19. El Florea, "Cu Privire la evolutia conceptului marxist naţiune," *Analele* Institutului de Studii Istorice si Social-Politice de pe lingă CC al PCR, XII, 6 (1967) pp. 66–79; Ana Gavrila, "Natiunea socialistă-etapa superioră in viaţa natiunilor," *Analele* Institutului de Studii Istorice şi Social Politice de pe lingă CC al PCR, XIV, 5 (1968) pp. 101–108. Cf. a speech by Ceauşescu at the 1972 National Conference of the Romanian Communist Party in *Romania on the Way of Building up the Multilaterally Developed Socialist Society*, V. 7 (Bucharest: Meridiane Publishing House, 1973) pp. 501–6; I. Madosa, "Independence – A Sine Qua Non for Actual International Cooperation," *Lumea* no. 9, 2–8 March 1979, pp. 21–2.

20. See Ceauşescu's Report to the Eleventh Congress of the RCP in *Congresul al XI-lea al Partidului Comunist Român* (Bucharest: Editura Politică, 1975) pp. 41–2. Cf. Romulus Caplescu, "An Important Contribution to the Assertion of the New Principles of Relations in the International Communist Movement, to Strengthening Solidarity in the Struggle for Security, Peace, and Social Progress," *Lumea*, no. 20, 14–20 July 1978, pp. 25–6; Constantin Florea, "RCP's Stand on New Phenomena and Trends in the Communist and Workers' Movement," *Era Socialistă*, no. 19 (1978) pp. 30–4.

21. "Statement on the Stand of the Rumanian Workers' Party Concerning the Problems of the International Communist and Working Class Movement," in William E. Griffith (ed.), *Sino-Soviet Relations: 1964–1965* (Cambridge: MIT Press, 1967) p. 284. Cf. Alexandru Puiu, *Comerţul Exterior şi Rolul Lui in Realizarea Programului de Dezvoltare Economică a României* (Bucharest: Editura Politica, 1974).

22. See, for example, N. Ecobescu, "A Ban on Nuclear Weapons – the Imperative Demand of the Peoples," *Lumea*, no. 1, 3 March 1978, pp. 10–12; "Disarmament – Top-of-the-Line Priority," *Lumea*, no. 16, 20–6 April 1979, p. 16; George Serafin, "European Security – Imperative of Continuity, of Constructive Efforts," ibid., pp. 8–9; *Scînteia*, 9 August 1980, p. 6; 11 October 1980, p. 3; see also the statement by Foreign Minister Stefan Andrei at the Madrid review meeting of the CSCE, *Scînteia*, 15 November 1980, p. 6.

23. For Ceauşescu's designation of Romania as a developing country, see his speech to a 1972 National Conference of the RCP in *Romania*, vol. 7, pp. 519–20. For a discussion of Romania's policies in this regard, see Ion Barac, "Romania and the Developing Countries," *Revue roumaine d'études internationales*, xi, 1 (35), 1977, pp. 55–72.

24. In September 1980, Foreign Minister Andrei said, ". . . some developed countries not only avoid taking part in the implementation of the new international order, but make widescale use of new forms that aim at the continuation of their exploitation of the less developed countries. . . . (T)he developed states, irrespective of their social–economic system, should show the necessary understanding as to the needs of the developing countries and pass on to resolved measures in view of building the new international economic order," Agerpress, 30 September 1980.

25. Barac, "Romania and the Developing Countries," p. 72. Cf. Ion Mielcioiu, "The Colombo Conference of the heads of state or government of the non-aligned countries, Romania's participation," *Revue roumaine d'études internationales*, xi, 1 (35), 1977, pp. 73–88.

26. See Ceauşescu's New Year's Message (Text), *Scînteia*, 4 January 1980, p. 4; cf. his opening address to the Socialist Unity Front Congress, *România liberă*, 18 January 1980, p. 3–a.

27. For a text of the resolution, see *The New York Times*, 15 January 1980, p. A8. The Romanians explained that they had wanted a UN resolution which would lead to "guarantees" that there would be no interference in the internal affairs of Afghanistan and "that no state will grant support to the antigovernment forces in that country." Bucharest Domestic Service, 15 January 1980.

28. See, for example, Ceauşescu's interview with the Swedish newspaper *Svenska Dagbladet*, in *Scînteia*, 5 November 1980, p. 1.

29. Indeed the multivolume (and growing) collection of Ceauşescu's speeches, reports, and remarks is entitled (since volume v) *Romania on the Way of Building up the Multilaterally Developed Socialist Society*.

30. See John M. Montias, "Romania's Foreign Trade: An Overview," in Joint Economic Committee, US Congress, *East European Economies Post-Helsinki: A Compendium of Papers* (Washington, DC: US Government Printing Office, 1977) pp. 865–85; Cal Clark and Robert Farlow, *Comparative Patterns of Foreign Policy and Trade: The Communist Balkans in International Politics* (Bloomington, Indiana: International Development Research Center, Indiana University, 1976), and Linden, *Bear and Foxes*, esp. Chapter 5, for discussions of this process.

31. See Josef C. Brada and Marvin R. Jackson, "Strategy and Structure in the Organization of Romanian Foreign Trade Activities, 1967–75," in *East European Economies*, pp. 1260–76.

32. By the end of 1979 Romania had been extended $905 million in officially-backed credits from Western sources. See National Foreign Assessment Center, *Soviet and East European Hard Currency Debt* (Washington: Central Intelligence Agency, 1980). See also Thad P. Alton, "Comparative Structure and Growth of Economic Activity in Eastern Europe," in *East European Economies*, pp. 199–266.

33. As of year end, 1982, Romania's hard-currency net debt stood at

$9.9 billion; see National Foreign Assessment Center, *Soviet and East European Hard Currency Debt,* and *Time,* 10 January 1983, p. 43.

34. See the discussion in Marvin R. Jackson, "Industrialization, Trade, and Mobilization in Romania's Drive for Economic Independence," in *East European Economies,* pp. 886–970; and in *Radio Free Europe Research* (hereafter RFER), 2 December 1980.

35. Virtually every recent speech of Ceauşescu's, whatever the audience or occasion, makes reference to inefficiencies, poor use of resources, delays, poor management, and "bureaucratic practices." A special concern has been a uniformly below-plan performance in agriculture. In a September speech to the People's Councils Congress, Ceauşescu said, "It is inadmissible that while many crops remain in the field, while some produce rots, you find the snackbars full, and scores of people, beginning with the mayor, at the city hall or at various institutions, instead of helping bring in the crops or working in the fields. And this is true not only of the communes, but also of the towns and the country." *Scînteia,* 13 September 1980, p. 2. Before the RCP Central Committee Plenum in October, Ceauşescu called for "military order and discipline in agriculture," *Scînteia,* 17 October 1980, p. 2.

36. See the Twelfth Congress speeches of Ilie Verdeţ (Prime Minister), *Scînteia,* 21 November 1979; Cornel Burtică (Minister of Foreign Trade), *Scînteia,* 23 November 1979; Paul Niculescu (Minister of Finance), *Scînteia,* 22 November 1979.

37. See Ceauşescu's Report to the Twelfth Congress, reprinted (in English) in "Ceausescu: 19 November Report to 12th RCP Congress," Foreign Broadcast Information Service (FBIS) *Daily Report,* Supplement, V. II, no. 238, supp. 038 (hereafter Ceauşescu, *Report*) pp. 11–20. As of early 1981 the final laws concerning the plan had not been enacted, thus permitting subsequent downward revisions in the targets.

38. See the speech to the Twelfth Congress by Virgil Trofin – who after the Congress replaced Vasilie Patilineţ as Minister of Mines, Petroleum and Geology – *Scînteia,* 21 November 1979, pp. 11, 12. At the Congress Ceauşescu announced the discovery of new oil deposits beneath the Black Sea. See Ceauşescu, *Report,* p. 12.

39. *RFER,* 12 August 1977, and 8 September 1978. Periodic reports have surfaced in the West about strikes and protests over working conditions, salaries, and food supplies. See Agence France Presse (Paris), 10 August 1980; *The New York Times,* 9 March 1981, p. A4.

40. See Ceauşescu, *Report,* pp. 6–9, 26–30; and *Scînteia,* 13 September 1980, pp. 1, 2.

41. *RFER,* 12 August 1977, and 8 September 1978.

42. An indication both of the need for increasing production in the energy sectors and of Romanian concern over the workers' movement in Poland was the party's decision to implement salary bonuses for workers in the oil, coal, and other raw material industries who exceed their production quotas; see *Scînteia,* 1 November 1980, p. 3.

43. See Montias, "Romania's Foreign Trade." See also *The Wall Street Journal,* 28 July 1982, pp. 1, 14.

44. Data presented by Paul Marer at an Academic Roundtable on Romania,

US State Department, 12 October 1977. In addition, Romania has also allowed the establishment of the greatest number of joint equity ventures with Western companies of any Comecon member. See *RFER*, 2 November 1979.

45. See Montias, "Romania's Foreign Trade," pp. 883, 885; Ceauşescu, *Report*, p. 25.
46. See Ceauşescu's speech to the CC plenum, *Scînteia*, 17 October 1980, p. 3; cf. *RFER*, 10 December 1980.
47. See John R. Haberstroh, "Eastern Europe: Growing Energy Problems," in *East European Economies*, pp. 379–95; cf. *The New York Times*, 21 November 1977, pp. 53, 55. *RFER* of 23 November 1979 quotes Reuters and UPI as reporting an undisclosed deal by which Romania was to have imported 350,000 tons of Soviet oil in 1979. Ceauşescu himself referred to an importation of nearly 1.5 million tons from the Soviet Union in 1980 (*Scînteia*, 17 October 1980, p. 3).
48. *Scînteia*, 17 October 1980, p. 3.
49. *RFER*, 23 March 1979, 2 November 1979, and 10 December 1980. In October 1978 the government also successfully concluded long negotiations with Canada for the purchase of a nuclear reactor, the first such sale to an East European state. *RFER*, 24 October 1978.
50. At the Twelfth Congress Ceauşescu stated that the earthquake had caused over $2 billion in damages and affected over 760 economic units. He also indicated that the Romanian people "were able to overcome the difficulties" and ultimately "insured the fulfillment" of the five-year plan. Ceauşescu, *Report*, p. 9.
51. *RFER*, 29 April 1977.
52. For obvious reasons sources for this view cannot be cited.
53. See, for example, *RFER*, 6 December 1977, 5 June 1978, 27 September 1978, and 4 May 1979.
54. See a discussion in Kenneth Jowitt, "Political Innovation in Romania," *Survey*, xx, 4 (Autumn 1974) pp. 132–151 and Trond Gilberg, "Romania: Problems of the Multilaterally Developed Society," in Charles Gati (ed.), *The Politics of Modernization in Eastern Europe* (New York: Praeger, 1974) p. 148. One extraordinary event which may reflect the existence of an opposition of uncertain size was the speech at the Twelfth Congress of Constantin Privulescu, a veteran party stalwart of 84, who rose to accuse Ceausescu of placing his own interests above those of the country, and who declared – while others were exulting in the General Secretary's leadership – that he would not vote for his reelection. See *RFER*, 28 November 1979. For Bucharest's scant reportage, see Agerpress, 23 November 1979. See also *RFER* on the disappearance of Stefan Voitec, a member of the RCP Political Executive Committee, 20 January 1981.
55. These changes are outlined in Linden, *Bear and Foxes*, pp. 280–1, n. 100; cf. *RFER*, 5 February 1980.
56. See the discussion in Jowitt, "Political Innovation in Romania," and Mary Ellen Fischer, "Participatory Reforms and Political Development in Romania," in Jan F. Triska and Paul M. Cocks (eds), *Political Development in Eastern Europe* (New York: Praeger, 1977) pp. 217–37.

57. Originally consisting of five members, this Bureau has grown steadily, and at the Twelfth Congress of the RCP was expanded to fifteen members. See *RFER*, 28 November 1979.
58. For two recent examples, see *Scînteia*, 27 November 1979, p. 3 and 30 November 1979, pp. 3, 4. At the same time the entire Ceauşescu family, and especially his wife Elena, have enjoyed wondrous success in their political careers. See *RFER*, 5 February 1980; *The New York Times*, 27 November 1979, p. 2.
59. See Daniel Nelson, "Sub-National Political Elites in a Communist System: Contrasts and Conflicts in Romania," *East European Quarterly*, x, 4 (Winter 1976) pp. 459–94.
60. "Less paper, less bureaucratism, and we will have more and better material goods!" Ceauşescu said in October (*Scînteia*, 17 October 1980, p. 2); cf. Bucharest Domestic Service, 26 September 1980; *Scînteia*, 18 December 1980, pp. 1, 3. For recent changes in the Romanian leadership, see *The Wall Street Journal*, 24 May 1982, p. 24.
61. Bucharest Domestic Service, 26 September 1980.
62. *Scînteia*, 18 October 1980, p. 3.
63. In December 1979, the Political Executive Committee approved a proposal from the Socialist Unity Front for increasing the number of constituencies where two candidates would run for seats in the Grand National Assembly. Bucharest Domestic Service, 12 December 1979. For a discussion of these elections, see Fischer, "Participatory Reforms and Political Development."
64. See the discussion in George Schöpflin, "Rumanian Nationalism," *Survey*, xx, 2/3 (Spring/Summer 1974) pp. 77–104; cf. Linden, *Bear and Foxes*, pp. 193–6.
65. Among the significant anniversaries celebrated in 1980, for example, was that marking "2050 years since the creation of the first centralized and independent Dacian state." See *Lumea*, 21 (23–9 May 1980) pp. 18–19; and 22 (30 May–5 June 1980) p. 26.
66. *RFER*, 22 June 1977.
67. See the letter to the Central Committee by Károly Király, former alternate member of the RCP Presidium and member of the Central Committee, in *The New York Times*, 1 February 1978, p. 23; cf. Manuel Lucbert, "La minorité hongroise de Transylvanie est mécontente de son sort," *Le Monde*, 5 May 1978, p. 4. At the Twelfth Congress Mihai Gere, candidate member of the Political Executive Committee, harshly rejected "false aggressive and ill-intentioned voices which resort to fabrications in order to distort our realities and try to set the Romanian, Hungarian, German, and other working people at loggerheads." See *Scînteia*, 22 November 1979, p. 5. For a review of government policies toward the Hungarians, see Mary Ellen Fischer, "Nation and Nationality in Romania," in George W. Simmonds (ed.), *Nationalism in the USSR and Eastern Europe in the Era of Brezhnev and Kosygin* (University of Detroit Press, 1977) pp. 504–21.
68. The three counties containing the largest German minorities (Braşov, Sibiu, and Timiş) together account for almost 14 per cent of Romania's industrial production. These counties' production figures represent,

respectively, 2.75, 1.59, and 1.16 times their shares of the national population. See *Anuarul Statistic al Republicii Socialiste România 1977* (Bucharest: Directia Centrală de Statistică, n.d.) pp. 94–5; comparison based on procedures used in Fischer, "Nation and Nationality," p. 517. As of 1966, 58.5 per cent of the German population was classified as workers, compared with 45.9 per cent of the Hungarian and 38.9 per cent of the Romanian; in contrast, only 20.6 per cent were engaged in farming compared with 45.2 per cent of the Romanian and 36.2 per cent of the Hungarian population. *Recensămîntul Populatiei şi Loucinţelor din Marţie 1966*, cited in Gilberg, "Romania," p. 140.

69. See Jacques Levesque, *Le Conflict sino-sovietique et l'Europe de l'Est* (Les Presses de l'université de Montréal, 1970) pp. 97–281; and Robert R. King, "Rumania and the Sino-Soviet Conflict," *Studies in Comparative Communsim*, IV, 4 (Winter 1972) pp. 373–412.

70. See Eugeniu Obrea, "Vigorous Assertion of National Independence Policies in the Service of Socialism and Peace," *Lumea*, 28 (15–21 September 1978) pp. 2–4.

71. In October 1978, that is, just after the first Hua visit, Ceauşescu entertained a Soviet delegation led by Foreign Minister Andrei Gromyko (Agerpress, 14–15 October 1978). And while Prime Minister Ilie Verdeţ was in Beijing in December 1980, Foreign Minister Andrei was in Moscow (*RFER*, 10 December 1980).

72. While such a policy had in fact been evident in US behavior toward Eastern Europe, it was never explicitly enunciated until the views of State Department Counselor Helmut Sonnenfeldt became public in March 1976 (*Washington Post*, 22 March 1976, p. 19). At a briefing for US European ambassadors in London the previous December, Sonnenfeldt had said, among other things:

> It must be our [U.S.] policy to strive for an evolution that makes the relationship between the Eastern Europeans and the Soviet Union an organic one. Any excess of zeal on our part is bound to produce results that could reverse the desired process for a period of time, even though the process would remain inevitable within the next 100 years. But, of course, for us that is too long a time to wait. . . . So our policy must be a policy of responding to the clearly visible aspirations of Eastern Europe for a more autonomous existence within the context of a strong Soviet geopolitical influence.

See the State Department summary of Sonnenfeldt's remarks (*The New York Times*, 6 April 1976, p. 14). Both President Ford and Secretary of State Kissinger were quick to try to modify both the wording and impact of this statement with statements of their own. See *The New York Times*, 6 April 1976, pp. 1, 14, and 7 April 1976, p. 16. For Romanian reaction to Sonnenfeldt's remarks, see *Scînteia*, 13 April 1976.

73. US Undersecretary of State David Newsom visited Romania from January 26 to 28, 1980, and met with both Ceauşescu and Foreign Minister Stefan Andres. *RFER*, 4 February 1980. In Ceauşescu's speech to the Socialist Unity Front Congress he called the situation "tenser than

at any time since World War II" and said, "We must prevent the current international tension from worsening relations in Europe." *România liberă,* 18 January 1980, p. 3–a.

74. For a discussion of the latter, see Jowitt, "Political Innovation in Romania," pp. 133–5.

75. Bucharest recently refloated the idea of creating a "zone of peace" in this region. See Agerpress, 13 March 1979. See also I. Madosa, "The Balkans – a Laboratory of European Security," *Lumea* 48 (28 November–4 December 1980) pp. 22–3.

76. Indeed, the last public dispute between Moscow and Bucharest erupted over the latter's refusal to increase its contributions to the WTO by increasing national defense spending. The Romanian rejection of this suggestion, put forth at a November 1978 meeting of the WTO Political Consultative Committee in Moscow, was promptly publicized heavily in Romania as were supporting resolutions by all relevant organs. See *Scînteia,* 25 and 27 November 1978; and Ceauşescu's speech to representatives of the Army and of the Ministry of Interior, 27 November 1978 (Agerpress, same date), and to the Plenary of the CC of RCP, 29 November 1978 (Agerpress, same date). The Soviet view of the Romanian position was expressed by Brezhnev in a speech on 5 December. "We are ready," he said, "for the most radical steps leading to disarmament, but at all stages of the struggle to achieve this end the principle of the equal security of the sides must be observed. We will not weaken our defense in the face of the growing military might of imperialism, whatever demagogic arguments are used to cover appeals for this." See *Pravda,* 7 December 1978.

77. According to *The Military Balance, 1979–1980* (London: International Institute for Strategic Studies, 1979), Romania has 28 fast attack gun boats and 20 torpedo-equipped hydrofoils built in China (p. 16).

78. For a discussion of "Active Romanian military defenses of foreign policy autonomy," see Aurel Braun, *Romanian Foreign Policy since 1965* (New York: Praeger, 1978) pp. 144–89.

79. See the discussion in Peter Bender, *East Europe in Search of Security* (Baltimore: Johns Hopkins University Press, 1972) p. 112.

80. For further discussion, see the chapter in this volume by William Zimmerman.

81. For a discussion of the significance of the Ukraine in Soviet views of Czechoslovakia in 1968, see Grey Hodnett and Peter J. Potichnyj, *The Ukraine and the Czechoslovak Crisis* (Canberra: Australian National University Press, 1970).

82. See Levesque, *Le Conflict sino-sovietique et l'Europe de l'Est,* among others, on this point.

83. In August *Scînteia* remarked, "Naturally, such actions as work stoppages, strikes, cannot solve the problems. On the contrary, they can only complicate them. . . ." 28 August 1980, p. 5. In October, though, Ceauşescu went further, speaking of "antisocialist elements and forces" in Poland and deriding "the so-called independent trade unions," ibid., 17 October 1980, p. 3.

84. *Scînteia,* 28 August 1980, p. 6; 5 November 1980, p. 6; 10 December

1980, p. 5. For the reaction to martial law in Poland see ibid., 26 December 1981, p. 6; 16 January 1982, p. 6.

85. *Scînteia,* 17 October 1980, p. 3.
86. *Scînteia,* 19 December 1980, p. 7.
87. *RFER,* 20 January 1981.
88. See Bogdan Mieczkowski's discussion of this problem in Poland; "The Political Economy of Consumption in Poland," *Polish Review,* xxiv, 3 (1979) pp. 68–85.
89. See *RFER,* 19 March 1979.

4 External Influences on Regime Stability in the GDR: a Linkage Analysis

MICHAEL J. SODARO

For the German Democratic Republic, the linkage between international developments and the domestic political system has traditionally been an intimate one. This has been especially true with respect to the vital connection that prevails between external factors and the internal stability of communist party rule. Perhaps more than any other ruling party in East-Central Europe, the Socialist Unity Party of Germany (SED) has been dependent on outside sources of support for its political viability. At the same time, however, the external environment has cast up an array of challenges to the stability of the SED regime, at times with the paradoxical result that both stabilizing and destabilizing influences emanate from the very same sources. It is on this crucial relationship between the international environment and regime stability in the GDR that the present study focuses.

Of course, it must be recognized that external factors are not the only determinants of the level of the GDR's internal stability. A host of other elements also come into play, including such domestically rooted phenomena as party and state organization, police repression, social structure and political culture. Without denying the impact of these internal forces, however, it is possible to explain a great deal about the SED's ability to maintain a relatively stable system of authority inside the GDR by referring to the GDR's ties with the outside world.

The analysis that follows aims to pursue some of these explanations by examining the impact on the GDR of influences emanating from five diverse external sources, all of which have in many respects increased their pressure on the East German regime in the course of the 1970s and early 1980s. These are: (1) the Federal Republic of Germany; (2) the Soviet Union; (3) the international economic system; (4) the Final Act of the Conference on Security and Cooperation in Europe (CSCE), signed in Helsinki in 1975; and (5) developments in the communist world, centering chiefly on Eurocommunism in Western Europe and the unprecedented events occurring in Poland in the early 1980s. In each case, the vantage point of the linkage analysis is from the "outside looking in," a focus that reflects the GDR's exceptionally high level of penetration by exogenous forces.

How have these factors made themselves felt inside the GDR in recent years? And what has been the extent of their influence on the stability of the SED regime? While the first of these questions can be answered with reference to statistical and other data, the answer to the second one can only be approximated. In the absence of precise measures for determining the degree of a communist regime's stability, or of its potential for instability, the analyst is forced to rely on qualitative judgments based on a reasonable assessment of how the available facts fit together. Perhaps the best we can do in attempting to understand how these foreign and domestic currents intersect is, first of all, to make clear distinctions between those external influences which tend to inhibit or obstruct the regime's attempts to build popular support at home, and which may therefore be considered tendencies that bear at least the potential for instability in the GDR, and those factors which may tend to facilitate or promote this delicate internal process of building popular support for the regime. Once these various factors have been identified, we can trace their effects on the economic and political systems of the GDR, and examine the SED's strategies for coping with them. It will then be possible to construct some alternative scenarios for the GDR's future development, and to make a critical evaluation of their relative plausibility.

In keeping with these considerations, the analysis that follows is divided into three sections. The first deals with the impact of external economic forces, and is particularly concerned with their domestic political ramifications. The second deals with external influences of a more specifically political nature. The final section sets forth three scenarios of possible future outcomes in the GDR, and addresses the question of whether the GDR is more stable now than a decade ago, or less so.

I. POLITICAL IMPLICATIONS OF ECONOMIC LINKAGES

(A) CONSUMER WELFARE: AN INTER-GERMAN COMPARISON

As is the case in other states of communist Europe, regime stability in the GDR depends to a considerable extent on the fulfillment of an unwritten "social contract" between the ruling elite and the citizenry. That is, in exchange for popular acceptance of communist party rule and willingness to work productively, the elite "agrees" to provide a wide range of economic and social benefits to the population. As the most productive state in communist East–Central Europe, the GDR has thus far registered remarkable successes in fulfilling both sides of this bargain. Whereas the question of the social contract is largely a domestic matter in most of the other states of the region, however, in the GDR it is infused with significant external complications. Owing to the bifurcation of German nationality into two states, and to the relatively high level of information about life in the Federal Republic available to residents of the GDR, many East German citizens are prone to compare their own socio-economic situation with that of fellow Germans across the border. Direct comparisons of this nature have been considerably easier to make since 1972, when the normalization of relations between the two German states (formalized in the Basic Treaty of December 1972) resulted in a tremendous influx of West German visitors to the GDR. These perceptions of comparative living standards in the two Germanies inevitably color the population's judgments of how successful the SED has been in keeping its part of the social contract, and thus bear directly on the SED's level of popular approval. Recognizing this fact, the SED's former leader, Walter Ulbricht, worked vigorously in the early 1970s to impede the process of detente in Europe, since he knew that the GDR would eventually be compelled to relax its visa restrictions on visitors from West Germany as a price for improved Soviet relations with the FRG. Ulbricht's obstructive tactics ultimately collided with overriding Soviet interests, and he was removed from power in May 1971.

From its very first weeks in office, the new SED leadership under Erich Honecker announced its intentions of making substantial improvements in the welfare of East German consumers. This policy represented a reversal of the priorities followed by Ulbricht, who in his later years was particularly concerned with high technology development.[1] Over the course of the 1970s, the SED made great strides towards meeting these pledges. Production of consumer durables, for example, rose appreciably during the decade. By 1979, 99 per cent of East German households owned a refrigerator (as against 56.4 per cent in 1970), and similar advances were recorded in the ownership of washing machines (53.6 per cent in 1970, and 80 per cent in 1979) and television sets (69.1 per cent in 1970, 90 per cent in 1979). Even private ownership of automobiles jumped from 15.6 per cent in 1970 to 36 per cent in 1979.[2] These gains were accompanied by substantial increases in state spending for social welfare programs. Between 1970–5, expenditures increased considerably over the previous five year period for such items as education (+ 40 per cent), health and social services (+ 32 per cent), and culture (+ 243 per cent).[3] In 1971, a veritable boom in housing construction began as the regime initiated plans to build over 950,000 new dwelling units and renovate over 400,000 older ones by 1980. In close conformity with these targets, housing construction between 1970–7 grew at the phenomenal rate of 62 per cent per year (compared with 5 per cent per year during the 1963–70 period).[4] Looking to the future, the SED in 1976 announced its intention to construct an additional 2 to 2.2 million units by 1990.[5]

In addition, personal income rose significantly in the 1970s, thanks to a policy of steadily increasing salaries for workers and collective farmers and raising pensions for retired persons. In all of these categories, the percentage increases registered in the years 1970–5 and 1975–80 were higher than those achieved under Ulbricht from 1965–70.[6] Furthermore, the Honecker regime kept prices relatively stable for most basic consumer necessities, a policy which proved particularly successful in the first half of the decade. By 1975, an East German family of four actually paid a smaller share of its income for food, rent, public transportation and utilities than in 1968.[7] While the domestic price increases necessitated in the second half of the decade by the growing costs of energy inevitably affected consumer welfare (as detailed below), prices for these basic necessities were still relatively stable at the start of the 1980s.

In view of these undeniable achievements, how did East German consumers compare with their West German counterparts in the decade of the 1970s? Comparisons of this type are always difficult to make with quantitative accuracy, but the available data reveal that the GDR made some positive gains vis-à-vis the Federal Republic in the 1970s, while at the same time remaining well behind the FRG overall.

On the positive side, the GDR in the first part of the 1970s managed to close the gap separating it from the FRG in such areas as personal income and purchasing power. According to estimates by the German Institute for Economic Research (DIW) in West Berlin, the average nominal income for GDR households (in East German marks) was 45 per cent of the West German figure (as expressed in deutschemarks). This represented a marked improvement since 1969, when the figure was 30 per cent. DIW's calculations also show that, when "shopping baskets" of similar consumer items are compared for the two Germanies, the mark actually had 3 per cent more purchasing power than the deutschemark.[8] Another category in which the GDR compares favorably with the FRG is food consumption. By 1975, the average East German consumer equalled or surpassed his West German counterpart in the consumption of pork, milk, butter, potatoes, bread and certain fresh vegetables.[9]

On the negative side, however, the record shows that the West German economy significantly out-performed the GDR in most consumer oriented categories throughout the 1970s. In spite of inflation and unemployment in the FRG, incomes, pensions and social welfare spending all rose to higher levels, and at times at higher rates, than in East Germany.[10] In addition, the GDR continues to suffer from a lasting inferiority to the Federal Republic with respect to the assortment and quality of consumer goods. The relatively high cost or unavailability of automobiles, stereo sets, labor-saving household devices, high quality clothing, fine foods and the like places the East German consumer at a distinct disadvantage in comparison with most West Germans.[11] While agricultural productivity is higher in the GDR than in certain other East European countries (notably Poland), it is still much lower than in West Germany.[12] Even the GDR's extraordinary growth in housing construction loses some of its luster when one considers that West German housing units are on the whole larger, better equipped and more easily obtainable than those now under construction in the GDR (though also much more expensive.)[13]

East German consumers thus improved their lot considerably in the 1970s, but still lagged far behind West Germans in a number of consumer categories. While these perceived lags may not be sufficient to trigger regime-threatening social disturbances, they are probably harmful to the SED's attempts to broaden its popular acceptance. At the very least, such relative deprivation vis-à-vis the FRG may sap public morale, thus further reducing work incentives and support for the regime.

(B) THE TWO-CURRENCY DILEMMA

In 1973, the East German authorities decided to allow residents of the GDR to receive up to 500 DM in foreign currency as gifts from Western sources. The regime then expanded the network of "Intershops," which provided Western goods and high-quality East German commodities in exchange for hard currency. The enhanced availability of valued deutschemarks has led to the creation of an illegal second market in the GDR, as East Germans privately exchange goods and services using the West German currency as a means of payment. Moreover, the influx of deutschemarks has divided East German society into "haves" and "have-nots," sparking resentment and jealousy among those citizens who do not have personal access to West Germans bearing hard currency gifts.[14]

While no exact data can be found on the amount of deutschemarks currently being transferred into the GDR in this fashion, it is presumed to run into the hundreds of millions. In 1978, an SED Politburo member stated that up to 700 million deutschemarks per year were being spent in the Intershops.[15] The magnitude of the political and social problems that follow is considerable. In May 1978, for example, public demonstrations took place in the East German town of Wittenberge involving clashes between the local police and citizens protesting the high price of articles in the Intershops.[16] In a subsequent interview with the *Saarbrücker Zeitung* in July 1978, Erich Honecker voiced his consternation at the West German media for portraying the Intershops as a sign of the failings of the East German economy. Although he had earlier asserted that the Intershops would be "no permanent companion of socialism," it was apparent from the tone and content of his remarks that he fully supported the two-currency approach.[17]

It was therefore somewhat surprising when *Neues Deutschland*, the SED daily, announced in August 1978 that GDR citizens would no longer be permitted to buy goods in the Intershops, and that the GDR mark would henceforth be "the only valid means of payment" in the country.[18] In all likelihood, however, it was Soviet pressure rather than anything else which brought about this change of course. The new policy was disclosed in *Neues Deutschland* less than two weeks after Honecker's annual summer meeting with Brezhnev in the Crimea. Apparently the Soviets expressed some jealousy of their own when referring to the excessive privileges of East German consumers.[19]

In spite of these Soviet pressures, the Honecker regime decided after a lengthy delay to reverse itself once again. When the new rules governing the use of hard currency in the GDR were finally published on 5 April 1979, they did not contain any provisions proscribing purchases in the Intershops by GDR residents. Instead, they merely required local citizens to exchange their deutschemarks for special checks issued at East German banks. These checks could then be used to purchase items at the Intershops. Only after probing by Western reporters did the GDR authorities further disclose that no personal identification would have to be displayed by East German citizens as they purchased their checks at the banks, and ultimately it became clear that no special measures would be enforced to ensure that the checks themselves did not become objects of exchange.[20]

The two-currency system thus remained in force, a vivid illustration of the FRG's direct impact on economic and social life in the GDR. By allowing East German citizens to continue using West German currency, the Honecker regime in effect acknowledged that withdrawing this privilege might provoke a popular backlash. Moreover, Honecker was also clearly reluctant to forego the large amounts of hard currency the GDR was banking through transactions at the Intershops. It is thus another curious irony of inter-German relations that the SED has condoned the circulation of Western currency in the GDR as a means of bolstering the internal stability of the communist regime.

(C) FOREIGN TRADE WITH THE WEST AND THE DOMESTIC ECONOMY

Just as worrisome to the SED leadership as these influences on East German consumers emanating from the Federal Republic, if not more so, is the prospect that international economic forces may compel the regime to trim the sails of its consumer welfare programs in the 1980s in order to balance imports and exports. In the course of the 1970s, the GDR allowed this balance to deteriorate to the point where, by the end of the decade, East Germany had accumulated a debt of $10.5 billion to the OECD (Organization of Economic Cooperation and Development) countries alone.[21] The largest single share of this deficit was incurred in trade with the FRG, and amounted to nearly 4 billion DM by 1980.[22] As in other areas, however, this mounting trade deficit, together with a variety of other economic exchanges with the Federal Republic, has had both positive and negative effects on the SED regime.

Viewed in a positive sense, the debt to the OECD countries may be looked upon as a long-term loan which has enabled the GDR to finance the purchase of much needed technology, grain and other goods from the West, while freeing domestic financial resources for investment in other areas (such as subsidies for consumer goods). In addition to the benefits derived from these deficits, the GDR has gained considerable advantages from economic dealings with West Germany above and beyond normal inter-German trade. Over the years, the GDR has benefited from special "swing" credits, visa charges, minimum foreign exchange requirements for visitors, road and other tolls, and other fees paid out by the government and citizens of the Federal Republic and West Berlin. In February 1978, the West German government disclosed that these payments and credits totaled more than 7.5 billion DM between 1970 and the end of 1977.[23] Added to this, the GDR obtains major economic advantages from its privileged access to European Economic Community markets owing to its special status in the Treaty of Rome.

In short, the sum total of trade deficits, credits and other transactions with the West constituted a rather substantial Western subsidy of the East German economy in the 1970s. Without it, the advances registered in consumer welfare in the last decade simply could not have been accomplished on the scale attempted by the Honecker regime.

In more negative terms, however, the adverse turn in trade balances represents a lingering sign of economic dependence on the West. So embarrassing have these deficits become that in 1975 the GDR ceased publishing data on the size of its trade imbalances, and the publication of its 1980 statistical annual was delayed by several months. The unfavorable direction of these trends is all the more apparent when one notes that, from 1963–70, the GDR had a net trade surplus of approximately 5 billion VM.[24]

It is also evident that the GDR cannot expect its trading partners in the West to permit East German deficits to rise indefinitely. This means that either a contraction in East German imports or an increase in the production of East German export goods will be imperative in the 1980s. Evidence from the second half of the 1970s indicates that the SED leadership is aware of this problem, and has taken appropriate steps to deal with it. Starting in 1977, for example, the capitalist industrialized countries' share of the GDR's total foreign trade fell to 23.8 per cent, down considerably from a peak of 28.3 per cent the previous year. In 1978, the figure dipped lower still (to 22.7 per cent), before rising back up to 25.2 per cent in 1979.[25]

Moreover, the GDR in 1978 reduced the rate of growth of its total trade volume, primarily by drastically cutting back imports.[26] Honecker himself announced that the "chief problem" to be addressed in the 1979 annual plan was "to raise the production and supply of the most profitable export products of our industry in significant quantities."[27] This was a far cry from the SED chief's assertion in the early 1970s that the "main task" of the GDR economy in the years ahead was to raise living standards.

Another problem stemming from the GDR's trade practices centers on its excessive reliance on the FRG. Too much dependence on the FRG for imports and economic assistance at least opens up the possibility that Bonn might seek to extract political concessions in return for economic benefits.[28] Implicitly acknowledging this danger, the East German leadership under Honecker has moved to diversify its Western trading patterns as much as possible. Following the establishment of relations with other OECD countries after 1972, East Germany began cutting back the FRG's share of its trade with advanced capitalist nations. Whereas the Federal Republic and West Berlin accounted for 41.9 per cent of the GDR's total trade with the industrialized capitalist states in 1970, by 1976 it comprised only 30.4 per cent of the GDR's trade with these countries.[29] However, a number of problems affecting the GDR's trade with other West European countries, including the mounting deficits and relatively high inflation rates, subsequently induced the East German leaders to revert to the FRG for more trade than they might otherwise have preferred. In 1977 and 1978, the Federal Republic's portion of the GDR's trade with the capitalist countries had risen back up to 35.6 per cent and 36.2 per cent, respectively, before falling back to 30.8 per cent in 1979.[30]

The fluctuations apparent in these figures reveal both the GDR's continuing desire to reduce the Federal Republic's portion of its trade with the West as well as the difficulties encountered in realizing this goal. By the end of the decade, Bonn still represented the GDR's leading Western trade partner, accounting for 8 per cent of its total trade turnover.[31] Even in 1980, in spite of the chill in inter-German political relations occasioned by the deterioration of East–West detente, trade between the two Germanies rose by 17 per cent over the previous year.[32]

Thus the GDR has experienced both beneficial as well as detrimental consequences from its foreign trade with the West in the 1970s and early 1980s. On balance, however, the impact on the

GDR's internal system must be regarded as predominantly negative. Ultimately the GDR's growing trade imbalances with the West can only have a frustrating effect on the aspirations of East German consumers, as more investment is pumped into the export goods sector and the GDR is increasingly compelled to live within its means. Already by 1980 there were indications that shortages of food and other consumer commodities were spreading in the GDR, a reflection, at least in part, of the new economic priorities imposed on the GDR leadership by international economic conditions.

(D) THE HIGH COST OF ENERGY

Clearly the rising cost of energy has aggravated these problems appreciably. In the 1970s, East Germany witnessed sizable increases in the amounts of energy it consumed and imported, while the price for these supplies, set for the most part by the Soviet Union, went up significantly.

Fortunately for the GDR, sixty per cent of its present energy needs are currently covered by domestic sources, mostly lignite. Plans to expand lignite production may encounter obstacles in the 1980s, however, as many of the remaining deposits are difficult to mine.[33] Meanwhile, energy usage in the GDR has risen noticeably in the past decade, and energy imports have spiraled upward accordingly. East German petroleum imports nearly doubled between 1970 and 1978, going from 10.3 to 19.9 million metric tons.[34]

As the chief supplier of these petroleum imports, the Soviet Union has been the principal direct source of the skyrocketing costs imposed on the GDR as it strives to meet its energy needs. In January 1975, Moscow doubled the price of oil, coal and natural gas exported to its alliance partners, and inaugurated a new index of annual price increases on the basis of a sliding five-year average of world prices. These and subsequent price hikes resulted in a 45–50 per cent increase in the price paid by the GDR for its energy imports between 1973 and 1978.[35] As a consequence, the GDR's terms of trade with the Soviet Union deteriorated sharply. Whereas in 1970 the GDR was able to cover its oil imports from the USSR with only 7 per cent of its total exports to that country, by 1980 nearly one-quarter of its exports to the Soviet Union went to finance oil deliveries, and by 1985 this figure is expected to climb to between one-third and forty per cent of the GDR's exports to the USSR. To make matters worse, the Soviets announced that the amount of its oil deliveries to the

GDR and other Warsaw Pact allies would not increase during the 1981–5 plan period.[36]

Meanwhile, the GDR remains almost completely dependent on the Soviet Union for oil. Despite serious attempts to conclude import agreements with Middle Eastern and other petroleum exporting countries,[37] the GDR by the end of the 1970s still imported nearly 90 per cent of its petroleum from the USSR. In fact, in 1978 this figure (89.4 per cent) was actually somewhat higher than in 1975 (88.8 per cent).[38]

The domestic impact of these price increases became strikingly evident in the latter part of the 1970s. To begin with, the GDR began to curtail the rate of its oil imports, a development which inevitably affects industrial growth.[39] Although the paucity of reliable data makes it difficult to calculate the precise effects of the costs and size of petroleum imports on the GDR's industrial production, energy-related problems were at the root of the GDR's inability to meet some of the principal goals of the 1976–80 five-year plan, and surely help account for the relatively lower growth targets planned for the 1981–5 period (see Table 4.1). In the first half of 1979, for example, energy shortages aggravated by severe winter weather and delivery bottlenecks resulted in a growth rate in produced national income (GDP) of only 2 per cent. Strenuous efforts were needed in the second half of the year to bring the annual figure up to 4 per cent, a result which fell short of the planned target of 4.3 per cent. The following year's final growth rate in national income (4.2 per cent) also failed to meet the projected goal (4.8 per cent).[40]

Of particular interest to East German consumers is the fact that production of manufactures, which includes many consumer items, has been declining steadily ever since 1975.[41] Most probably this shortfall has reflected the need to divert greater investments into other sectors of the economy, with export goods and energy items taking precedence over the production of consumer goods.[42] In another category of vital interest to consumers, salaries and pensions have grown at slower rates since the late 1970s, and in January 1976 the regime introduced a phased-in schedule of price increases for raw materials and industrial goods.[43]

As the preceding overview of various trends indicates, the GDR has been palpably affected by adverse influences stemming from the international economy. These negative tendencies represent only part of the story, however. In a more positive vein, it must be noted that, as the 1980s began, the East German economy continued to

TABLE 4.1   *Recent five-year plans and results*
(figures represent percentage growth)

	1971–75 Plan Results (1970 = 100)	1976–80 Plan (1975 = 100)		1981–85 Plan Targets (1980 = 100)
		Targets	Results	
Produced national income	130	127.9	122	128–130
Industrial goods production	137	134	128	128–130
Industrial labor productivity	129	130	126	128–130
Construction industry	138	137.2	123	118–120
Individual trade turnover*	128	121.5	122	120–122
Net money income of the population	127	121.4	119.8	120–122
Investments	135	128	128	111–112†

* Includes certain foods, luxury consumables (candy, etc.) and consumer manufactures sold domestically.
† Computed by the author on the basis of figures in *Neues Deutschland*, 18–19 April 1981.
SOURCES   "Abschwächung der Wachstumsimpulse," *DIW Wochenbericht*, 6/81 (5 February 1981); *Neues Deutschland*, 18–19 April 1981.

show steady progress in a number of key areas. Even though many plan targets could not be met, the fact remains that in 1980 East Germany's produced national income grew at a rate of 4.2 per cent and in 1981 it grew at the planned rate of 5 per cent. Whether future results fall short of the planned goals or not, these figures are impressive when set beside the lower growth rates prevailing elsewhere in the Soviet bloc. Despite built-in systematic barriers to energy conservation in East German industry, the SED could boast that industrial energy consumption had declined by more than initially projected in the late 1970s and 1980.[44] Even more importantly for the central question of political stability, East German consumers have continued to receive an assortment of economic and social benefits. In addition to the wage and pension increases mentioned earlier, shift workers and working mothers saw their work time reduced to a 40-hour week in the late 1970s. Maternity leave and paid vacation time for workers were also extended. Moreover, housing construction actually exceeded the GDR's grandiose plans for the 1976–80 period by 63,000 units, and Erich Honecker announced at the SED's Xth Party Congress in April 1981 that, in keeping with previously proclaimed ambitions, up to 950,000 additional units would be built or renovated by the end of 1985.[45]

Most significantly of all, the SED remained committed to a policy of price stability for basic consumer goods, many of which have not risen in value in twenty years. At the Xth Party Congress, Honecker reaffirmed earlier pledges to keep prices stable "in the future" for many consumer essentials (such as rent, food items and certain services). Prices for new or very expensive products would rise enough to cover costs.[46] To maintain this commitment to price stability, the GDR by 1981 was devoting an estimated $10 billion a year to state subsidies for food and consumer manufactures, and an additional $2 billion to housing subsidies.[47] Meanwhile, the regime intensified its efforts in the late 1970s and early 1980s to "hide" consumer inflation by shifting a growing portion of durable goods and foods from ordinary stores to so-called "Exquisit" or "Delikat" shops, where items are classified as "luxury" goods and sold at higher prices.[48]

The picture that emerges from this sketch of the East German economy is therefore mixed. While international disturbances have definitely made their mark, the GDR has thus far managed to withstand their impact rather successfully, thanks in large measure to gains in labor productivity.[49] Thus there were no signs either in 1981 or even in 1982 of the kind of headlong plunge into economic and social disintegration that wracked Poland in the 1970s and subsequently. As Table 4.1 shows, growth in critical economic sectors in the GDR was slower in the second half of the 1970s than in the first, but respectable gains were still visible. The plan directives for 1981–5 issued at the Xth SED Congress called for even more modest growth rates in most areas than the previous five-year plan, but, here again, national income is expected to rise by more than 5 per cent per year. As a consequence, many East German consumers, surveying their situation at the start of the new decade, could conclude either that things were "getting worse, though slowly," or that they were "getting better, only more slowly than before." Depending upon which aspects of consumer welfare they chose to look at, either of these statements could be justified. The crucial question for the SED, however, was whether the pressures arising out of the world economy in the 1980s would allow the GDR to fulfill even the relatively scaled down growth targets written into the 1981–5 plan. In this respect, the slashes in the growth rates for investments projected for the 1981–5 period are not a propitious omen for the future (see Table 4.1).

II. THE DOMESTIC IMPACT OF EXTERNAL POLITICAL INFLUENCES

(A) EXPANDED INTER-GERMAN CONTACTS

The number of citizens from the Federal Republic and West Berlin visiting the GDR and East Berlin has increased astronomically in recent years, rising to a figure of 8.1 million in 1979. In addition, some 1.4 million East German pensioners were permitted to visit West Germany or West Berlin in that year, along with an additional 41,500 GDR residents having urgent family business in West Germany. Direct telephone links between the two Germanies have also multiplied since the introduction of new direct dialing procedures. In 1970, only 700,000 calls were placed in the FRG and West Berlin to the GDR and East Berlin; by 1979, the number had risen to over 19 million.[50]

While the GDR has found it difficult to impede this stream of contacts without violating the Basic Treaty and subsequent implementation agreements with Bonn, it has reacted to the new circumstances in several ways. The SED's most direct action to date has been to discourage travel into the GDR by increasing visa fees and minimum currency exchange requirements for most categories of private visitors from the West. New regulations along these lines were first introduced in 1976. Later, in October 1980, the GDR suddenly quadrupled the currency exchange requirement for Western visitors, raising them to a minimum of 25 DM. This measure was taken in the wake of the intensified East–West tensions of that year, and may in part be viewed as an East German response to Chancellor Helmut Schmidt's earlier cancellation of a summit meeting with Honecker and as a sign of the SED's nervousness about events in Poland. In any event, the move was effective in stemming the flow of Western citizens to East Germany. Between October 1980 and March 1981, the number of individuals crossing into East Berlin from

West Berlin declined by 55 per cent over the same period a year earlier.[51]

Meanwhile, the SED authorities have sought to shield the East German population from Western political and cultural influences by reinforcing ideological values. During the 1970s, SED propaganda, communicated not only by the mass media but also by the educational system and party organizations, intensified its commitment to establishing a sharp ideological "delimitation" (*"Abgrenzung"*) between the GDR and the FRG. East German citizens are subject to a veritable barrage of official commentary which pits the socialist, peace-loving and eminently successful GDR against what is portrayed as the imperialist system of West German late capitalism. Attitudes of real hatred towards the FRG are continually inculcated in the citizenry, and particularly the children, throughout the entire political socialization process. At the same time, the SED leadership has redoubled earlier efforts to develop a sense of separate GDR nationhood, completely divorced from any lingering attachments, sentimental or otherwise, to the Federal Republic. In the absence of extensive survey data, it is difficult to measure the extent of the population's receptiveness to this campaign. It has been reported, however, that a poll of East German youth conducted by the SED in the late 1970s showed that 75 per cent of those between the ages of 16 and 25 considered themselves to be "Germans," not East Germans.[52]

One aspect of the *Abgrenzungspolitik* deserves special mention. As part of its endeavor to instruct East German youth in the need to defend the "socialist fatherland" against the putative aggressive machinations of the FRG, the GDR announced in 1978 that compulsory military instruction for children in the 9th and 10th grades would soon be introduced. The official announcement of this measure evoked staunch criticism from religious leaders in the GDR. The hierarchy of the Lutheran church voiced its strong disapproval of the militarization of East German youngsters in an official statement that was read out in all pulpits in the GDR. Later, representatives of the church met with Honecker to discuss this and related issues directly. The SED tried to dampen the dispute by granting the church greater opportunities to propagate the faith and train clerics, but it did not give way on the question of military education for children. The case illustrates how readily a foreign policy issue, that of *Abgrenzung* vis-à-vis the Federal Republic, can influence domestic politics in the GDR.

(B) WEST GERMAN JOURNALISTS

Following the normalization of inter-German relations in 1972, the GDR liberalized its regulations governing the activities of West German journalists working in East Germany. In the latter half of the 1970s, however, the SED leadership increasingly soured on its earlier willingness to allow Western journalists freer rein in the GDR. A series of incidents took place which induced the SED to prevent the reportage of "bad news" from the GDR by restricting the rights of reporters from the FRG. Several journalists were eventually expelled from the country, and in January 1978 the GDR closed down the office of *Der Spiegel* in East Berlin following that journal's publication of a "Manifesto" allegedly written by SED dissidents (see below).

Harsher measures followed a year later. In April 1979, new regulations were enacted which placed tighter restrictions on the ability of Western journalists to function in East Germany.[53] Among other things, the new rules required reporters to obtain official authorization before conducting any interviews or opinion surveys. Despite official protests from West German officials, the GDR now appears intent on keeping foreign reporters within strict bounds in the future.

(C) THE FEDERAL REPUBLIC AND EAST GERMAN DISSIDENTS

Another phenomenon of the 1970s was the increasing willingness of East German writers to get around the strict censorship system by having their works published in the FRG. Those taking advantage of this opportunity included such critics of the regime as the late Robert Havemann, Rudolf Bahro, and a growing number of novelists and poets whose writings had been rejected by East German censors for being unduly critical of life in the GDR. In spite of the publicity these writings have received in West Germany, however, the ranks of the East German dissident community remain rather small. Severe repression, including an arsenal of recently augmented laws proscribing the publication abroad of material considered harmful to the GDR, has combined with the SED's relatively successful cooptation of at least part of the intelligentsia to keep internal dissent within manageable proportions for the regime.[54]

Moreover, the SED has discovered that West Germany provides a convenient "safety valve" to which dissident artists and intellectuals can be banished. Perhaps the most sensational of these cases involved the East German songwriter Wolf Biermann, whose GDR citizenship was revoked in 1976 while he was in the Federal Republic. Over the next few years, several dozen prominent writers, actors and other artists were either expelled to West Germany (as in the case of Bahro) or encouraged to emigrate. The SED authorities apparently decided it was preferable to allow these regime critics to publicize their views in West Germany rather than permit them to attack the system from within. Exiling East German dissidents has thus become one of the SED's most effective ways of keeping them isolated from other potential anti-regime elements inside the GDR, and represents another curious example of how the Federal Republic exerts both destabilizing and stabilizing influences on the East German political system.

Another manifestation of West German influence on GDR dissidents concerns the peace movements that have been particularly vocal in the two countries since 1980. In both German states, prominent cultural figures and religious leaders have joined with ordinary citizens to express their misgivings about the growing East-West arms race in Europe and to voice their anxieties *as Germans* concerning the dangers of a superpower conflict on German soil. In spite of the obstacles to public protest that exist in the GDR, a number of East German intellectuals have taken advantage of officially sanctioned meetings and the Western media to condemn both NATO and the Warsaw Pact countries for sharing responsibility for the latest escalation of nuclear missile deployments in the European theater. In addition, thousands of GDR citizens have attended meetings sponsored by their churches to discuss issues relating to the role of the military in East German life.[55] To be sure, it cannot be said that the East German opposition to the arms race simply represents an offshoot of the West German peace movement. On the contrary, anti-militarist sentiments in the GDR have strong indigenous roots, especially in local dissident and religious milieux. Nevertheless, it seems clear that disarmament has become such a prominent issue in the GDR in recent years at least in part because of the wide publicity the peace movement in the FRG has generated. Whether this converging sense of national identity on the part of East and West Germans who are critical of their governments' ties to the superpowers will grow in the future is a matter that bears watching in the 1980s.

(D) THE EFFECTS OF HELSINKI

Perhaps the most telling effects of the Helsinki accords on the GDR's domestic system center on the massive increase in the number of East German citizens who have applied for exit visas, in hopes that the SED will observe the "freedom of movement" provisions of Basket III. Estimates vary on the size of this group of would-be émigrés, ranging from a generally accepted lower figure of about 100,000 to claims that as many as 200,000 have applied to emigrate since 1975.[56] To date the GDR authorities have not been particularly inclined to honor the Helsinki guidelines. Over the long run, however, public pressures for an easing of the restrictions on travel to the West may grow, and the GDR's signature on the Helsinki Final Act may prove to be a stimulus to domestic instability rather than just the guarantee of the GDR's international legitimacy it was originally intended to be.

Two other areas affected by the Helsinki accords concern the role of Western journalists in the GDR, and the political demands advanced by East German dissidents. In each case, Basket III contains clauses which oblige the signatory states to grant these groups greater freedom to function. Moreover, both groups have referred to the CSCE agreement in pressing their case for broader professional freedom in the GDR. Neither has met with much success. In short, the SED leadership does not feel constrained to implement those aspects of Basket III which it finds unpalatable. Given the lack of any enforcement mechanism, the GDR feels it can safely ignore the human rights clauses of the Final Act.

(E) EUROCOMMUNISM

The Eurocommunist movement, which derived its impetus from the revisionist proclivities of the Italian, Spanish and French communist parties in the early to mid-1970s, has been viewed by some Western observers as containing the germ of a revisionist infection that might eventually sweep across Eastern Europe. Like other states in the region, however, the GDR has proved to be largely immune to Eurocommunist viruses. Although dissidents like Havemann and Bahro had praise for at least some aspects of Eurocommunism in their writings, there did not seem to be any extensive wave of sympathy for the West European revisionists in the SED. One of the few manifestations of Eurocommunist tendencies to surface in the

GDR occurred in January 1978, when the West German magazine *Der Spiegel* printed a "Manifesto" allegedly composed by a group of SED party members seeking fundamental change in the GDR.[57] The document called for extensive political and economic reforms, and explicitly referred to some of the notions advanced by communists in Western Europe. The flurry of controversy which the "Manifesto" stirred up swiftly died down, however, as the authors of the document never revealed their identity, and no follow-up action on their part took place. It therefore seems improbable that a reformist movement capable of effecting a split within the ranks of the SED currently exists. The declining political fortunes of the Eurocommunist parties in their own countries evident since the late 1970s may have reduced their influence in Eastern Europe even further.

(F) THE IMPACT OF EVENTS IN POLAND IN THE EARLY 1980s

The economic and political disruptions which shook Poland once again in the summer of 1980 has had obvious implications for all the communist states of East–Central Europe. In particular, the unprecedented legalization of an independent trade union ("Solidarity") and the process of renewal that took place inside the Polish United Workers' Party until the imposition of martial law in December 1981 inevitably placed all the ruling elites in the region on guard against signs of similar unrest in their own countries. For the SED, any movement in the direction of strikes or similar demonstrations of mass discontent in the GDR would be utterly intolerable. It is for this reason that the East German regime acted more quickly than most other Warsaw Pact states in making known its disapproval of the changes occurring in Poland, and quickly voiced its sympathy for the martial law regime.[58]

Fortunately for the SED leadership, East German workers have thus far shown little inclination to emulate their Polish comrades. On the contrary, Western journalists have reported a significant amount of anti-Polish sentiment among many GDR workers, reflecting both traditional ethnic antagonisms as well as animosity directed at Polish consumers who periodically cross the border to buy up goods not readily available in Poland.[59] The GDR leadership seems to have given subtle encouragement to these nationalistic sentiments. On 15 February 1981, Erich Honecker made a speech in which he referred to the eventual possibility of the reunification of Germany under a socialist system. This was the first public reference to reunification by an SED official in years, and may have been intended as an implicit reminder to East German citizens that their political destiny remained in Germany, and that only by supporting the SED could they hope to realize the ultimate goal of national unity.[60]

In the final analysis, however, the GDR's main line of defense against a possible spread of "the Polish sickness" into the GDR is a sound domestic economy. The events in Poland, even in spite of the respite from political unrest achieved thus far as a result of the Jaruzelski regime's repressive measures, thus place additional pressure on the GDR to keep growth up and consumer prices down. At the same time, the SED is aware of the need to stay in touch with working class opinion, while its leaders simultaneously strive to dampen unwarranted popular expectations with periodic reminders that "we can distribute only what is first produced."

Beyond these considerations, the GDR has other compelling reasons to hope that domestic order can be reestablished in Poland, preferably by the Polish authorities themselves. A Soviet invasion would inevitably result in a freeze in East–West relations of indefinite duration, with incalculable economic consequences for the GDR, while continued instability slows down Polish deliveries to the GDR of coal and other needed resources.[61]

III. OUTLOOK FOR THE 1980s: THREE SCENARIOS

How might the trends that have been traced thus far work themselves out in the 1980s? No assurances can be given for the accuracy of the following projections, but at least we can hazard some judgments about the relative likelihood of various possible occurrences. The three scenarios that follow are arranged in descending order of probability. All are predicated on the assumption that various international economic conditions affecting the GDR, such as the price of petroleum and of most imports from the West, will not improve in the immediate future, and may even get worse. In addition, all focus on the attitudes towards policy change that may be expressed by three major groups: the mass of the population (characterized broadly as "consumers"); the dissidents in the cultural elite; and the SED hierarchy.

(A) THE "MORE OF THE SAME" SCENARIO

In this scenario, the tendencies delineated in Parts I and II proceed along more or less the same path they have followed in the final years of the 1970s and the first years of the new decade. That is, East German consumers will continue to see some improvements in their purchasing power and in the availability of new housing and other basic consumer items, but no substantial closing of the gap in living standards between themselves and the average consumer in the FRG. Most importantly, in this scenario the political authorities make sure that consumer prices for essential commodities inside the GDR remain stable. Rising costs are covered by ever-increasing state subsidies for consumer goods. Similarly, the regime maintains its commitment to construct at least 2 million new housing units by 1980 (or, if need be, housing construction is cut back only marginally below this goal). Meanwhile, imports are held to the low levels they reached after 1977, while more investment is pumped into the export industry. As a result, growth in the production of industrial goods for East German consumers slows down. The result is a continuation of the fairly quiet acceptance of things by the bulk of the East German populace, an attitude that may be reinforced by news of rising inflation and unemployment in the Federal Republic.

Meanwhile, dissent among intellectuals and others in the cultural elite continues to assert itself, but, as in the recent past, the regime handles the problem with sufficient flexibility to avoid serious repercussions. No politically viable reform movement of any significance develops which might link the consuming masses with the dissidents. At the same time, no real push for radical change emerges within the SED elite.

(B) THE "CONSUMER INFLATION" SCENARIO

The chief hallmark of this series of possible developments is that the SED leadership, under the pressure of rising costs, feels constrained to introduce price increases for basic consumer commodities, such as rent, utilities, clothing and even the most widely consumed foods. As a consequence, the East German consumer sees his purchasing power and real income decline for the first time in years. Shortages of essential commodities aggravate the situation. In addition, the priority given to the export sector, combined with a general decline in economic growth resulting from the need to cut back imports of Western technology and to conserve energy, requires the regime to reduce expenditures substantially for both housing construction and consumer industrial goods. A general feeling then sets in among millions of East German citizens that living standards are getting "worse," instead of "better, but more slowly than before."

How will East German consumers react? The answer to this question depends on a number of variables whose realization cannot be foreseen with any certitude. Much depends, for example, on the size of the price increases, the commodities for which they are effective, the manner in which they are annouced to the public, and so on. Certainly the SED leaders will wish to avoid the mistakes committed by the Polish authorities in 1970, 1976 and 1980. For example, efforts may be made to raise prices gradually and perhaps to shift the brunt of the inflation to higher-salaried groups.

In any event, at least three developments are possible in the face of price increases and widely shared perceptions of a downturn in living standards. First, there could be generally passive acceptance of the new situation. While consumer grumbling would certainly occur and public morale would dip, popular discontent would not assume the form of overt manifestations of dissatisfaction, such as strikes, demonstrations, and the like. A second possibility is precisely such an outburst of consumer discontent. The form it takes might involve conscious attempts to emulate the Polish experiences of 1970, 1976, or, in the most extreme case, 1980. Even worse from the regime's point of view, a third eventuality can be imagined as an offshoot of the second. That is, the sudden explosion of mass anger induces dissidents and students to rush to the aid of the popular forces. In this case, the twin causes of consumer frustration and elite dissent, heretofore kept separate, would intersect, presenting the SED leadership with a challenge to its authority of crisis proportions. In the throes of these events, the SED leadership might have to back down and, like the Poles in these years, rescind the austerity measures. Meanwhile, it is assumed in this scenario that the SED hierarchy holds together, and no major "defections" to reformist elements takes place among party functionaries. This assumption does not hold, however, in the scenario to be considered next.

(c) THE "PRAGUE SPRING/POLISH SUMMER" SCENARIO

As its name implies, this scenario would involve some of the main features of the Czech reform movement of 1968 or of the Polish "renewal" that started in 1980. Among other things, this presupposes the intersection of three separate movements for change: popular elements representing mass dissatisfaction with material living conditions (as well as a large measure of anticommunism and anti-Russian feeling); dissidents from the cultural elite, including a sizable number of students; and well-placed SED functionaries demanding major reforms, perhaps along the lines of the "Manifesto."

Theoretically, an East German "Prague Spring" could develop very rapidly, following catalytic events such as public demonstrations by workers or angry consumers, or, alternatively, it could emerge gradually, in the context of a slow but visible economic stagnation. In either case, the emergence of a broad-based coalition of this kind would constitute the most acute threat to the stability of the SED regime yet considered.

Of the three scenarios just outlined, the ones most likely to transpire over the course of the next decade are the "more of the same" scenario or, quite possibly, some variant of the "consumer inflation" scenario. Prospects for the realization of the "Prague Spring/Polish Summer" scenario appear to be practically non-existent at present. For one thing, the mass of East German consumers and leading dissidents from the cultural elite have yet to show clear signs of making common cause. More importantly, the SED does not appear to contain a reformist wing of any consequence. In addition, the Jaruzelski government's crackdown on dissent in Poland starting in December 1981 has already demonstrated that there are limits to a communist regime's tolerance of domestic political turmoil in Eastern Europe. The principle reason for including this scenario here is to explain why one should be inclined to discount it. Given the long-standing tranquility of the East German working class, the relative homogeneity of the SED elite, and the continuing ability of the East German economy to grow by more than 4 per cent per year while providing economic and social benefits, however modestly, to the consumers,[62] it appears that the decade of the 1980s will probably witness either "more of the same" or, at the worst, the passive acceptance by the East German masses of socio-economic stagnation.

In any event, one of the chief questions which the SED leadership may have to confront in the decade ahead is the problem of whether to introduce price increases for basic consumer needs. A related problem concerns the government's ability to make good on its promises of major new housing construction. Certainly the leading authorities will want to defer making hard choices on these issues for as long as possible. Whatever the outcome, the GDR must in any case look forward to a decade of rising international prices, more deficits, fewer imports, a freeze on Soviet oil exports, higher domestic costs, declining investment rates, more attention to producing goods for export, and lower rates of growth in consumer-related industries. The result will quite possibly be a period of lower growth rates in national income than the GDR has seen since the early 1960s. How the SED leadership handles the potentially volatile politics of these conditions will determine whether the GDR remains the bedrock of political stability it has been over the last two decades.

Perhaps the most paradoxical conclusion to emerge from this study centers on the question of whether the GDR is more stable at the outset of the 1980s than a decade earlier, or less so. Although the pluses and minuses of this question cannot be calculated with any precision, it seems that, on the whole, the political influences on the GDR stemming from the outside world have tended to be more supportive of the SED regime than destabilizing in nature, while the economic influences have been mixed, including both powerful stabilizing as well as potentially destabilizing elements. The paradox that underlies these tendencies derives from the fact that, over the past decade, it is the Federal Republic of Germany that has become a primary source of stabilizing influences, thanks above all to its recognition of the GDR and to its generous infusions of economic assistance of various kinds, while the Soviet Union has in effect become a major source of destabilizing impulses by virtue of its economically debilitating energy policies. Of course, West Germany continues to exert a strong attraction over the East German population by its very existence as an economically advanced, democratic state, and the USSR (which maintains nearly 400,000 troops in East Germany) remains the ultimate guarantor of the GDR's survival as a communist state. What has changed in the course of the 1970s however, is that Bonn, which once sought to isolate the GDR by denying it formal recognition, has lately acquired a large stake in the GDR's political stability, since only a secure East German leadership can feel strong enough to procede with expanded contacts between German citizens. Meanwhile, the Soviets have been increasingly willing to risk political instability in East–Central Europe by imposing onerous economic costs on its Warsaw Pact allies. A dramatic shift has thus occurred in the principal external sources of stability and instability on the German Democratic Republic. It thus appears that the future of internal stability in the

GDR in the 1980s will remain inextricably linked with external political and economic forces that are difficult, if not impossible, to control.

NOTES AND REFERENCES

1. On Ulbricht's perceptions, see Michael J. Sodaro, "Ulbricht's Grand Design: Economics, Ideology, and the GDR's Response to Detente," *World Affairs*, vol. 142, no. 3 (Winter 1980), pp. 147–68.
2. See Doris Cornelsen, "The GDR in a Period of Foreign Trade Difficulties: Developments and Prospects for the 1980's," in *East European Economic Assessment*, Part 1 (Washington: Joint Economic Committee of the US Congress, 1981) p. 311.
3. Deutsches Institut für Wirtschaftsforschung, *Handbuch DDR-Wirtschaft* (Reinbeck: Rowohlt, 1977) p. 333. (Hereafter cited as *Handbuch DDR-Wirtschaft*.)
4. Cited in Hans-Dieter Schulz, "Der Verteidiger hat das Wort," *Deutschland Archiv*, 4/1978, p. 338. (Hereafter this source will be cited as DA.)
5. *Handbuch DDR-Wirtschaft*, pp. 145–6. See also Manfred Melzer, "Wohnungsversorgung und Wohnungsqualität in der DDR," ibid., 9/1978, pp. 963–8, and Michael Langhof, "Zum Bedeutungswandel der Wohnungspolitik der DDR," ibid., 4/1979, pp. 1390–1404.
6. *Handbuch DDR-Wirtschaft*, p. 219; Cornelsen, "The GDR in a Period of Foreign Trade Difficulties," p. 303.
7. *Handbuch DDR-Wirtschaft*, p. 229.
8. Ibid., pp. 230–1.
9. Ibid., p. 234.
10. Statistisches Bundesamt, *Statistisches Jahrbuch für die Bundesrepublik Deutschland* (Bonn: 1972, 1975, 1978). (Hereafter this source will be cited as *Statistisches Jahrbuch der BRD*.) See also Bundesministerium für innerdeutsche Beziehungen, *Zahlenspiegel* (Bonn: 1978).
11. The fact that state investments in repairs and services in the GDR declined 80 per cent between 1970 and 1975 is just one indication that progress in some consumer categories must be paid for with shortcomings in others. See *Handbuch DDR-Wirtschaft*, p. 333. See also Charlotte Otto-Arnold and Heinz Vartmann, "Das Kaufkraftverhältnis zwischen der D-Mark und der Mark der DDR Mitte 1981," in DA, 5/1982, pp. 513–9.
12. By 1981 an average agricultural worker could feed 18 persons in the GDR, 34 in the FRG, and 7 in Poland. See Dan Morgan, "East Germans Produce More Meat but Rely Heavily on U.S. Grain," *The Washington Post*, 24 April 1981, p. A37.
13. The average dwelling unit in the FRG has 75 square meters, as opposed to 59 in the GDR. By the mid-1970s, 64 per cent of the West German units had three rooms or more, while over 80 per cent of the East German units had three rooms or fewer. Even after completion of the goals of the 1971–5 period, only 17 per cent of the GDR's housing units had central

heating, and fewer than half had indoor toilets. See *Handbuch DDR Wirtschaft*, pp. 142–4.

14. On these points, see Hartmut Zimmerman, "The GDR in the 1970's," *Problems of Communism*, vol. XXVII, no. 2 (March–April 1978) pp. 38–9.

15. Hans-Dieter Schulz, "Vor dem Einkauf schnell zum Bank," DA, 5/1979 p. 452; ND, 14 December 1978.

16. See DA, 6/1978, p. 670.

17. The interview is reprinted in DA, 8/1978, pp. 881–8. See also Dettmar Cramer, "Abschied vom Intershop?," DA, 9/1978, p. 898.

18. ND, 8 August 1978.

19. For speculation as to Soviet motives, see Cramer, "Abschied vom Intershop?," pp. 897–8.

20. See Schulz, DA, 5/1979, pp. 451–3. For an excellent survey of Soviet–GDR relations, see Angela Stent, "Soviet Policy Toward the German Democratic Republic," in Sarah M. Terry (ed.), *Soviet Policy in Eastern Europe* (forthcoming).

21. *The Economist*, 22 March 1980, p. 78. By the end of 1982, the GDR's debt stood at $14 billion. See *Time*, 10 January 1983, p. 43.

22. For the figures, see Arthur A. Stahnke, "The Economic Dimensions and Political Context of FRG–GDR Trade," *East European Economic Assessment*, Part 1, p. 340. See also Ronald G. Oechsler, "GDR Trade with the Industrial West Since 1975: Performance and Prospects," in *East European Economic Assessment*, Part 1, pp. 325–39.

23. Computed from official West German figures, reprinted in DA, 5/1978, pp. 529–33.

24. See Hans-Dieter Schulz, "Kann die SED Führung jetzt pfeifen?," DA, 6/1979, p. 564. The Valutamark (VM) is the currency in which the GDR conducts its foreign trade. In 1976, 1 VM was equal to 0.72 DM, and in 1978 1 VM was equal to 0.634 DM.

25. Computed from data in *Statistisches Jahrbuch der Deutschen Demokratischen Republik 1979* (East Berlin, 1979) p. 232. (Hereafter this source will be cited as *Statistisches Jahrbuch der DDR 1979*.) Also, *Statistisches Taschenbuch der Deutschen Demokratischen Republik 1980* (East Berlin, 1980) p. 91. (Hereafter this source will be cited as *Statistisches Taschenbuch der DDR 1980*.)

26. Total trade grew by only 6 per cent in 1978, a figure that was half of the average annual percentage growth in trade in the period after 1970. Significantly, imports increased by a mere 1.7 per cent while exports went up by 10 per cent. See "DDR-Aussenhandel: Importrestriktionen bei unzureichendem Exportvermögen" (West Berlin: DIW Wochenbericht 47/49, 1979) pp. 478–80. See also Maria Haendcke-Hoppe, "DDR-Aussennandel unter dem Zwang zum Erfolg," DA, 3/1982, pp. 262–9.

27. *Neues Deutschland*, 25 May 1978. (Hereafter this source will be cited as ND.)

28. For a study of West German efforts to use trade with its Eastern neighbors as political leverage, see Angela Stent, *From Embargo to Ostpolitik: The Political Economy of West German–Soviet Relations*,

1955–1980 (New York: Cambridge University Press, 1981); for an analysis of this question as it relates to inter-German trade, see Stahnke, "The Economic Dimensions . . ."

29. Computed from data in *Handbuch DDR-Wirtschaft*, p. 233.
30. Calculated from figures in *Statistisches Jahrbuch der DDR 1979*, and in *Statistisches Taschenbuch 1980*.
31. *Statistisches Taschenbuch 1980*, p. 91.
32. "Innerdeutscher Handel: Eingeengter Expansionsspielraum" (West Berlin: DIW Wochenbericht 12/81, 1981) p. 137.
33. See the article by State Planning Commissioner Gerhard Schürer in *Einheit*, 12/1978, pp. 1245 ff., and Werner Gruhn, "Zur Energiepolitik der DDR," DA, 11/1979, p. 1160. At the Xth SED Party Congress, Honecker stated that indigenous energy sources accounted for 60 per cent of the GDR's total energy consumption, but this figure was down from the 67 per cent level reported in the GDR in the late 1970s. See ND, 12 April 1981.
34. "DDR-Aussenhandel . . . ," p. 480.
35. Hans-Dieter Schulz, "Ein neuer Wachstumsverlust," DA, 1/1979, pp. 6–7. Soviet oil prices for the GDR are one-half the world market price. See Honecker's speech in ND, 12 April 1981.
36. See "Handel DDR-UdSSR im Zeichen verminderten Wachstums" (West Berlin: DIW Wochenbericht, 7/80, 1980).
37. For an analysis of the GDR's efforts to obtain oil from Third World producers, see Michael Sodaro, "The GDR and the Third World: Supplicant and Surrogate," in Michael Radu (ed.), *Eastern Europe and the Third World* (New York: Praeger, 1981).
38. Computed from data in *Statistisches Jahrbuch der DDR 1979*.
39. Between 1970–75, East German oil purchased abroad grew by an average of 10.8 per cent per year; in 1978, they grew by only 4.6 per cent. Computed from data in *Statistisches Jahrbuch der DDR 1979*.
40. "DDR-Wirtschaft im Strukturwandel" (West Berlin: DIW Wochenbericht, 6/81, 1981) p. 68.
41. For figures, see Doris Cornelsen, "Wachstumseinbüssen infolge extremen Witterungsbedingungen," DA, 10/1979, p. 1085. In 1981, domestic consumer trade grew by only 2.5 per cent, falling short of the goal of 4 per cent. See ND, 16–17 January 1982.
42. Honecker himself noted at the Xth SED Congress that, between 1976–80, 60 per cent of all industrial investments went to energy items. ND, 12 April 1981.
43. For a list of these scheduled increases, see Cornelsen, "The GDR in a Period of Foreign Trade Difficulties . . . ," p. 321.
44. ND, 12 April 1981.
45. Ibid. Housing construction in 1981 also exceeded the planned targets for that year. See ND, 16–17 January 1982.
46. ND, 12 April 1981. See also Honecker's earlier pledge to maintain price stability at the 11th plenum of the SED Central Committee in December 1979, in ND, 14 December 1979.
47. If state subsidies were to be undertaken in the United States on the same scale as in the GDR, the equivalent figures would be $120 billion per

year for food and consumer goods and $24 billion for housing. See Dan Morgan, "E. Germany Feels its Welfare Program Makes Labor Strife Unlikely," *The Washington Post,* 15 April 1981, p. A30.

48. "Abschwächung der Wachstumsimpulse" (West Berlin: DIW Wochenbericht 6/81, 1981) p. 74.

49. Honecker attributed 90 per cent of the recent growth in national income to increases in labor productivity. ND, 12 April 1981.

50. *Jahresbericht 1979* (Bonn: Bundesministerium für innderdeutsche Beziehungen, 1980) pp. 18, 20.

51. *The Washington Post,* 27 March 1981, p. A9. For statistics on interGerman travel in 1981, see DA, 3/1982, p. 237.

52. *Der Spiegel,* 1 October 1979, p. 105.

53. For the documentation, see DA, 7/1979, pp. 773–84.

54. For an extended discussion of the GDR's treatment of dissidents, see Michael J. Sodaro, "Limits to Dissent in the GDR: Fragmentation, Cooptation and Repression," in Jane L. Curry (ed.), *Dissent in Eastern Europe* (New York: Praeger, 1983).

55. For more detail on the GDR peace movement, see ibid. See also the documentation in DA, 3/1982, pp. 313–36 and 5/1982, pp. 542–7.

56. See the estimates in Werner Volkmer, "East Germany: Dissenting Views in the Last Decade," in Rudolf L. Tőkés (ed.), *Opposition in Eastern Europe* (London: Macmillan Press, 1979) p. 121.

57. For the text, see *Der Spiegel,* 2 January 1978, pp. 21–4, and 9 January 1978, pp. 26–30.

58. For an analysis of GDR commentary on the Polish events, see the articles by Peter Jochen Winters in DA, 10/1980, 1/1981, and 3/1982.

59. *Der Spiegel,* 20 October 1980, p. 21.

60. ND, 16 February 1981.

61. Dan Morgan, "E. Germans Cast Uneasy Eye Toward Poland," *The Washington Post,* 11 April 1981, p. A21.

62. According to official sources, produced national income in the GDR rose by 5 per cent in 1981, but by only 3 per cent in 1982. See ND, 16/17 January 1982 and 15/16 January 1983. The 1983 plan calls for a growth rate in this category of 4.2 per cent. See ibid., 4/5 December 1982.

Part II

The Role of Specialist Elites

5 The Scientific–Technological Revolution and the Role of Specialist Elites in Policy-making in Czechoslovakia

SHARON L. WOLCHIK

The role of experts or specialist elites in the making of policy in socialist states is a question which has received a good deal of attention since these states were established. It is also a question which has become increasingly important in the past decade, for scholars and policy-makers in Eastern Europe and the Soviet Union, as well as observers in the West, have argued that the continued economic development of these societies will depend on the efficient utilization of specialized knowledge. In the pages to follow, I discuss some of these expectations concerning the proper function of expertise and those who possess it in policy-making. I then evaluate the role which specialists have played in Czechoslovakia and the factors which have influenced that role during various periods, with particular emphasis on the making of demographic policy. Finally, I discuss the outlook for specialist influence on policy-making in Czechoslovakia in the 1980s and the implications of this outlook for the political system.

THE SCIENTIFIC–TECHNOLOGICAL REVOLUTION AND MODERNIZATION

Analysts in Eastern Europe and the Soviet Union agree with the

111

expectations of certain West European and American scholars that specialists will play an increasingly important role in policy-making in socialist states as these states become more developed economically. However, their framework for discussing such issues and their main areas of concern differ. East European and Soviet discussions of the role of experts tend to be couched in terms of the scientific–technological revolution. Drawing on terminology which was introduced first in the Soviet Union, these analysts argue that economic progress in the future will depend heavily on the extent to which scientific knowledge and technical expertise can be generated and incorporated into the day-to-day working of the economy and society.[1] From this perspective, the chief concern is how efficiently such knowledge and expertise can be utilized in the making of public policy.

Western observers also point to the needs of economic development and modernization as the primary factors leading to increased participation of experts in decision-making in these societies. The argument is often made, for example, that greater reliance on objective, rational criteria in the making of decisions and greater attention to the input of specialists are key factors in overcoming the difficulties which socialist elites face in achieving desired levels of economic development or running advanced industrial economies.[2] However, Western scholars also point to a second set of influences which may lead to an increased role for specialists in decision-making, that is, the impact which modernization has had in increasing the resources of specialists as well as the need for their skills. Thus, certain analysts argue that modernization has produced greater social diversity in socialist states and established the groundwork for the development of group identities and interests on the part of specialists.[3] Given this perspective, Western scholars have tended to be more concerned with the implications which greater specialist participation in decision-making would have for the continuation of current political systems than have analysts in Eastern Europe and the Soviet Union. This focus on the potential political consequences of greater specialist input in policy-making and the corresponding problem of political control of specialist activities was particularly evident in the 1960s, when many Western analysts argued that an increased role for specialists would eventually lead to a decrease in the communist party's control in certain areas of society, if not to political liberalization or democratization.

Discussion of the role of specialists in Czechoslovakia has reflected both of these perspectives. Radovan Richta and other members of the interdisciplinary team which the Communist Party of Czechoslovakia commissioned in the early 1960s to study the requirements of the scientific–technological revolution in Czechoslovakia outlined the former argument in *Civilization at the Cross-roads* and set the stage for further discussion. Arguing that the effective use of scientific knowledge would be the key factor in how well the Czechoslovak economy produced in the future, Richta and his colleagues called for the elimination of barriers to the utilization of such knowledge and urged the development of measures to encourage persons who possessed expertise to further develop and use their skills.[4]

On the basis of these and similar formulations, which legitimized the role of experts without challenging the leading role of the party or the continued monopoly of power by current party leaders, specialists in Czechoslovakia came to play an increasingly important role in the formation of public policy as well as in stimulating the period of debate among intellectuals which predated the actual political reform of the late 1960s. As debate became more open, certain intellectuals called for the recognition of social diversity and argued that the interests of particular social groups might continue to conflict with each other even under socialism.[5] Basing their arguments on this new view of the nature of socialist society, specialists and professionals argued for greater autonomy to practice their professions and, during the reform era itself, for the right to advocate and defend professional interests. They also continued to press for an increased role in policy-making.[6]

The role which specialists and intellectuals played in setting the conditions which eventually led to the reform era in Czechoslovakia, as well as in the making of public policy during this period, is well documented. Economists, jurists, historians, and writers, to take but a few examples, took extremely active roles in bringing problems to the attention of party leaders, formulating possible policies, and advocating particular alternatives.[7] During the reform era itself, many experts put themselves at the disposal of the reform leadership. As Vladimir Kusin notes, "The Dubček leadership could, from the very beginning, count on unprecedented expertise, such as the previous regime was partly denied and partly refused to accept. . . . (F)ew regimes had ever been able to rely on such formidable theoretical support."[8]

To what extent does the current Czechoslovak leadership enjoy similar benefits? While we know a great deal about the activities of experts during the reform era, far less attention has been given to the role of experts in policy-making since that time. The effects of "normalization," or the reversal of most aspects of the reform process, which have been evident since the early 1970s, and the very active role which many experts and intellectuals played in that process may be presumed to have created less favorable conditions for the exercise of influence by specialists in Czechoslovakia than existed in the mid- to late-1960s. At the same time, however, the situation which led to increased specialist input at that time, including severe economic problems, has not changed. Thus, as they enter the 1980s, Czech and Slovak leaders are confronted with many of the difficulties common to the region, including poor economic performance and a declining ability to satisfy popular aspirations for improvements in the standard of living. Recent discussions of economic policy, as well as the limited economic reform focusing on improving efficiency and limiting the use of scarce energy and other resources which went into effect in January 1981, reemphasize the importance of taking a scientific approach to decision-making in the economic and other spheres.

Czech and Slovak leaders will therefore continue to face the dual problem noted above: how to use the knowledge of specialists effectively and at the same time prevent greater specialist input and autonomy from threatening the existing political order. The pages to follow examine the role which specialists have played in the making of policy in one area during several periods in Czechoslovakia in order to evaluate the likelihood that communist leaders will meet both of these challenges successfully in the 1980s.

Numerous analysts of policy-making in the United States and other countries have argued that the process by which policy is made, the type of conflict involved, and the number and kind of political actor likely to take part all vary according to the "issue area," or type of policy.[9] Thus, specialists, as well as other groups and individuals outside the circle of top political elites, are more likely to play a significant role in the making of certain kinds of policy than they do in others. In socialist countries specialist input appears to be most likely on those policy issues which are problematic, that is, in which there is no obvious, easily-agreed upon solution, but not sensitive ideologically, that is, those which do not threaten either the existing political order or the power of top political leaders.[10]

The likelihood of specialist influence on policy-making also appears to be conditioned by two other important sets of factors: the nature and resources of the specialists and the political climate. Thus, specialists with greater resources, including highly valued expertise, a higher degree of group identity and cohesion, and access to top political decision-makers, appear to have a greater chance of influencing policy than those less favored. At the same time, both the likelihood that specialists will attempt to influence policy and the willingness of political leaders to solicit or tolerate specialist intervention in policy-making are clearly influenced by the general political climate in socialist states. This climate may be expected to influence the kinds of tools which specialists use to intervene in policy-making, as well as the extent of specialist intervention.[11]

DEMOGRAPHIC POLICY AS A POLICY ISSUE

The impact of these factors is evident in the role which specialists have played in the formation of demographic policy in Czechoslovakia. As in other arenas, specialist influence in this policy area has gone through a number of stages which differed in terms of the extent of such influence, the number and kinds of specialists involved, and the tools of influence used by specialists.

As the variety and frequency of measures adopted illustrate, demographic policy is an important and problematic issue in Czechoslovakia. Elite concern centers around the low birth rates, which date from the mid-1950s. To a certain extent, this decline in the birth rate, which persisted with slight variations to the late 1960s, paralleled the drop in rates of natural increase which occurred in many Western countries as they industrialized. However, in Czechoslovakia, as well as in several other East European states, the decline in the birth rate has been greater than the level of economic development alone would suggest and reflects the additional impact of certain aspects of the strategy of economic development chosen after the establishment of communist-led systems, including high employment rates of women in the productive ages, severe housing shortages, and insufficient child care facilities and services. The liberal abortion law introduced in Czechoslovakia in late 1957 also contributed to the decline in the rate of reproduction.[12]

The consequences of such low birth rates include the aging of the population and the reduction of the future labor force. The latter effect is particularly disturbing to Czech and Slovak leaders because the country is already experiencing a labor shortage. In addition, the fact that rates of reproduction in Slovakia, although also declining, remained higher than in the Czech Lands, raised the possibility of eventually upsetting the ethnic balance.

Measures to improve the birth rate also, however, have their costs, as Czech and Slovak elites were to discover. Pro-natalist policies which encourage women to pay more attention to their maternal roles and in practice remove young women from the labor force for extended periods of time decrease the number of persons in the current labor force. They also pose problems for economic managers and enterprise directors who must accomodate the maternity leaves and return of women in the childbearing ages; success in increasing the number of children born also puts additional pressure on already scarce services and child care facilities.[13] In addition, determined efforts to increase the number of births also pose certain medical problems and raise the possibility that unwanted children will not receive a proper upbringing. The problematic nature of policy decisions in this area, then, and the resulting need for specialists to evaluate the relative merits of various approaches, may be expected to create favorable conditions for specialists to have an input in policy-making.

At the same time, demographic policy does not involve issues which are particularly sensitive in ideological terms. With the exception of the early post-Second World War period, discussion of the birth rate problem did not involve any major contradiction of Marxist–Leninist ideology. Nor did it represent a threat to the leading role of the communist party or the power of incumbent party leaders. Specialist elites could thus depict policy questions in this area as largely technical ones, that is, issues which should be decided on the basis of judgments made by those with the specialized knowledge to evaluate population trends and the probable impact of various policy measures. For both of these reasons, then, this area is one where we might expect experts or specialist elites to exert a good deal of influence on policy-making.

In contrast to many policy areas, the outcome of policy decisions in this area does not directly affect the professional or institutional interests of the groups most involved in the making of policy, even though certain social groups do gain or lose as the result of the decisions adopted. Thus, although specialists such as demographers and economists were expected to put forward policy proposals which reflected their institutional affiliations, I expected policy conflict to center far more around analytical issues. Given the technical nature of the issues and the type of conflict involved, I also expected research and persuasion of relevant state and party elites on technical grounds to be the chief tools which experts would use in intervening in the policy-making process. In fact, the nature of the conflict and the resources which specialists used both varied a good deal, depending in large part on changes in the political climate.

STAGE ONE: FORMULATING THE PROBLEM

This stage, which dated from approximately 1956 to the early 1960s, saw certain specialist elites, most notably demographers and statisticians working in the State Statistical Office, bring the birth rate problem to the attention of political leaders. In order to do this, they had to overcome the barriers posed by both ideological constraints and the undeveloped state of demography as a discipline or profession in the early 1950s. As in other socialist states, the political elites in Czechoslovakia, as well as members of the intelligentsia, accepted the view that the establishment of a socialist system would be accompanied by spontaneous population growth.[14] Thus, policy-makers discussed pro-natalist measures in the immediate post-war period, particularly in terms of how best to overcome the negative population impact of the war, but they enacted very few concrete measures to encourage childbearing. This policy continued after 1948, when communist elites began the process of encouraging rapid economic development and transforming society. The constitution of the new Czechoslovak state officially recognized the state's responsibility to provide financial aid to families with children, and a system of children's allowances was set up. However, these payments were small, and the allowances were seen as part of the general social welfare system rather than as specifically pro-natalist measures. The few analyses of the reasons why the population was not increasing as rapidly as expected pointed to the continued influence of the poor demographic conditions of the interwar period and the negative effects of the war itself on the health of men and women of childbearing age.[15]

The undeveloped state of demography as an academic discipline during this period also inhibited a more realistic assessment of the causes of population problems at this time. Although demography had been taught in Czechoslovakia since 1897 and as an independent university level subject since 1923,[16] few professors lectured on the subject until the late 1950s and early 1960s. Demography suffered from the same conditions which affected the other social sciences during the Stalinist period. Under these conditions, demographers were unable to conduct empirical research or question the official explanation for negative population developments. As a textbook for demography students published in 1969 notes, the task of demographers during this period was to "attack Malthusianism, clarify the class character of capitalist states, expose bourgeois demography as an instigation to genocide, and expose the apologetic nature of all social sciences under capitalism."[17]

Change in this state of affairs came about as the result of two different sets of developments. First, the birth rate continued to decline, despite elite expectations; particularly after 1953, it became increasingly obvious that previous expectations and explanations concerning population issues were not adequate. The change in the political climate in Czechoslovakia which occurred after the XXth Congress of the Communist Party of the Soviet Union facilitated this realization, for demographers and other specialists were able to use the slight relaxation of ideological pressure which occurred during this period to conduct the first empirical investigations of the causes of population problems. The first of these researches was organized by the State Statistical Office and carried out in 1956. Based on a nonrepresentative sample of women between the ages of 20 and 39, the study focused on the women's family plans, employment status, and factors influencing their desire to limit family size.[18] This study was followed by others which investigated fertility levels in newly built housing developments in Prague and other population-related issues.[19]

The development of an empirical orientation toward population questions was aided by the establishment of the State Population Commission in 1958. Whereas the earliest empirical studies were made possible by the slight relaxation of ideological pressure in the intellectual sphere after changes in the political arena, the catalyst for the establishment of the Population Commission was the adoption of the 1957 law legalizing abortion.[20] A measure which Czech and Slovak elites enacted soon after the Soviets and several other East European leaders had liberalized abortion, the law was later justified as a means of preventing the harm to women and families caused by the growing number of illegal abortions in Czechoslovakia. Part of the law called for the formation of a commission to oversee its operations.

The Commission itself, which originally consisted of 20 specialists and representatives of mass organization,[21] was important for several reasons during this period. First, members of the Commission organized a number of additional studies of population issues. In cooperation with the State Statistical Office, the Commission sponsored research on expenditures for children; the adequacy of urban and rural living conditions; marriage, contraception, and abortion; the success of students with working mothers; and numerous studies of women's situation at work and at home.[22] The results of these studies, many of which were confirmed by later, more methodologically sophisticated surveys, formed the basis of a more realistic approach to population issues.

The State Population Commission also appears to have contributed to the growing self-awareness of demographers and the development of demography as a profession. Members of the Commission wrote the first post-Second World War textbooks for use in new courses on demography in several university departments, and the number of courses also increased, particularly in faculties of natural sciences and economic geography departments.[23] In 1959, the State Statistical Office began publishing a specialized journal, *Demografie,* four times a year to report the results of demographic researches. It also issued several collections of demographic research results in 1959, 1961, and 1962.[24]

As the result of these developments, demographers began to acquire both the legitimacy and the tools to enter policy debates concerning the population problem. But their opportunities to use these tools to influence policy during this period appear to have been quite limited.[25] Certain specialists were able to conduct research, and an institution was available to serve as a forum for articulating policy prescriptions and contacting members of the political elites. The active participation of demographers and other specialists in the formation of population policy, however, would have to await a more fundamental change in the political climate.

STAGE TWO: DEBATING THE ALTERNATIVES

Whereas demographers and specialists in the statistical office and elsewhere working on population-related issues were the main specialists involved in discussing demographic policy in the 1950s, in the 1960s debates over these issues came to involve a number of other individuals, including other specialists, such as economists, psychologists, and sociologists, as well as managers, educators, physicians, other health-care professionals and representatives of the mass organizations. For a short period of time, larger groups of citizens were also involved, most particularly members of the women's organizations.

The nature of specialist involvement in the policy-making process also changed during this period. Whereas the main role of experts during the 1950s and early 1960s was to bring a new problem to the attention of the political elites, specialists in the 1960s took active roles in arguing for the adoption of various population measures and evaluating the success of policies after they were adopted. In doing so, they continued to use scientific expertise as a primary tool of influence; however, particularly in the mid- to late-1960s, they also used other resources, including ties with certain factions of the political leadership and links with broader groups of citizens, to support their positions.

The role which specialists played in the making of demographic policy at this time was conditioned by three main influences. First, the early 1960s saw a continuation of the development of demography as a separate and legitimate discipline. Particularly after 1964, when sociology also was reestablished as an academic field, demography was introduced as a subject of study in an increasing number of higher educational institutions. In contrast to the earlier period when demography lectures were given primarily in natural science faculties as part of regional geography curricula, most courses were now given in philosophy departments or in newly established departments of sociology or social science.[26] The growing recognition of demography as a profession also was reflected in the creation of the Czechoslovak Demographic Society as part of the Academy of Sciences in 1964, as well as in several professional conferences organized in the mid-1960s.[27] As reports on these conferences and a review of the subjects published in the demographic journal *Demographie* indicate, demographers were conducting research on a broader range of subjects than in the late 1950s. The studies conducted during this period also began to reflect the better training of researchers in the field and increased familiarity with the preoccupations and techniques of Western demographic research.

The growing professionalization of demographers was given added impetus by the more general changes taking place among intellectuals in Czechoslovakia in the 1960s. As noted earlier, the period immediately preceding and leading up to the reform period in the late 1960s in Czechoslovakia was one of intense activity among intellectuals. As part of this process of questioning earlier practices, certain specialists came to argue for greater autonomy to practice their professions and, in many cases, claimed the right to define and defend their own professional interests in contrast to those of other professions or social groups. At the same time, certain members of the political elite, faced with pressing difficulties in many areas of society and economics, now welcomed specialist input in decision-making. This greater receptivity on the part of political leaders is most evident in the numerous teams of scholars which the party commissioned to study different social problems.[28] In this climate, demographers, including those originally trained in other disciplines, as well as other specialists, strengthened the institutional bases of their professions and took a more active role in policy debates.

A final factor which was favorable to greater intervention by specialists in the making of demographic policy during this period was the continued decline in the birth rate. Despite increases in the family allowances in 1959, the number of live births continued to fall and reached 15.7 per 1,000 population in 1961.[29] Elite concern over this trend was reflected in the consideration of population issues at the 12th Congress of the party in 1962 and in the adoption of certain pro-natalist measures at that time.[30] It was also reflected in the reorganization of the State Population Commission which was expanded in 1963 and given greater power to influence the preparation of population measures.[31] The Commission continued to be responsible for supervising the abortion law and preparing educational materials to foster positive attitudes toward parenthood. In addition, Commission members were also charged with organizing research on a variety of demographic issues, evaluating population trends, making suggestions to the political elites concerning population measures, and checking the effects which legislation would have on the living standards of families with children.[32]

The increased authority of the Commission was reflected in the 1964 decision to allow its periodic reports to be printed rather than circulated in mimeographed form as they had been during 1958–9 and 1962–3.[33] As part of its work, the Commission sponsored an increasing number of surveys and research studies during this period, including several which examined changes in the status of women and the impact of these changes on fertility patterns.[34] Commission members, as well as other specialists interested in demographic questions, used the results of these surveys to support various policy prescriptions in the mid to late 1960s. In the more open conditions which prevailed during this period, numerous other specialists, including economists, psychologists, and educators, as well as managers, representatives of economic enterprises, and officials of the ministries and mass organizations, also took part in the discussion of population issues.

This process went through two fairly distinct phases. During the first, specialist elites used professional meetings, articles in specialized journals, formal and, presumably, informal contacts with the political elites, to raise previously undiscussed issues and point out possible conflicts which might arise from the adoption of particular policy measures. This phase, which to some extent should be seen as a continuation of the stage discussed earlier, saw a gradual extension of the limits of debate on many types of social issues, as well as a more open expression on the part of specialists of a desire to take a more active role in the formation of policy. At the same time, however, debate over various policy alternatives remained confined to the elite level.

In the mid to late 1960s, the number of groups involved in discussion of population issues increased. Although the most important actors continued to be political and specialist elites, debate over the consequences and desirability of various population measures spread beyond the elite level to include certain members of those groups which would be most directly affected by the outcome of the debates. In these conditions, certain specialists came to serve as a conduit for bringing the desires of citizens to the attention of political decision-makers.

The debates over demographic policy in the 1960s centered around several issues. First, specialist elites and policy-makers debated the best means of increasing the birth rate, including the relative merits of positive incentives and such measures as restricting the grounds for abortion or access to contraceptives. Specialists also discussed the role of women in contributing to the low birth rate and how best to deal with the fact that women were both workers and mothers. A related issue involved the costs and benefits of supporting women to remain at home to care for small children or expanding public child care facilities. Finally, specialists and policy-makers considered the economic aspects of various pro-natalist measures, including the immediate and long-term economic costs of having sizeable numbers of women withdraw from the labor force to have children.[35]

In the course of these debates, specialists formed informal coalitions with other experts and members of the political elite to support particular policy positions. At times, these coalitions also included representatives of the mass organizations and members of broader social groups. One of the most important of these coalitions in terms of its impact on the making of demographic policy included members of the State Population Commission, sociologists and demographers employed in state research institutes, such as the Research Institute for the Study of Public Opinion and the Research Institute on the Living Standard in Bratislava, and intellectuals who were members of the Women's Committee. Particularly during the late 1960s, specialists and officials from these organizations worked to encourage party leaders to take action on a wide variety of population-related issues. They also served to translate the desires of women as reflected in survey research and public opinion polls carried out on a number of demographic questions to political decision-makers.[36]

This and other coalitions often included specialists from a variety of different disciplines, and experts with the same speciality frequently held opposing views on particular demographic issues. There were at times certain common aspects to the analyses of experts in the same discipline which contrasted with those of other specialists. Most demographers, for example, appear to have favored the use of positive incentives to encourage childbearing and opposed restricting the grounds for abortion; on the whole, demographers were also sympathetic to efforts of leaders of the women's organization to improve women's situation and ensure women's right to work. At the same time, however, opinion among demographers was extremely divided concerning the best solution for care of small children, and certain demographers adopted positions which, in their opposition to the employment of women with small children, were closer to those most often taken by economists.[37]

From the 1950s on, similar policy perspectives and personal acquaintance were more important factors in the formation of policy coalitions than disciplinary training or institutional affiliation. Specialists in Czechoslovakia, that is to say, did not, even during the reform period, take part in policy-making in this issue area as interest groups. Rather, even though members of certain of the professions and specializations involved did participate in organized action to further the interests of their particular occupational group, their participation in policy debates concerning population issues occurred in the ad hoc, informal coalitions Franklyn Griffiths argued would characterize specialists' intervention in policy-making in communist states.[38]

At the same time, it is interesting that the group of specialists who appear to have the greatest influence on the making of population policy in Czechoslovakia has remained remarkably stable since the early 1960s, despite normalization and the many changes associated with the end of the reform period. Working through established channels, such as the Population Commission and the various research teams established to conduct research on population issues, as well as through informal contact with members of the party and government elite, many of the same individuals continue to be involved in discussion of policy in this area.

The impact which specialists had on the formation of policy during this period is evident in a number of the pro-natalist measures adopted in the late 1960s and early 1970s. Research conducted by demographers and sociologists formed the basis for the adoption of certain policy measures, including increased aid to families with young children and young married couples; expanded paid maternity leave; and increases in children's allowances and the one-time payment after the birth of a child.[39] Formally recommended by the Population Commission, these measures were adopted by the government and form the core of the government's pro-natalist policy. Demographers and other specialists who opposed restriction of the grounds for abortion, however, were less successful in influencing policy. Despite the efforts of numerous specialists, and in contradiction to the results of survey research which showed the majority of Czech and Slovak women to be against restricting abortion, severe limitations on access to abortion were imposed in the late 1960s and early 1970s.[40]

STAGE THREE: POLICY EVALUATION AND IMPLEMENTATION

The end of the reform era in Czechoslovakia has created, in general, less favorable conditions for specialists to influence policy than existed in the 1960s. The reemphasis of the leading role of the party, renewed emphasis on ideology, and the explicit rejection of many of the theoretical innovations of the late 1960s, particularly those concerning the role of social groups and the nature of social relations in a socialist society, have reduced both the legitimacy of specialist intervention in policy-making and the resources of specialists. Certain specialists who played a major role in the debates of the 1960s, particularly those who were active in the reform movement, are no longer in their previous positions. Others have been removed from formal positions of responsibility, but continue to practice their specialties in less visible research positions. The massive personnel changes which occurred in most social science faculties as well as in the research institutes in the early 1970s also may be expected to have decreased the growing sense of professional identity and common interests which was developing among members of certain professions. In addition, most experts now also have far less opportunity to serve as purveyors of mass desires to political elites, at least directly.

However, despite these limitations, specialists continue to take part in the making of policy in this area at both the policy planning and policy evaluation stages. Thus, while greater care must be given to framing research questions in acceptable Marxist–Leninist terms, empirical research continues on a broad variety of population related issues. Researchers at the Institutes on the Living Standard and Public Opinion in Bratislava, for example, completed several major surveys of the impact of pro-natalist measures on family life and women's status in the mid-1970s. Sociologists and demographers employed in the section of the Federal Ministry of Labor and Social Affairs established in 1969 to deal with questions relating to women and the family conducted other surveys on demographic questions, and the Population Commission also has sponsored several research projects. The Research Institute on Public Opinion in Prague recently carried out several short-term polls related to population issues, and long-term research on demographic trends and population questions is included as one of the main research tasks in the most recent five-year research plan.

The coordinating body for this research, as well as the focal point for specialists' participation in the making of policy in this area, remains the Population Commission. After a brief period when it did not function, the State Population Commission was reconstituted as the Government Population Commission in 1971. Now headed by a vice-premier of the Federal government, the Commission continues to be charged with monitoring the effects of population policy and fostering pro-natalist attitudes on the part of the population. Comprised of representatives (usually deputy ministers) of the various ministries involved in making population policy, including Health, Labor and Social Affairs, Culture, Education, and Finance, representatives of certain mass organizations, such as the unions and the women's organization, and specialists from the universities and research institutes, the Commission meets several times a year to discuss and evaluate population policies. Much of the actual research work of the Commission appears to be carried out by experts working in other research institutes; the Commission, and particularly its Secretariat, which is housed in the Federal Ministry of Labor and Social Affairs, serve as a coordinating body. In addition, several permanent sub-committees have been set up to deal with particular aspects of population policy.[41]

Debate continues on many of the issues discussed in the 1960s, with several important differences. First, certain solutions to the demographic problem which were discussed during that period, including sending women with young children back to the home, are no longer publicly advocated. Specialists, as well as party leaders, reaffirm women's right to work when discussing population policy, despite the fact that the actual solution chosen, that is, paying young women to stay at home with their children until they reach the age of three, means that most women in the child-bearing ages are out of the labor force for substantial periods of time. Similarly, experts no longer openly challenge the wisdom of prohibiting women from having abortions. Nor, with very few exceptions, do specialists question the desirability of a pro-natalist approach. Differences of opinion undoubtedly continue to exist on all of these issues, but they are seldom expressed in public channels.

Within these limits, demographers and other specialists continue to play an important role in evaluating and proposing modifications to existing population policies. Through work on government-ordered research projects and in teams of experts assigned to analyze particular population developments, these experts collect and interpret the data which form the basis for choice of policy measures. By their contacts with members of the governmental and party elites, they also help determine which problems need investigation and how much attention should be given to particular issues. At present, much of the input of specialists in this area is directed toward increasing the effectiveness of the existing set of pro-natalist measures. Asked by the government to conduct a review of population policies and recent demographic trends in late 1981, for example, the Government Population Commission proposed only minor modifications of current programs. But, while most experts who have an input in this area appear to share the view of those affiliated with the Population Commission that the basic direction of the existing policies is correct, it is possible that a shift may occur in the relatively near future, as ministry officials, as well as individual experts appear to be heeding the cautions put forward by certain demographers concerning the difficulty of fundamentally altering underlying demographic trends through a program of incentives.

THE OUTLOOK FOR THE 1980s

What conclusions can we draw from the above analysis of the role of experts in the making of demographic policy regarding the questions raised at the beginning of this chapter? To what extent, that is, will communist elites in Czechoslovakia be able to utilize the specialized knowledge of experts effectively in the making of public policy in the 1980s? And how will they deal with the potential challenges to the current political order which greater autonomy and increased specialist input may pose?

In terms of the first issue, the outlook seems, at least in this policy area, to be fairly positive. In contrast to many of the changes which occurred in Czechoslovakia during the late 1960s which were later reversed, greater reliance on specialists in the formation of demographic policy is one aspect of the reform process which persists. Although certain limits have been placed on the way in which specialists take part in policy-making as well as on the alternatives which may be considered, numerous formal and informal mechanisms exist to channel specialized knowledge into the making of demographic policy. The continued labor shortage, as well as the recent slight decline in the birth rate, indicate that this policy area will continue to be perceived as problematic, and, consequently, as one in which expert input is needed. Given the relatively non-sensitive, technical nature of population issues, one cannot automatically generalize these results to other policy areas. However, the routine consultation of experts on population issues suggests that Czech and Slovak leaders may be willing to allow a good deal of specialist input in the making of policy in similarly non-sensitive areas.[42]

The outlook also seems favorable for communist elites in terms of the second issue raised above. Despite, or perhaps because of, the legacy of 1968 and the great involvement of demographers and other experts in the reform period, the increased role of experts in the making of policy in this area does not appear to pose any real problems of political control for party leaders. If we are to judge by their activities in the 1970s, the Demographic Society and the Government Population Commission will continue to serve as focal points for demographers and specialists working on demographic questions and will reinforce the professional identity of this group of specialists. However, there is little evidence that even a significantly greater degree of professional identity or group autonomy would be problematic for current leaders. As Manfred Grote has noted in a perceptive discussion of the role of technocratic elites in East Germany,[43] communist elites in many countries have been fairly successful in incorporating the most important groups of specialists into the existing system by satisfying their professional desires, granting them material benefits and social prestige, and preventing them from linking up in any significant way with other possible sources of discontent or catalysts for change. Thus, individual experts in Czechoslovakia may express dissenting opinions or challenge the existing political system. But there is little reason to expect the specialists most involved in the formation of policy in this or other areas to generalize their desire for greater professional autonomy or more involvement in the policy-making process to other areas of life. Currently, significant portions of the intellectual community in Czechoslovakia may accept the political system more as the result of force than out of conviction. In the future, Czech and Slovak leaders may be successful in obtaining a more genuine acceptance of the current order, based, as appears to be the case in certain other East European countries, on appreciation of personal and professional benefits.

The current situation in Czechoslovakia suggests, then, that there is no necessary link between greater autonomy for professionals or a higher degree of involvement of specialists in policy-making and political change in socialist states, at least in the short run.[44] In view of the role of specialists in the one policy area examined, communist elites in Czechoslovakia may well be able to obtain the kinds of specialized knowledge needed in policy-making while at the same time maintaining the existing political system and their own power in it in the 1980s. Of course, greater specialist participation does not necessarily lead to more effective policy. But it does ensure that policy choices are based on information and analyses other than those of the top political elite alone.

NOTES AND REFERENCES

I would like to thank the International Research and Exchanges Board and the National Council for Soviet and East European Research for their financial support of part of the research for this chapter.

1. See H. Gordon Skilling, *Czechoslovakia's Interrupted Revolution* (Princeton University Press, 1976) pp. 125–9 for a discussion of the origin of the term and references to Soviet and Czechoslovak works using this terminology; see Erik P. Hoffman, "Changing Soviet Perspectives on Leadership and Administration," in *The Soviet Union since Stalin*, edited by Stephen F. Cohen, Alexander Rabinowitch and Robert Sharlet (Bloomington, Ind.: Indiana University Press, 1980) pp. 71–92 for a discussion of recent Soviet perspectives on the impact of the scientific–technological revolution on policy-making.
2. See, for example, R. V. Burks, "Technology and Political Control in Eastern Europe," in Chalmers Johnson (ed.), *Change in Communist Systems* (Stanford University Press, 1970) pp. 265–311.
3. See Chalmers Johnson, "Comparing Communist Nations," in Chalmers Johnson (ed.), *Change in Communist Systems*, pp. 1–32 and Richard Lowenthal, "Development vs. Utopia in Communist Policy," in Chalmers Johnson (ed.), *Change in Communist Systems*, pp. 33–116 for discussions of some of the unintended consequences of economic development in communist states.
4. Radovan Richta and collective, *Civilization at the Crossroads* (Prague: International Arts and Sciences Press, 1969). See Skilling, *Czechoslovakia's Interrupted Revolution*, pp. 126–9 for a discussion of this work.
5. Zdeněk Mlynář and Michal Lakatoš were particularly active in formulating these ideas. Similar views were also expressed by sociologists and other scholars at numerous seminars and conferences held in Czechoslovakia in the mid-1960s. For examples of new views on the nature of socialist society see the essays presented in Pavel Machonin and collective, *Sociální struktura socialistické společnosti* (Prague: Nakladatelství Svoboda, 1966).
6. See Skilling, *Czechoslovakia's Interrupted Revolution*, Parts III, IV and V for a detailed analysis of the role of various groups of experts and specialists immediately before and during the reform period.
7. Numerous other scholars have examined the activities of various experts in this period. In addition to Skilling, see, for example, Andrzej Korbonski, "Bureaucracy and Interest Groups in Communist Societies: The Case of Czechoslovakia," in Lenard J. Cohen and Jane P. Shapiro (eds), *Communist Systems in Comparative Perspective* (Garden City, N. Y.: Anchor Books, 1974) pp. 358–78; Galia Golan, *Reform Rule in Czechoslovakia: The Dubček Era, 1968–1969* (Cambridge University Press, 1973) and *The Czechoslovak Reform Movement: Communism in Crisis, 1962–1968* (Cambridge University Press, 1971); and Vladimir Kusin, *The Intellectual Origins of the Prague Spring* (Cambridge University Press, 1971) and *Political Groupings in the Czechoslovak Reform Movement* (New York: Columbia University Press, 1977).
8. Kusin, *Political Groupings*, p. 118.
9. My analysis of factors which facilitate specialist intervention in policy-making in communist states draws heavily on the analyses of the policy-making processes in communist states set forth by William Zimmerman

in "Issue Area and Foreign-Policy Process: A Research Note in Search of a General Theory," *American Political Science Review* LXVII 4 (December 1973) pp. 1204–12 and Donald R. Kelley, "Interest Groups in the USSR: The Impact of Political Sensitivity on Group Influence," *Journal of Politics,* 34 (1972) pp. 860–88.

10. These expectations, as well as others which have guided this study, are set out in greater detail in Sharon L. Wolchik and Jane L. Curry, "Specialists and Professionals in Policy-making in Czechoslovakia and Poland," proposal submitted to the National Science Foundation, 15 February 1980. The larger study of which this chapter is a part also provides more detail concerning the policy decisions discussed in this chapter.

11. H. Gordon Skilling, "Groups in Soviet Politics: Some Hypotheses," in Skilling and Franklyn Griffiths, (eds), *Interest Groups in Soviet Politics* (Princeton University Press, 1973) pp. 19–45 discusses the impact of these factors on the participation of various types of groups in policy-making in the Soviet Union.

12. The number of live births per 1,000 population decreased from a post-Second World War high of 24.2 in 1947 to 21.2 in 1953; this ratio continued to decline throughout the 1950s and 1960s, reaching 14.9 in 1968. Vladímir Srb, *Demografická příručka* (Prague: Nakladatelství svoboda, 1967) p. 183 and *Statistická ročenka ČSSR* (Prague, 1970) p. 91.

13. See Jerzy Berent, "Causes of Fertility Decline in Eastern Europe and the Soviet Union," *Population Studies* XXVI (March 1970), 1: 35–58 and (July 1970), 2: 247–50; Alena Heitlinger, "Pro-natalist Population Policies in Czechoslovakia," *Population Studies,* XXX, 1: 123–35; Československé výskumný ústav práce a sociálních veci, Bratislava, *Mezinárodní srovnání populační politiky* (Prague: CVUPSV, 1974); "Přehled demografického vývoje a populační politiky évropských socialistických statu," *Zprávy státní populační komise,* 1966, 4: 3–40; and Sharon L. Wolchik, "Demography, Political Reform, and Women's Issues in Czechoslovakia," in Margherita Rendel (ed.), *Women, Power and Political Systems* (London: Croom Helm, 1981) pp. 135–150 and Henry P. David and Robert J. McIntyre (eds), *Reproductive Behavior: Central and Eastern European Experiences* (New York: Springer, 1981) for detailed analyses of the demographic situation in Czechoslovakia and other East European countries.

14. See Helen Desfosses, "Demography, Ideology, and Politics in the USSR," *Soviet Studies,* XXVIII (April 1976), 2: 254–56 for a discussion of the impact of ideology on demographic analysis in the Soviet Union; see Wolchik, "Demography, Political Reform, and Women's Issues," p. 137 for a discussion of this influence in the CSSR.

15. See Helena Švarcová, *Populace a společnost* (Prague: Státní nakladatelství politické literatury, 1959) for an early Czech analysis of population trends; Švarrová modified many of these views and criticized the influence of Stalinism on demographic analyses in *Populace* (Prague: Nakladatelství politické literatury, 1966).

16. Vladímir Srb, Milan Kučera, and Ladislav Ružička, *Demografie* (Prague: Svoboda, 1971) p. 49.

17. Ibid., p. 21.

18. See Srb, *Demografická příručka*, pp. 214–18 for a brief summary of the results of this study.
19. Ibid., pp. 219–28.
20. Srb, Kučera, and Ružička, *Demografie*, p. 581.
21. Ibid.
22. The results of these studies are summarized in Srb, *Demografická příručka*, pp. 224–48. More detailed reports may be found in *Demografie* and *Zprávy státní populační komise*.
23. See Srb, Kučera, and Ružička, *Demografie*, pp. 50–1 for information concerning the expansion of courses in demography and their location during this period.
24. Srb, Kučera, and Ružička, *Demografie*, p. 49 provide an inventory of works published during this period. Compared to later periods, the results of demographic research were not widely distributed.
25. An example of this limited influence is the enactment of the law liberalizing abortions, which appears to have been adopted over the objections of numerous demographers, who were concerned about the potentially negative effects this law would have on the birth rate.
26. Srb, Kučera, and Ružička, *Demografie*, pp. 50–1.
27. Srb, *Demografická přírucka*, p. 6.
28. See Skilling, *Czechoslovakia's Interrupted Revolution,* Ch. 4 and Kusin, *Political Groupings,* pp. 113–22 for a discussion of these research teams.
29. *Statistická ročenka ČSSR,* 1970, p. 91.
30. See Heitlinger, "Pro-natalist Population Policies in Czechoslovakia," pp. 130–1 for a review of these measures.
31. Srb, Kučera, and Ružička, *Demografie*, p. 582.
32. Heitlinger, "Pro-natalist Population Policies in Czechoslovakia," pp. 130–1.
33. Srb, Kučera, and Ružička, *Demografie*, p. 40.
34. See, for example, Jiří Prokopec, "Vdáná žena v rodině a zaměstnání," *Zprávy státní populační komise,* 1962, 2, pp. 60–1; Milan Kučera, "Orientační sonda o příčinách vzéstupu porodnosti v roce 1963," *Zprávy státní populační komise,* 1964, 1: 9–12; Vladímir Wynnyczuk, "Výsledky sondaže o prodloužené mateřské dovolene ve výbraných okreséch," *Zprávy státní populačni komise,* 1964, 4: 20–8 and Jiří Prokopec, "K nové úprave předpisu o úmělém přerušení těhotenství," *Zprávy státní populační komise,* 1963, 4(1): 24–6.
35. Many of these debates also involved reconsideration of the position of women under socialism. See Hilda Scott, *Does Socialism Liberate Women?* (Boston, Mass.: Beacon Press, 1974), ch. 6; Alena Heitlinger, *Women and State Socialism* (Montreal: McGill-Queen's University Press, 1979), chs. 15, 16; and Sharon L. Wolchik, "Politics, Ideology, and Equality: Changes in the Status of Women in Eastern Europe," Ph.D. dissertation, the University of Michigan, 1978, ch. 7 and 8 for discussion of these debates. See Wolchik, "Demography," for more detailed discussion of the various poles in debates over population issues.
36. See Wolchik, "Politics, Ideology, and Equality," ch. 7 for illustrations of the actions of specialists in this regard.

37. See Heitlinger, "Pro-natalist Population Policies in Czechoslovakia," Scott, *Does Socialism Liberate Women?* and Wolchik, "Politics, Ideology, and Equality," ch. 7 for discussions of these perspectives; see Wolchik, "Demography," pp. 140–2 for examples of similar attitudes expressed by demographers.

38. Franklyn Griffiths, "A Tendency Analysis of Soviet Policy-Making" in Skilling and Griffiths (eds), *Interest Groups in Soviet Politics,* pp. 335–377.

39. See Walter Vergeiner, "Czechoslovakia," in Sheila B. Kamerman and Alfred J. Kahn (eds), *Family Policy: Government and Families in Fourteen Countries* (New York: Columbia University Press, 1979) pp. 108–16; Heitlinger, "Pro-natalist Population Policies," pp. 130–5; and *Population Policy in Czechoslovakia* (Prague: Orbis, 1974) for information concerning concrete pro-natalist measures adopted in the late 1960s and early 1970s.

40. Numerous social science surveys showed that most women were against restriction of the grounds for abortion. Articles and seminar reports indicate that most demographers also opposed such restrictions. See, for example, the views expressed in "Zkracený zaznam z jednání celostátního seminaře k problemům zákona o úmělem přerušení těhotenství," *Zprávy státní populační komise,* 1968, 3 and in Marie Krchová, "Zákon o úmělem přerušení těhotenství a jeho vliv na populační vývoj," *Zprávy státní populační komise,* 1971, 2: 52–4. Nonetheless, a law passed in 1973 prohibits abortion for all but medical reasons.

41. See Vergeiner, "Czechoslovakia," p. 112 for information concerning recent projects.

42. As Walter D. Connor noted in a comment on this chapter, the effectiveness of policy measures in achieving desired goals or solving particular problems is not necessarily increased by greater input from specialists. Pro-natalist policies based on recommendations made by specialists led to a greater increase in the birth rate in Czechoslovakia than earlier measures adopted without such input, but other factors, including positive changes in the number of women in the childbearing years, undoubtedly also had an influence.

43. Manfred Grote, "The Socialist Unity Party of Germany," in Stephen Fischer-Galati (ed.), *The Communist Parties of Eastern Europe* (New York: Columbia University Press, 1979) pp. 167–200.

44. The developments which led to the Prague Spring, as well as the cooperation between intellectuals and workers in Poland in 1980–1, indicate that such a link may be one outcome of greater professional autonomy for certain groups. While it is also possible that the long-term consequences of such autonomy may challenge the existing system, the recent experience of Czech and Slovak leaders, as well as of leaders in several other East European countries, indicates that the two may be relatively compatible for the foreseeable future.

6 Polish Journalists in the 1980s

JANE L. CURRY

Information, the mass media, and the very nature of journalism in post-war Poland were major issues for the striking Polish workers in August, 1980. Their demand for a freer mass media ranked in importance with their demands for the right to strike and to form free trade unions.[1] During the eighteen months between the strikes and the declaration of martial law, control of the media was a major focus of conflict. Although they had not served as the primary formulators of popular thought and action during this period (as they had in previous liberalization movements[2]), journalists were locked in conflict between popular demands and their own desires to produce an informative and critical media and the unwillingness of the Party leadership, especially the conservative factions, to give up control – particularly of the truly mass media like television. That Party leadership was also not willing to concede to either Solidarity's or journalists' demands for changes in the legal regulations of the media and party guidance of its programming. Finally, the declaration of martial law focused directly on control of the media: all but two dailies were closed down initially; television was completely taken over by the military; and the Interpress press agency was disbanded. Journalists were detained not only for their connections with Solidarity but also for their professional work and their participation in the Polish Journalists Association; large numbers were fired; and the journalism work of the Solidarity period was subject to sharp attacks.

In response, journalists have continued a silent battle. Most journals could not be reopened for months because their staffs either refused to submit to loyalty oaths and political reviews or were unable to pass these reviews. Because of the opposition of the Association of journalists' leaders and the support they received from the membership, the Association was the first and, in the initial six months of martial law, the only professional organization disbanded completely.

From the strikes through the imposition of martial law, journalists' actions were, in large part, those of professionals. That they had been perceived as professionals held back by the Gierek leadership was clear from the fact that workers attacked the highly developed censorship system that had been built up under Gierek without attacking Polish journalists and the work that they attempted to do. In fact, they pressed relentlessly for access not to the Western press or even to the "uncensored" press which had been published by various dissident groups since 1976 but to the mass media of Poland. The result of the August demands and the initial government concessions was a burgeoning of lively and highly critical discussion as well as the publication of a massive amount of information that had never been available before. The providers of this information and the participants in most of the discussions, however, were not the workers who "liberated" the mass media but the professional journalists who had worked under Gierek's repressive system, the less repressive system of Gomulka, and the moment of freedom that existed in 1956.

Evidence of journalists' level of professionalism was also visible in the period after the Gdansk agreements were signed. Although journalists came to represent a wide variety of viewpoints and ideologies in the media, they shared common perceptions of what their role and level of autonomy should be. Individual journalists and groups of journalists also expressed common policy goals and desires vis-à-vis the entire information system and regarding their roles as journalists in policy making, even though they were split in their ideological affiliations. As a result, on issues related to media control and the determination of what should appear in the media, they were often at odds not only with those in the political leadership who wanted a traditional press but also with Solidarity itself. When splits occurred within the profession concerning issues directly related to the media, these tended to reflect a battle between older journalists and younger journalists trying to push into the profession.

On both sides of the political spectrum, individual journalists continued to act out roles they had seen as part of their professional work when the press was more controlled. They were critical links and negotiators between the embattled leadership and the strikers.[3] As attempts were then made to create new, credible leaders at various levels, journalists also appeared as viable options even as they insisted on maintaining their professional positions.[4] Later, under martial law, journalists were targets of attack by the government for their statements and activities. Others shared with military officials connected with Jaruzelski the prominent positions in the Party leadership of that regime. In these roles, they were not only spokesmen but also participants in regime decisions. The splits revolved around what political policy journalists or journals should advocate and how much self-control had to be exerted over media content to prevent another Czechoslovakia or the kind of mass turmoil that would bring heavy repression. This, it can be argued, was a political issue rather than a professional one.

Journalists' actions in the early 1980s called into question assumptions commonly made in the West about the role of journalists in communist politics. On the one hand, traditional assumptions about the success of socialization in these societies and the development of "red-experts" were not borne out by the events of the 1980s. Although under Gierek journalists (and other less "political" professionals) had clearly not been able to be the "structural basis for a free and independent citizenry in a world threatened by bureaucratic tyranny" (the role they are expected to perform in the West),[5] they hardly proved to be bastions of support for communism. Once the workers' strikes had forced a change – at least *de facto* – in the controls on the profession, journalists acted almost instantly to "protect the interests derived from their occupational roles,"[6] no matter what their broader political ideology. This professionalism continued in the refusal of the majority of established journalists, as opposed to those on the fringes of the profession, to submit to martial law strictures that essentially required them to hold jobs totally on the basis of political criteria and give up all notions of professional rights and autonomy.

However, their professionalism did not give them the kind of influence in the policy process that one would expect in a situation where the political leadership proclaimed a strong commitment to modernization. The dependence of journalists on their readers to "liberate" them from the controls of the Gierek media system (which aimed at economic modernization) in the 1970s, as contrasted with their ability to stimulate popular criticism by engaging in media criticism in the mid–1950s and early 1960s (when the society was far less modernized) raises questions about how, in a modernizing society, professionals can find themselves with progressively less impact on policy and less control over their own work. In fact, the media discussions which took place in Poland before martial law was imposed emphasized the weakness of professionals and specialists vis-à-vis strong bureaucratic interests. The inability of professionals to do more than absent themselves in protest or embrace martial law totally further demonstrates the inability of specialists and professionals to counter the political leadership and the bureaucracy it controls, at least on more political issues in Poland.

Finally, the question of the future of the Polish media and professionals like journalists under continued martial law or post-martial law governance remains. This question involves more than merely what policy comes out of the factional battles within the leadership. After all, the popular significance of the media and its control has been demonstrated and recognized by the Party leadership, media personnel, and the population. But these groups have come to different conclusions on what should be done. How these questions are resolved is a major long-term question and will certainly remain the subject of tension. The demographic shift in the profession from long established journalists to younger journalists who entered the profession in the 1970s and came into their own during the 18 months of Solidarity's prominence will be a second major factor in determining the future of the Polish media. For in journalism, as in other professions, the generational shift will be dramatic and put relative unknowns into power.

THE NATURE OF THE JOURNALISM PROFESSION AND JOURNALISM PROFESSIONALS

The journalism profession in Poland has, since its reorganization at the end of the Second World War, been both highly political and extremely professional. Its politicization as a tool of the Communist Party is clear in Lenin's original model of the press as "not only a collective propagandist and collective agitator, but also a collective organizer."[7] The journalists' role was further expanded by Stalin to include what have remained integral elements of the communist authorities' perception of media work "to educate the public,"[8] "to facilitate the construction of a new life,"[9] and to serve as "the most trusted transmission belt [to] take a decision and carry it to the very midst of the people."[10]

Most Polish journalists, in contrast, see their professional role as equally politically significant but far more politically independent. In their own words, they should not only be the chief and most trusted sources of information for the population, but should also serve as a "loyal opposition party in the British sense" and as a trusted ombudsman for the society.[11] When they were surveyed and interviewed in 1976 and 1979, journalists universally made it clear, as they had in their discussions in the 1950s and 1960s and once again in their discussions after August 1980, that this role was seriously hurt by outside pressures and controls.[12] The nonrecognition of their work and of their proposals by the political leadership was equally troublesome for them.[13]

The consistency and strength of journalists' convictions about their role has been a product of their high level of professionalism.[14] Group identification and interaction is higher among journalists than among any other professional or occupational group which has been studied in Poland.[15] It involves: (1) a professional community based on informal patterns of interaction and a set of values unique to the profession;[16] (2) the feeling that they should be "recruited and licensed on the basis of their technical competence rather than their ascribed social characteristics";[17] and (3) the feeling that they have the right to independence and autonomy and that they, and not their clients, should be able to make judgments on how they can best serve their clients' interests.[18] Survey research and interview data indicate that all of these characteristics existed among journalists in the 1970s and also as early as the Stalinist period in Poland. Their strength is as much a product of the political pressures which the political leadership placed on the profession and on individual professionals as of professional training or professional group regulation.

Journalists' behavior as professionals and as a professional group is also an outgrowth of the demography of the profession. By the end of the 1970s, the journalism profession was primarily a profession of recruits from the Stalinist period. Even after the jump in recruitment in the 1970s to stem the aging of the profession and to fill the positions created by the expansion of the media, two-thirds of the 6,000 journalists registered with the Association of Polish Journalists were over 40 in 1977.[19] How this demographic picture will change in the post-martial law period is not yet apparent. Of the top professionals and chief editors prior to martial law, all were older. For these journalists the formative events which shaped their attitudes were the euphoria and openness of the Polish October in 1956, the gradual stabilization under Gomulka, the turmoil of the late 1960s, the hope of the early Gierek period, and the bureaucratic control of the last half of the Gierek years. The experiences, gains, and losses encountered in their professional life during each of these periods carried over into succeeding periods and affected their demands, behavior, and perception of viable options. In the changes that occurred between August 1980 and December 1981, these journalists have continued to be the leaders of the profession, and they were joined by their colleagues of earlier years who had been blacklisted under Gierek. At the same time, the younger generation of journalists – individuals who had little hope of attaining editorial positions under normal circumstances – pressed for new leadership and for more unrestrained criticism. They also tended to collaborate with other young professionals more often than with their senior colleagues. It is this younger generation, schooled in the "propaganda of success" of the Gierek years and initiated in the dramatic changes of the 1980s, who will come to dominate the profession in the 1980s and 1990s, no matter what the political leadership tries to do to transform the media.

When martial law was instituted, few journalists in either of these two groups were trustworthy enough for the military regime to staff the mass media. Instead, a third, "lost" generation of journalists tended to emerge. This group appears have included many individuals who entered the profession in the late 1950s or early 1960s, in the time of stability under Gomulka. At the time this group entered the profession, there were few openings for journalists in any prestigious papers, and there was little to encourage individuality. As a result, they were either forced to take regional posts or to remain at low prestige and low visibility jobs in the profession. Some of these individuals appeared in the late 1960s when a factional battle within the party offered them a chance to take positions as older journalists were forced out in the anti-Semitic campaign. On the whole, the positions of these journalists were eclipsed in the 1970s with the strict press control of the Gierek era and the liberalism of the Solidarity period. However, they were available to take positions under martial law – the first time that the profession was so cleansed that there were prominent, visible positions for them. What remains to be seen is whether their prominence is a reflection of support for martial law or merely their desire to use an opportunity to advance in their careers. Although we will not know until some of the control on the press is diminished, some of their attitudes may be different simply because of their different professional history.

THE PAST

While the situation in which journalists found themselves in August 1980 was new, their reactions and demands were products of long years of experience. Once it became possible to do so, journalists took action on the same issues on which they had focused in the past: (1) access to information and the ability to publish that information; (2) recognition of the profession and the press as a significant and even an indispensable element in the policy-making and administration process; and (3) the garnering and protection of material benefits for the profession. Their experiences in the post-1956 period and under the controls of the Gierek period, however, led them to seek very different and more institutionalized solutions. The clear dependence of the profession on its readers' pressure for a more open press also seemed to liberate the profession from its usual reluctance to make public demands as a group and to discuss the problems of their profession in the mass media. Whereas journalists in the past relied largely on informal agreements with the political leadership or on individual solutions to more general professional problems, they sought to protect their gains from future retrenchment by developing new professional and general legal structures to protect the profession from the difficulties of the last thirty years. As a result, to end these reforms, the martial law regime was faced with either ignoring the newly passed censorship law or disbanding the entire journalists' organization.

Historical memory for most journalists at the top of the profession in the past, and, as a result, for the professional community as a whole, began in the Stalinist period. At that time journalists were constantly cross-pressured between the ideological statements and demands of the political leadership, and the realities of daily life: meeting with dissatisfied readers, being treated as "the enemy" by managers and bureaucrats, and struggling for survival on very low earnings. This conflict between ideology and reality created a sense of professional community and professional goals even though, in this period, there were few opportunities to articulate demands. Instead, journalists and editors fell into unspoken patterns of action to protect their personal interests. Editors, caught between conflicting leadership demands for highly politicized staffs and for regular and efficient publication, simply ignored the productive journalists' inattentiveness to political action.

In the four years between the actual establishment of a Stalinist press system and the initial winds of de-Stalinization in 1954, journalists did not act to influence information policy or to reduce the political demands on their time. They lived with the uncomfortable contradictions between the Party's demands that they investigate and the government bureaucrats' unwillingness to give them access to pertinent information, and between the expectations that they would serve as community political leaders while at the same time acting as productive professional writers. When they were met on their first assignments to government offices with signs saying "Journalists not welcome here,"[20] journalists were trapped by the need to write something publishable and their own sense that they should investigate bad situations. If, in fact, they surmounted the barriers to information and their own caution, journalists and editors still faced strong reactions to their criticism.[21] Their responses were dual. On the one hand, they tended to retreat and "color reality rather than reporting on problems and failures."[22] On the other hand, they began deliberately to build ties as individuals with Party and state officials in their area who would rely on them for information and help them in their own work. This pattern of professional and policy-related action through private channels to individuals in the leadership on any given level propelled them further into Party work and also established a permanent pattern of professional action through informal and personalized channels.

Once the floodgates of de-Stalinization began to open in the mid-1950s, journalists pressed openly and articulately for real changes in their professional position and in general information policy. This occurred at all levels and involved demands for participation *as journalists* in various policy debates in a variety of forums ranging from private, one-to-one professional discussions and closed meetings of the Polish Journalists Association to public media discussions. Although journalists as members of the intelligentsia played a role in opening these floodgates, their reactions were much the same as they were to be twenty-five years later, with one critical exception: journalists in the mid-fifties were so caught up in a rapidly changing situation that they failed to institutionalize their gains.

As de-Stalinization gained momentum, journalists found themselves in a fluid situation in which the institutions which had once controlled them simply collapsed. The economic crisis and the failure of confidence in the system ultimately required journals to become self-supporting. New professional editors were brought into many journals to make them more popular. Party leaders who had allied themselves with journalists to bring in Gomulka took over the Press Department.[23] After the Poznan demonstrations in the summer of 1956, the employees of the censors' office resigned *en masse* in reaction to the lack of consistent directives and support from the Party bureaucracy and, ultimately, in a protest against censorship as an institution.[24] Since Party officials and bureaucrats were being attacked by the press and the public, few dared subject themselves to further condemnation for ignoring journalists. When they did, journalists simply took action against them in the press and in their association meetings. Journalists thus found themselves controlling their own professional life in a situation where there were no viable institutions left to fight. Instead, they were brought into positions of political authority in local and national politics as some of the only untainted candidates. They even talked of running their own candidates for parliament and acted on broader policy questions as representatives of their profession.[25] They also acted as experts regulating their own work rather than risking Soviet intervention or giving in to their readers' insatiable hunger for information.[26]

Journalists' hopes had been pinned on Gomulka's new leadership to maintain and promote their new gains. In reality, Gomulka was a liberal about the profession only in his lack of interest in it as a political force.[27] Prominent journalists were able to provide far more information and broader, sharper criticism than they could in the Stalinist period (or under Gierek). But in spite of their open and active pressure, they were not able to get results from their criticism or make gains in material benefits. In the area of information access, journalists got some token legal guarantees without enforcement provisions.

In the area of bettering their material conditions, journalists acted on a number of fronts. Much of their lobbying effort was public and deliberate. The professional Association leadership acted, by their own reports, like any Western associational interest group. They participated as professional representatives in the negotiations for each new salary code. The Association leadership, despite the fact that it did not legally represent journalists in questions of benefits, took a public stance independent from the publishers and the Union of Professional Workers on Books, the Press, and Radio (a vertical union which included all employees in these agencies).[28] When the agreement which emerged did not fulfill their expectations, they made it clear in the profession's journal that they were not in full agreement with the measure and that it was "not the ideal law and no one will see it as such."[29] To strengthen their bargaining position in this and subsequent negotiations, the Association leaders commissioned an independent study of the material and social situation of journalists.[30] The results of the study were then constantly used as proofs that the poor material conditions of the profession hurt its ability to produce reports of interest to the Gomulka leadership[31] and to maintain the minimal health requirements promised by the leadership.[32]

When no gains were made by the leaders, they attempted to placate their members by establishing temporary programs funded by the Association. Individual journalists also changed their work patterns to maximize their earnings. The impact of all of these individual actions on the quality of the mass media was then cited by the Association leadership as evidence of the need to improve conditions. Meanwhile, the editors, on whom the Association placed part of the responsibility for easing individual journalists' situations, manipulated their budgets to pacify the journalists and provide some incentives. The results, however, helped but did not solve the problems of middle and entry level journalists – the very "lost" generation that now dominates the media.

In the areas of information access and the ability to publish, journalists fought a guerilla battle. As individuals, as professional representatives, as staff groups, and as members of a professional association, journalists used all of their professional resources to force some change. Since the Gomulka leadership's lack of interest in the media made the enactment of real structural changes impossible, the battle was fought on an issue-by-issue basis. This was further encouraged by the fact that individual professionals and journals were in competition with one another to get information and publish it in order to increase their readership.

Because the political elite was very porous in this period, access to information was dealt with as an individual problem. Journalists went to their editor or their Association representative to get an advocate to force recalcitrant officials to give them information. Alternatively, well-placed journalists went to their own political patrons. In some cases journalists went public and published articles attacking the low-level bureaucrats who had denied them information. Ultimately, it was assumed that good journalists could get information on their own – even if it required more time.

The ability to publish information was a far more critical professional issue in this period. It was not only a question of professional authority over their own sphere of expertise but an economic question because journalists were paid only for what they published. However, even in the Gomulka years, discussions of this troubling issue had to be conducted outside public channels. No article could be published implying that there was censorship in Poland. In fact, the very regulations and decisions of the censors were not made public to the professional community nor were they regularized or predictable.[33] Those who knew what was cut and what could be pushed through were at the top of the profession.

Journalists were troubled not only by the problems created for them by outside intervention in their professional decisions on what to write, but also by the unpredictability of the process.[34] There was, however, little support for legalizing the Main Office of Control and its functions as this was felt to give too much legitimacy to the censorship process and to reduce the field of maneuver open to individual editors by specifying what could and could not be censored. Without any legislation, individual editors and prominent journalists felt that they could use their personal contacts in the Party to override decisions on important issues for them and rely on the censors' office to shield them from responsibility for their attempts at publishing critical material.

To protect themselves, journalists engaged in self-censorship and also in various informal devices to discourage or circumvent censorship of their articles. A tradition was developed of sending censors articles only after the entire journal had been set in type. This gave the censors a chance to see the articles in the context of the entire layout, and, at the same time, gave them far less time to debate with the editors. It also put them in the uncomfortable position of knowing that any decision requiring the editors to reset the pages would cost the journal large sums of money.[35] Editors also used the porous and factionalized Gomulka elite to find protectors and allies.[36] Some even attempted to court their censors by talking to them and socializing with them. In these activities the editors were taking advantage of the decentralized structure of the Main Office, a structure which had been instituted to prevent internal uprisings like the revolt in 1956.

Formal action took place on a much more limited scale. Journalists and editors with no personal power complained to the Association leadership about their difficulties with censorship. Censorship was attacked on the floor of national and regional Association meetings.[37] The Association leaders argued with the accessible political leadership that, at the very least, a more predictable and rational censorship system than the existing haphazard process was necessary. By their own accounts, none of their discussions had any effect.[38]

In trying to increase their impact in the policy process, journalists used both public and private channels. On the one hand, they used their personal ties to advocate specific policies by going to accessible policy makers with information they had collected and presenting their case. Their demands were usually for more governmental commitment to social welfare and economic development. These concerns stemmed in large part from their vantage point as the most trusted ombudsmen in Polish society. They also stemmed from their professional inclination to seek solutions to problems and to report on changes.[39] At times, journalists admitted that their reports to the policy makers were skewed to force action on issues which they as professionals thought were critical.[40]

Journalists also pressed for their published criticism to be more effective. They used the media to attack low-level administrators for not responding to their criticism. They also were active as a professional association and as individuals in the formulation of an Administrative Code which required institutions to respond to criticism within a specified period. Since the original Code did not make clear distinctions between media complaints and those of individual citizens, journalists continued to criticize it in their writings while their Association leaders brought the problem up regularly with their contacts in the leadership. As a result, journalists got a revision of the Code which they considered a minor gain.[41] In this area, as in the area of material gains, professional leaders reported their lobbying openly and specifically in professional meetings and professional publications.

By 1964, however, it was clear to journalists that their ability to lobby as a group and work through individual contacts in the leadership was not bringing them the kind of position that they sought as professionals. As a result, they became involved in higher-level political battles. This was encouraged by the fact that some factions appealed directly to journalists' interests as a professional group. Both Edward Gierek (then the head of the Katowice regional Party organization) and Mieczyslaw Moczar (at least titular head of a national Party faction)[42] deliberately courted the profession as Western politicians do. They appealed to their interests in increasing their earnings, improving information access, ensuring greater access to publication, and increasing the profession's policy-making role. Gierek spoke at numerous journalists' meetings and met privately with many journalists. He continually pointed out the special position of the profession in his region.[43] The Moczarist grouping took a far more active approach. Often without insisting on total ideological support, members of the faction used their links with the Ministry of Interior to aid individual journalists with travel, extra resources, information, additional publications, leverage with the censors' office, and the advocacy of their policy concerns.[44] In addition, as Moczarists attacked long-established journalists, they opened new channels of professional mobility.[45]

Middle and low-level journalists then used this broader political ferment to benefit themselves: in the period prior to 1967 there was a major turnover in the profession. As journalists and editors were fired because of their Jewish background, new individuals whose mobility had been blocked took over. The delegates to the 1968 National Association Congress were for the most part new faces particularly from areas outside of Warsaw.[46]

In the late 1960s journalists were interested in finding an alternative to Gomulka's *status quo* policies if not to the Gomulka leadership itself. They sought a leader who would not only be more receptive to their professional interests but who would also press for modernization in the economy and society. Since the situation was much less fluid and the profession far more established, they used professional vehicles to push for a leadership change. The most deliberate and well-known case of this was the presentation of a plan by the editors of *Polityka* to a small number of alternative Party leaders, including Edward Gierek, in 1969.[47] The editor of *Polityka* at that time was Meczyslaw Rakowski, a well-connected political figure who subsequently became a member of the Party Central Committee and, in 1981, deputy prime minister in charge of labor and the economy, a post he maintained after the imposition of martial law. The plan was intended to do far more than set out the themes *Polityka* would cover in the next year. It was intended to suggest alternative policies to Gomulka's and encourage the Gierek faction to move to take power, as well as to encourage *Polityka*'s alternative candidates to take positions acceptable to this group of journalists. The plan itself was subsequently reflected in Gierek's initial statements and was thought in the early 1970s to have been an aid in giving Rakowski and his staff a special position.[48]

Clearly the *Polityka* document and other professional support of Gierek did not trigger the change in leadership, but they did encourage him and his supporters. Journalists saw Gierek's takeover as the solution to their problems. Few knew about the press system in Katowice.[49] What they understood was that Gierek had made Katowice not only the most industrialized region in Poland, but also the most prosperous, and that journalists had high positions in the Gierek leadership there.[50] Furthermore, Gierek made clear the value he placed on the profession by appealing immediately to journalists to make suggestions for policy changes and by talking about the need for better propaganda and communication. One of his first meetings after taking over was with the Association leadership during which he promised, without leadership prompting, to increase investments in the media and to give journalists the kind of salary benefits that they had sought for ten years.[51] But the honeymoon proved short for the profession. Journalists quickly came to see that his understanding of "better communciation and propaganda" assumed Party rather than professional control. As a result, there was only a short period in which the press was able to initiate policy discussions and engage in criticism. Thus, in the initial Gierek years, journalists saw the regime take important strides toward fulfilling their interests in modernization; but they also found themselves increasingly constricted by the Party leadership. Once the economic situation worsened, journalists found themselves almost totally blocked from making public criticism and from having any interchange with the leadership.

The weakness of the journalism profession during this period was a result of the strengthening of the control institutions which took place under Gierek. In addition, the leadership changes which followed his takeover and the regularization of the authority of institutions of control further diminished the possibilities for journalists to turn to friends within the Party for protection. Gierek brought in his own group of "Silesians" with whom established journalists had had little contact and insisted on far more unity within the leadership than Gomulka had been able to achieve. These changes, coupled with the desire by elites at all levels to avoid the ramifications of the economic failure which began in the mid-1970s, gave journalists fewer options than they had had since the 1950s.

The institution-building of the Gierek years markedly decreased journalists' ability to get information and to publish the information they had managed to collect. In the area of information access, a number of proclamations requiring administrators to provide information to journalists were issued, but sanctions were not applied to violators of these new rules. As the economic situation worsened, administrators were increasingly reluctant to give information to journalists even on a private basis for fear that it would be transmitted through private conversations, "secret bulletins," or public channels. Disaffected members of institutions also became less informative as they saw that journalists were powerless to use the information they gave. Finally, in what was touted as a move to increase journalists' access to institutions, a system of institutional press agents was set up. Although regional journalists without contacts in the center were now in a better position to get basic information from ministries, the actual effect of the change was to filter and control the journalists' contacts and access.

In the areas of censorship and political interference, the profession as a whole was in a weaker position than it was under Gomulka. The Main Office of Control was more dominant in the editorial process than ever before. Its staff was far larger than it had been in the 1960s. And, according to individuals who had worked in the Main Office of Control in the 1960s, the specificity and number of regulations had multiplied dramatically.[52] Because of the structures set up under Gierek, the regulations and political decisions of individual censors were far more immutable than ever before. The regulations came directly from the Press Department and no other individuals or institutions could intervene in the censors' decisions directly.[53] The Press Department also was given the final voice on media-related issues, and other Central Committee departments lost their rights even over the publications in their area. This gave journalists only one institution of appeal (unless they had contacts in the Politburo): the very Central Committee department which gave the original directions to the censors. In addition, many of the leaders with whom journalists had worked since the 1950s were displaced by Gierek's men from Silesia. Few established journalists had any ties with these men. As a result, there were not even informal channels to protect journalists from censorship by the newly expanded and centralized control institutions. Even journals with politically and professionally well-placed editors were highly censored and their appeals had little impact.[54]

Coupled with the shoring up of control institutions, there was an increased intensity and compulsion in the direction given to the media. The Central Committee Press Department expanded from some ten "instructors" from 1950–70 to over 50 "instructors" and a large support staff under Gierek.[55] Each instructor was assigned a group of journals to review regularly and also to visit, assign tasks, and participate in their periodic planning sessions.[56] On the scale of the media as a whole, Press Department officials did more than just supervise the Main Office of Control. They also organized meetings for journalists on various topics and events and played a major role in the selection and appointment of editors. Finally, they also began to produce detailed directives on how events such as the Helsinki Conference, the Pope's visit, Party Congresses, and the American Bicentennial should be handled.[57] While it is clear that their inroads in individual decisions were far more limited than their goals, these inroads were significant for the profession. By 1979, interviews even with well-known journalists indicated that they felt powerless against the new institutions of control.[58]

The growth of institutions of control and direction was clearly effected without the journalists' participation and approval. In fact, in many areas, journalists and even well-placed editors were unaware of the changes until they were already in place. As these institutions were being built up, the regime came forth with promises that the profession would be an integral element in policy-making, a role it had long sought for itself. Journalists were invited to use private channels to bring information and their expertise into policy discussions. In the early Gierek years, they were included on committees setting out long-range plans. Closed "press conferences" with Gierek and other officials were held where journalists could raise issues and get answers.[59] But as the economic situation worsened, criticism was less welcomed by the Party leadership. Journalists in the mid-1970s were essentially excluded from even internal discussions.[60] Old channels for funneling information to the leadership were eliminated by the Press Department, Press Department officials were promoted in the late 1970s, and journalists were increasingly excluded and restricted. The mass media reflected this in its increasingly unilinear and unrealistic contents.[61]

SOLIDARITY: LIBERATION AND REPRESSION

The workers' strikes of late summer 1980 clearly discredited the media policy of the Gierek leadership. Journalists responded to the options provided by the August agreements on two levels: they began to write much more openly[62] and they pressed for changes in the professional organization and in professional life. In the first six months after the August accords, established journalists who had been in the profession since the 1950s took the lead in criticism. As the *odnowa* (renewal) movement spread and increased its demands, young journalists who had just entered the profession began to play leadership roles or to edit new and increasingly critical journals. The middle generation, however, basically continued its work. They were not in positions to lead in criticism nor were they free to fill new roles. In spite of their past weakness, they were both tainted and divided.

Soon after the Gdansk agreements were signed, journalists began to talk openly about the problems of the Gierek media policy. The journalist who had been considered the "most influential" by his colleagues in the 1976 survey, Karol Malcuzynski, summarized the views which were being expressed by his colleagues when he spoke to fellow Sejm deputies on 5 September 1980:

> For years the mass media have declined. The concept and the practice by which they were controlled was fundamentally false. In the mid-1970s, the propaganda of success – which was primitively conceived and crudely implemented – became an obstacle to discussion and consideration of economic and social costs of [Gierek's policy of rapid economic development]. . . . From 1976 to 1980 this propaganda was nonsensical. At first this propaganda was irritating, but there came moments when it bordered on a provocation of the people. Central direction of the mass media was carried to the extreme, resulting in complete control not only of information but also of commentary. With few exceptions, it was impossible not only to use one's own thoughts but even to use formulations that departed from the prescribed models. . . . With each passing year, censorship was more active. In this chamber, there are twelve journalists, including several chief editors. They can recount not just tens but hundreds of examples of censorship that border on the ridiculous.[63]

In condemning the past media system, journalists readily admitted that an internal censor had been developed "through years of silence, pressure, and respectful gallantry about things which should have been clearly formulated."[64] The result, journalists made clear, was that the mass media went unused and disrespected. No aspect of the Gierek press policy or its results went uncriticized by journalists in the mass media and in their own meetings and discussions. Opposition to its continuation was clear to the new leadership.[65]

After the disappointments of 1956 and 1970, however, active journalists were unwilling to depend on the beneficence of a new leadership. Instead, they began in September to restructure their own organization and to work on a draft of a press law to regulate censorship. They did this while the Gierek press institutions were still in place.[66] At the same time, journalists continued their traditional patterns of professional behavior. They wrote the kinds of stories which they had always wanted to write or those they had written in the past only to have them rejected by the censors. They openly admitted to censoring themselves in order not to encourage Soviet intervention and civil disorder. Moreover, as before, prominent editors and journalists played roles in political organizations. Many of those who became involved as activist journalists had been prominent in the Gomulka era and blacklisted in the Gierek period. The organizations they helped lead included Solidarity advisory groups, Party organizations, and professional organizations.[67]

In setting up a control system with which they could live in the 1980s, journalists generally recognized that

> (n)o reasonable person in Poland with a sense of responsibility demands today the complete abolition of censorship. What is needed is to limit its area of responsibility, its powers, and its criteria of evaluation, and to establish a procedure for appealing its decisions.[68]

To do this, journalists worked on establishing a press law which would not only specify what information and media could be censored (as an item included in the government draft of the proposed new law, albeit with more restrictions), but also subordinated the office of censorship to the Parliament, provided for a relatively independent appeals process, specified a time limit for reviewing materials after they were submitted, and narrowed the number of periodicals and areas of discussion which could be censored.[69] In the "popular" draft composed by journalists and other professionals along with Solidarity representatives at the end of 1980, journalists got added provisions which gave them input into the selection and monitoring of personnel in the Main Office. This combination of demands reflected the journalists' growing sense of themselves as professionals who were the only ones qualified to determine the appropriate controls for professional work as well as their sense of the limits of Soviet tolerance. For this reason, journalists opposed the demands and attempts by printers in Solidarity to show their readers where works had been censored by printing blank spaces or a series of dots.[70] This, for journalists, was a reduction in their professional image. In the end, the journalists' draft provided the standard for most of the law.

In the initial period after the August accords it was equally important to journalists to resolve the problems of their professional life. Almost immediately after the accords were signed, local organizations of the Association of Polish Journalists began to press for the convening of an "Extraordinary" congress of the Association. That Congress was called for the end of November 1980, and preparatory meetings were held in October. During this period, journalists voiced their concerns not only about the establishment of legal control of the mass media, but also about the transformation of their own organization. Their concern was focused primarily on restructuring the organization so that it would be a force which would intervene and protect journalists' professional autonomy vis-à-vis their editors and the political authorities. Statutes were also included which made the leadership of the organization more directly responsible to the members of the profession through open elections. Finally, the profession took on itself the rights of a professional union which henceforth was to have a legally guaranteed role in all negotiations over working conditions, pay, and professional legislation. This was a role which it had earlier assumed on a *de facto* basis. In contrast to what happened in 1956, however, the Association in 1980 moved rapidly and independently to establish its new order by making the changes in its own statutes.[71]

In the final major area of journalists' traditional concerns – access to information – the gains registered by Solidarity appeared to have already solved the problem. Freedom of information for the striking workers meant as much an end to censorship as the opening of administrative channels to the public. Yet, while this was the least pressing issue for journalists in this period, journalists acted to reinforce their gains. The new provisions of the Association required the leadership to intervene when information was being held back. Journalists pressed for, and got the *de facto* right to vote on candidates for chief editor of their papers. While this had many other ramifications, it also gave journalists a potential sanction to be used in forcing their editors to battle for their access to information. The journalists recognized that, if they were able to control censorship, they would be able to use their own columns as weapons against bureaucrats who withheld information from them. Finally, willingly or unwillingly, journalists were increasingly drawn into cooperating with the workers on a more equal footing. This meant, in part, at least a temporary decrease in the superiority and isolation of the profession.

By January 1981 these institutional changes were either already in place or would have been in place were it not for the continuing upheavals in the political situation. Most of the media was using its new-found independence and autonomy to discuss issues long held dormant by the Gierek-era control mechanisms. The future of the profession and of the media, however, remained an open question. The domestic political and economic problems created an atmosphere in which many journalists felt it was necessary to engage in sharper and sharper criticism of the present and the past. This brought journalists into direct conflict with the Party bureaucracy which had long controlled the press and which continued to act as it had in the 1970s: sending orders to censors, intervening in television work and overriding editorial decisions. It also resulted in increased instances of censorship. All of this discouraged and radicalized those journalists who were outside the circle of the establishment leadership. Some journalists moved to "internal" publications of professional and union organizations that were, according to the provisions of the new law, exempt from censorship. These journals became leading public organs. Older journalists like Stefan Bratkowski, caught between their inability to satisfy or lead the workers and their failure to get sufficient concessions from the Party leaders, moved from focusing on purely informational concerns to broader political action. This brought them into conflict with the Party authorities and lessened their professional gains although not their professional positions.[72] A few like Mieczyslaw Rakowski switched from being journalist–politicians to politicians with their own journal.[73] And finally, the ultimate professional control, that is, the charge that unrestricted journalistic freedoms might provoke a Soviet invasion, seemed to ring more and more hollow. In December 1980, editors had used translations of American warnings that an invasion was about to take place to threaten journalists into self-censorship. By spring and early summer 1981, these threats of a Soviet invasion had been made so often that they lost credibility.[74] This development, coupled with the ferment in the Party and the society, radicalized young and senior-level journalists even as threats made by the Soviets themselves increased before the Party Congress set for July 1981.

The year following the August events represented an entirely new era in professional life in Eastern Europe. For the first time professionals were the beneficiaries and not the benefactors of the working class. Not only were journalists forced to "catch up" to the workers, but they also lost some of their social prestige and special privileges.[75] Even in the area of information control, an issue clearly within their professional expertise, journalists were forced to compromise not only with the government but also with the Solidarity leadership. All of these changes clearly represented an unprofessional dependence of journalists on society, which replaced the unprofessional dominance of journalists by the Gierek leadership.

The declaration of martial law ended journalists' attempts at protecting their gains by institutionalizing them through legislation. It also limited their ability to act openly as professionals. Those journalists "liberated" by Solidarity's gains and active in pressing for radical reform were detained and removed from their positions. Initially, all journals but the central Party daily and the military daily were closed down. Polish television, although it had never been free enough of Party control to broadcast the many information programs its staff sought to produce, went from civilian to military control. And one of the two major press agencies was eliminated. Under these conditions, the newly passed law on censorship was simply nullified by the "state of war." Individual journalists and editors found themselves on salaried leave or fired.

Even as they were defeated, however, there was evidence of the continuing commitment of many journalists to the profession and the importance of a supportive media to Poland's rulers. Journalists traditionally seen as leaders in the profession who had not joined the Jaruzelski regime or who were not detained or in hiding did not resign themselves to being subjugated.[76] Large numbers of Poland's established journalists, if they were given the opportunity to return to journalism work after subjecting themselves to a loyalty test, are reported to have refused to do so. As a result, even journals that did reopen and had not taken radical stands after August 1980 (the most prominent of which was *Polityka,* edited for 25 years by Deputy Prime Minister Mieczyslaw Rakowski) could not assemble enough of their staff to have a listing of names on the masthead. Even on those journals that did reopen later, established journalists who returned made some critical statements or, when this was not possible, limited themselves to esoteric, nonpolitical topics.

The political leadership demonstrated, first of all, the seriousness with which it took the mass media by shutting it down. In the weeks that followed, it found itself unable to reconstitute the media as it had planned because of journalists' reactions. The results were threefold. First, even before Solidarity was directly attacked, Party and government officials strongly criticized the media and the journalism profession. Large numbers of journalists were also detained. Second, journals were either not reopened as had been planned or they were produced by undersized staffs of largely unknown or discredited journalists. And, third, because of its commitment to "renewal," the entire Association of Polish Journalists was disbanded.[77] It thus became the first professional organization to be eliminated in Poland since the Second World War.

None of this has useful parallels in earlier events in Poland or elsewhere in Eastern Europe. At this writing, six months after the declaration of martial law, the course of events is not even clear in Poland. Journals are just beginning to appear. A new organization of journalists has been formed, the Journalists Association of the Polish Peoples' Republic, but it had only put out a declaration of loyalty that did not present any information about its plans or its membership. Journalists who are writing are known as professionals who rose in 1968 by making strong attacks; as established journalists who elected to return out of personal necessity or agreement with the necessity for martial law (the smallest group); or staffers who had remained on the staff but had not become professionally prominent either because they entered the profession in the early 1960s when there were no openings or because they had not distinguished themselves as writers. Their numbers are as yet far more limited than the normal professional cadres. How the media will be "normalized" under these conditions is an open question for the Polish regime as well as for outside observers. Unless large numbers of journalists involved with the Renewal return, the Polish media will be dominated by a generation which has essentially known professional life in Poland as a life where opportunity is blocked by the stability of the older generation and, under Solidarity, the "brashness" of newcomers. Whatever the outcome, however, the massive attack on the profession and the political power's victory over journalists do not bode well for professional leadership and pressure for autonomy in the 1980s.

NOTES AND REFERENCES

This article is based in part on research done in Poland in 1976 under the sponsorship of the International Research and Exchanges Board and in 1979 while on an interviewing project for the Rand Corporation. I am particularly grateful to these organizations for their assistance in this research; to the Polish journalists who answered my questions openly and patiently; to Sol Wank for his reading of the original version of this manuscript in March 1980; and to Matthew Frederick for his assistance in the preparation of the introduction.

1. Item 3 of the Gdansk demands read "upholding the freedom of the press, opinion, and publications guaranteed in the Polish constitution, . . . the mass media are to be made accessible to representatives of all faiths." In the agreement signed 31 August 1980, one of the first provisions was for the government to present to the parliament a draft law controlling censorship.
2. Their influence on popular upheavals in Poland (1956 and 1970), Hungary (1956), and Czechoslovakia (1968) has been well documented in works such as: Paul Zinner, *Revolution in Hungary* (New York: Columbia University Press, 1962) and *National Communism and Popular Revolt in Eastern Europe* (New York: Columbia University Press, 1956); Josef Maxa, *A Year is Eight Months* (Garden City: Doubleday, 1970); Frank L. Kaplan, *Winter Into Spring: The Czechoslovak Press and the Reform Movement* (Boulder: East European Quarterly, 1977); Robin Remington, *Winter in Prague* (Cambridge: MIT Press, 1969); and H. Gordon Skilling, *Czechoslovakia's Interrupted Revolution* (Princeton University Press, 1979).
3. In the early months of the transformation in Poland, leading Catholic and non-Catholic journalists were represented on the negotiating teams for both the government and the strikers. Often, these advisors would have had close personal ties with one another and would be able to work out agreements because of their personal relationships. In February 1981, when the printers threatened to go on strike over the continuation of strict prepublication censorship, it was the head of the journalists' association who was the liaison between the printers and the Minister of Justice, Jerzy Bafia.
4. The most prominent of these individuals, Mieczyslaw Rakowski, the chief editor of *Polityka,* kept his editorship of this liberal socio-political weekly when he became Deputy Prime Minister.
5. Terence Johnson, *Professions and Power* (London: Macmillan, 1972) p. 16.
6. Joel J. Schwartz and William E. Keech, "Group Interest and the Policy Process in the Soviet Union," *American Political Science Review,* LXIII, no. 3 (September 1968) p. 850.
7. V. I. Lenin, "What Is To Be Done?" in *Collected Works,* vol. I (Moscow: Progress Publishers, 1967) p. 233.

8. Bernard A. Ramundo, "They Answer To *Pravda,*" *The University of Illinois Law Forum* (Spring 1964) p. 106.
9. Ibid., p. 115.
10. Mark Hopkins, *Mass Media in the Soviet Union* (New York: Pegasus, 1970) p. 104.
11. Interview data collected by the author in 1975–6 under the sponsorship of the International Research and Exchanges Board.
12. In 1976, of the 200 journalists who returned surveys sent to their offices, 105 said that the main negative characteristic of the profession was that it was too politically risky and 119 said that the work had too fast a pace. Opposition to political pressures on the profession is clear not only from the complaint that journalism is "politically risky" but also from the incidence of criticisms such as: "too many chances to make enemies" (66 listings on a multiple listing questionnaire) and "too many difficulties in getting and publishing information" (55 listings).
13. Interview data, 1976.
14. In the case of Polish journalists and Western professional groups like lawyers in the United States, this professionalism does not preclude a high level of political involvement and politicization.
15. Stefania Dziecielska, *Sytuacja Spoleczna Dziennikarzy Polskich* (Wroclaw: Ossolinium, 1962) p. 191.
16. Joseph Ben-David, "Professions in the Class System of Present Day Society," *Current Sociology,* XII, 1963/64, p. 249.
17. Elliot Friedson, *Professional Dominance: The Social Structure of Medical Care* (New York: Atherton Press, 1970) p. 96.
18. Ibid.
19. Zbigniew Krzystek, "Kim Jestesmy?," *Prasa Polska* (August 1977) p. 3.
20. "Nie wolno kneblowac zdrowej krytyki," *Prasa Polska* (February 1949) p. 24.
21. Interview data, 1976.
22. Henryk Korotynski, "O niektorych zywotnych zagadnieniach naszej prasy," *Prasa Polska* (November 1953) p. 7.
23. Interview data, 1976.
24. Jane Curry, *The Media and Intra-Elite Communication in Poland: The System of Censorship* (Rand Corporation: December 1980), p. 5.
25. Jerzy Mond, "Uwagi o refleksje o 'Terenie'," *Prasa Polska* (November 1956) p. 4.
26. Journalists organized their own Board of Review for post-publication censorship which brought journalists and government representatives together. They also limited their reports when Wladyslaw Gomulka called them in and attacked their writings for encouraging a Soviet invasion. This was reported to the national congress of the Association which was meeting in Warsaw from 30 November to 2 December 1956) Stenogram, Walny Zjazd.
27. Jane Curry, *The Media and Intra-Elite Communication in Poland: Organization and Control of the Media* (Rand Corporation: December 1980) pp. 3–13.
28. T. R. "Plenum i uklad," *Prasa Polska* (May 1964) p. 1.
29. Ibid., p. 3.

30. Tadeusz Kupis, *Zawod dziennikarskie w P.R.L.* (Warsaw: Ksiazka i Wiedza, 1966) p. 1.
31. Ibid., pp. 207–8.
32. Tadeusz Kupis, "Dziennikarskie Zdrowie" in T. Kupis, *Dziennikarskie Sprawy* (Warsaw: Ksiazka i Wiedza, 1976) pp. 191–201.
33. Jane Curry, *The Black Book of Polish Censorship* (New York: Random House, 1983) and interview data.
34. Interview data and Stenograms, Walny Zjazd, 1960, 1964, and 1968.
35. Interview data, 1976. (One of the "reforms" in 1955 was to make all but the actual PUWP organs responsible for becoming financially self-supporting.)
36. Interview data, 1976 and 1979.
37. Stenograms, Walny Zjazd, 1960, 1964, 1968.
38. Interview data, 1976.
39. For a more complete description of journalists' attempts to influence policy, see J. Curry, "Polish Journalists in the Policy Making Process," in Maurice D. Simon and Roger E. Kanet (eds), *Background to Crisis: Policy and Politics in Gierek's Poland* (Boulder, Colorado: Westview Press, 1981).
40. Interview data, 1976.
41. Zbigniew Kwiatkowski, "Uchwala rzecz wazna," *Zycie Literackie* (19 March 1978) p. 12.
42. Interview data, 1976 and 1979.
43. *Prasa Polska*, 1964–70, and interview data, 1976.
44. Interview data, 1976.
45. Interview data, 1976.
46. The delegates to the National Congress who were elected during 1967 were almost totally new. It was this Congress which met during the March events but which had been selected far earlier. Most of its members were low and middle level journalists who had been able to move up because of the purges at higher levels.
47. "Problemowy Plan Pracy Redakcje 'Polityka' Rok 1969."
48. The text of the plan and the topics it covers are almost identical to Gierek's initial policy statements.
49. Interview data, 1976. (Gierek had ruled his section of the country so independently and separately from the central authorities that he was known as the Polish Lumumba. Along with that went the fact that few Katowice journalists went to Warsaw and few Warsaw journalists had contact with Katowice.)
50. Interview data, 1976. (One of the chief advisors to Gierek in the 1960s was Maciej Szczepanski, at that time the editor of *Trybuna Robotnicza*.)
51. Curry, *Organization and Control of the Media*, p. 16.
52. Interview data, 1979.
53. Ibid.
54. The statistics compiled from 1974 to 1976 show that it is the socio-political weeklies which were the most heavily censored. With the exception of *Wiez* and *Tygodnik Powszechny*, journals of the Catholic intelligentsia, most of the censored items were from journals tradition-ally considered to represent leading elements of the PUWP. They are

the journals with editors who had enough authority for journalists to be willing to take risks in the hope that the editor would protect them from censorship. The journals cited with some regularity for having the highest rate of censorship in that period were: the dailies, *Slowo Powszechne* and *Zycie Warszawy*, and the socio-political weeklies, especially *Polityka*. By 1979, *Polityka* was thought to be the most censored journal in Poland with the possible exception of *Tygodnik Powszechny*.

55. Interview data, 1976.
56. Ibid.
57. Curry, *The Black Book of Polish Censorship*.
58. Interview data, 1979.
59. Ibid.
60. Ibid.
61. Ibid.
62. Chris Pszenicki, "Polish Publishing 1980–81," *Index on Censorship*, 1/1982, pp. 8–11.
63. The full text was carried by DPA, the West German news agency, on 7 September 1980.
64. Jerzy Wilmanski, "Nie tylko censor," *Prasa Polska* (October 1980) p. 17.
65. "Nadzwyczajny Zjazd Delegatow SDP," *Prasa Polska* (December 1980) p. 6.
66. Dariusz Fikus, "Niech kazdy mowi, co ma na sercu," *Prasa Polska* (February–March 1981) p. 7.
67. John Darnton, "Warsaw Printers' Union Is a Thorn in Censors' Side," *New York Times* (7 February 1981) p. 1.
68. Karol Malczuzynski, as quoted in Jane Leftwich Curry and A. Ross Johnson, *The Media and Inter-Elite Communication in Poland: A Summary Report* (Rand Corporation: December 1980) p. 14.
69. "Ustawa o kontroli publikacji i widowisk," *Prasa Polska* (January 1981) p. 7.
70. Interview data, 1981.
71. "Statut SDP zatwierdzony," *Prasa Polska* (January 1981) p. 11.
72. Bratkowski was called before the Party Control Commission and criticized. The censorship draft was originally due in November 1980. It was ultimately delayed, partly by disagreements and partly by the press of other events, until August 1981.
73. He is now the deputy prime minister and, in the Extraordinary Congress, ran for First Secretary of the PUWP as a liberal candidate.
74. Interview data, 1981.
75. "Polish Journalists Move to Salvage Their Reputation," *New York Times* (10 November 1980) p. 24.
76. Three of the most respected journalists of the 1960s and 1970s (Wieslaw Gornicki, Jerzy Urban, and Mieczyslaw Rakowski) were prominent in the Jaruzelski regime. But, with the exception of Jerzy Urban's attacks on other journalists' lack of historical memory in their attacks on non-journalists who had benefitted from the Gierek system, they did not engage in direct public attacks on their fellows.
   Other prominent journalists who had headed the Journalists' Associa-

tion during the Solidarity period were detained, went into hiding or did not write because of their activities during the Solidarity period.

77. "The Normalization of Poland's Journalists," *Radio Free Europe Research,* Polish Situation Report, no. 73/82 (2 April 1982).

7 Intellectuals and their Discontent in Hungary: Class Power or Marginality?

RUDOLF L. TŐKÉS

The 1970s marked the rise of the "second generation" of post-war dissident/critical intellectuals in Eastern Europe. The first generation, with which members of the new generation did not, as a rule, claim ideological kinship, had been the great and near-great rebels, nay-sayers and the revisionist Marxist philosophical loners of the 1930s and the 1940s who could not find accommodation with the harsh realities and the politics of Stalinist expediency of the 1950s. Djilas, Kolakowski, Lukács and Brecht addressed broad moral and ethical issues as these surfaced in the early "difficult" years of socio-political transformation in Eastern Europe.[1] Ideological conscientious objectors are never welcome in a one-party state, and critical writings about the moral turpitude of the New Class, the ethical indefensibility of historical determinism, the idiocy of the cult of personality clothed in the doctrine of socialist realism and the dictatorship of the anti-intellectual apparatchiki were suppressed and their authors forced into premature retirement from public life.

It is still unclear whether and in what way the writings and the general political legacy of these early dissenters have shaped the thinking of the next generation of critical East European socialist intellectuals. For most, with the exception of some of the Prague Spring ideologues, Rudolf Bahro, the Lukács School and perhaps Robert Haveman, Marxism ceased to be a theory capable of providing intellectually defensible and empirically valid answers to the basic problems of East European society and politics.[2] For many, questions of economics, planning, principles of distribution of surpluses which had been extracted from the population in the preceding decades of

160

forced industrialization and collectivization became the central issue of the 1970s. In the last few years the critical intellectuals' interest shifted to new concerns. These include questions of the quality of life, culture and intellectual identity in the age of dying ideologies and consumerist regime policies. Though they are the main bene-ficiaries of its results, many intellectuals are alarmed by consumerism as the regime's main legitimacy-building device. This has prompted a new round of polemics about the fate of cultural and spiritual values in a period of regime preoccupation with energy, foreign trade and industrial productivity.[3]

The purpose of this essay is to offer an informal normative frame-work for the discussion of the issues, participants and outcomes of dissident politics in Eastern Europe; to outline the rather special circumstances which shaped the form and content of intellectual discontent in Hungary in the late 1960s and early 1970s; to introduce and discuss the notions of "class power" and "marginality" of the intellectuals as advanced by a new sociological study by Iván Sze-lényi and György Konrád; and to develop a partial test of the Szelényi-Konrád hypotheses by juxtaposing these against the re-sults of a 1979 Hungarian *samizdat* opinion survey.

DISSENT AND DISCONTENT: CAUSALITY AND CONCEPTUALIZATION

Some years ago in a study of the politics of dissident interest articu-lation I speculated that certain kinds of dissent, coming from "instru-mental-pragmatic" critics of the regime, might contribute to peace-ful or, at any rate evolutionary, change in the Soviet Union.[4] With Andrei Sakharov in internal exile and the rest of the prominent dissidents driven abroad or effectively silenced at home, now it seems abundantly clear that my reasoning was based on wishful thinking about the potentials of critical policy recommendations of scientists, economists and liberal intellectuals to help foster political liberaliza-tion in the USSR. I also underestimated the illiberal pragmatic consensus that unites all Communist elites against innovations that could upset the political balance of power through the admission of low-status groups into the policy-making process.

Systemic similarities notwithstanding, the East European situation is appreciably different from that which obtains in the USSR. Nation-alism and latent or overt anti-Soviet feelings are central to popular beliefs and the proximity of the West and Western cultural influences tend to exacerbate anti-regime sentiments. However, to reduce East European dissent to anti-Soviet outbursts and to anomic expressions of national xenophobia is to miss the essential point, which is the coming of age of post-totalitarian societies of Eastern Europe. These societies are quite unique as they are creations of 35 years of sustained Communist party and government efforts to establish economically developed, politically stable and socially highly stratified national entities as parts of a Soviet-dominated international alliance system.

The political transformation of this area in the last third of a century and popular resistance to changes from above have taken place in four stages: (1) initial breakthrough and scattered violent resistance (1944–48); (2) high Stalinism, forced mobilization, large-scale dislocation of the populations and similar measures which climaxed in the crises of 1956; (3) post-totalitarian consolidation, partial economic, but no political reforms and the crises of this process (1960–70); and (4) accommodation and consensus-building which is characterized by an increasingly widespread struggle for power, status and access among all active and passive participants of the political process in Eastern Europe in the last ten years.

Because of wide accessibility of the necessary documentary evidence, the availability of rich interpretative literature on post-war East European politics and the unprecedented openness with which the regimes and their critics argue their case, it is now possible for students of political change, and of dissent in particular, to advance new explanations about these matters.

In the broadest sense, one may regard dissent as a consequence as well as the cause of change in the development of Communist-type systems. The causes and consequences of change in Communist systems have been subjected to intensive scrutiny by several Western scholars.[5] Their findings are useful but are of marginal applicability for the purposes of this study. Therefore, I shall focus on the general phenomenon of dissent by viewing it as central to the establishment and continuing political legitimacy of a Communist state.

In the most fundamental sense, it had been dissent and dissatisfaction with the pre-Communist political, economic and cultural order that made successful Communist revolutions possible. Here I am not concerned with the very important differences between "indigenous" and "derivative" revolutions, but submit that *both* kinds of revolutions took their ideological and political departure from a set of legitimating principles. These, for the want of a better term, may be conceptualized as aspects of a "social contract," between the victorious Communist party elite and the people whom they sought to enlist to join the march toward the building of socialism and communism.[6] The "social contract" had many components, but the essential ones offered a set of tradeoffs: for the basic social welfare package of "bread, land and peace," members of the population were to forego (as most Russians in 1917 and many East Europeans in 1944–5) the dubious benefits of Western-style liberal democracy and the kinds of classical democratic freedoms that did not come to most East Europeans' attention until the late 1970s in the form of Western demands for the implementation of the Basket Three provisions of the Helsinki Agreements of 1975.

The precedents of 1953 (East Berlin), 1956 (Budapest and Warsaw) and 1968 (Prague) have convincingly demonstrated to all East Europeans that so long as the USSR has vital security interests in this area no drastic changes would be tolerated in the realm of political, economic and social institutions. This, within the given framework of the military, political and ideological dependency of the East European regimes on the USSR, provided for only one substantive area, that of social-welfare policy, which the regimes could utilize to legitimate their rule. However, a more general definition of the social contract between the people and the regime after 35 years of uninterrupted industrialization, economic development and one-party rule must include components that transcend issue of "bread" and basic sustenance. These include demands not merely for more of the same, but for a growing range of needs which are perceived as *rights* and expectations for their prompt satisfaction by the regime. The infinite elasticity of needs and the very finite political and economic resources that the East European states possess to satisfy them provide, in my view, the framework in which dissent of all kinds is articulated in contemporary Eastern Europe.

Dissent or dissatisfaction with existing conditions goes well beyond familiar interactions between the Communist regime and its articulate libertarian foes. Dissatisfaction with existing conditions also pertains to one's opportunities, class status, career mobility and personal prerogatives in the workplace and in the social arena.[7] For these reasons, contemporary dissident politics in Eastern Europe may best be characterized as disputes over the *current implementation* of the original social contract. These manifest themselves as formal and informal contestation among all members of the post-totalitarian society to benefit from central allocation and distribution of power, status, material, cultural and psychic benefits. The stakes, in most cases, are tangible (income, perquisites, access to consumer goods, leisure time and cultural benefits and opportunity to travel in the West), and in other cases intangible (social mobility, rank, status, access to restricted information and other psychic rewards of being at, or on the way to the top of, the socio-political pyramid).

Disputes and contestation over the implementation of the basic social contract takes place on three levels. On the *first* level the matter involves a widespread but, with the exception of the still unfolding Polish developments of 1980–3, extremely one-sided clash of wills between the political haves and the political have-nots: the party apparat, the top state bureaucracy, the economic, military, cultural, educational and scientific elites on the one hand, and the rural population, the unskilled workers, the old, the uneducated, the infirm and economically marginal elements of the society on the other hand. The stakes are essentially economic and concern wages, food supply, housing, transportation, social and welfare services, but also non-economic, such as social mobility of the young through unimpeded access to higher and specialized education and equal treatment under the law. Since the summer of 1980 these demands have been forcefully articulated by the leaders of the Polish independent trade union movement,[8] but in the preceding thirty-five years the have-nots' grievances had rarely found organized expression – unless these had been taken up by the Catholic Church, by a socially conscious writer, crusading journalist, or radical sociologist.

The *second* level of contestation over the meaning and implementation of the social contract takes place between the humanistic, nationalistic, religious and New Left-type intellectuals on one hand, and the technocratic, administrative and communications-specialist university graduates to which much of the state and central party apparat belongs, on the other. This is by far the most visible level of confrontation and it takes place mostly through authorized publications (such as small-circulation specialist journals and the like), but also through informal lobbying and self-published unauthorized channels. Ostensibly, the issues revolve around the *interpretation* of the social contract, but in fact concern access to top policy-makers. The latter are asked to adjudicate conflicting elite claims for a politically secure, economically advantageous and ideologically flexible working environment and improvements on the existing structure of elite privileges and perquisites. In this context questions of censorship, quality of life and other existential issues are secondary, and, in the final analysis, expendable debating points. Not all East European poets are liberals and not all East European technocrats are conservatives, but, as a rule, both appear to be united in the quest to have influence on policy-making and in maintaining a political and economic distance between themselves and the non-elites.

The *third* level of contestation is over the *operationalization*, through authoritative decisions about resource allocations, of the social contract. It takes place between established or ad hoc alliances of various policy groups within the top party elite. Although the details vary in each East European state, each policy group, clique or faction maintains extensive contacts with the key participants of policy debates at the level below. Since the 1960s internal security channels of information about the political have nots' demands have been supplemented by more specific public opinion surveys by Central Committee, Academy of Sciences or radio/TV-based expert sociologists.

The above outlined threefold hierarchical pattern of participation in discussions concerning the implementation, interpretation and operationalization of the social contract is based on the regimes' communications monopoly and the policy of denying members of low-status social groups direct access to newspapers, radio and television. Although the very existence and continued vigor of the East European samizdat has, in a symbolic way, broken the censors' stranglehold on the freedom of expression, the fact is that with Poland's single exception, self-published writings have never reached the average worker or peasant. Foreign broadcasts (RFE, BBC, VOA) have been helpful to convey dissident messages to the average East Europeans, but they are no match for the authenticity of self-published writings. In Poland since 1976 however, self-published books, journals, leaflets have proliferated to the extent that uncensored literature has had a demonstrable impact on the thinking and overt behavior of hundreds of thousands, and in 1980, millions of people. Thus, at least in that country, a clear case can be made for the revolutionary consequences of the newly created horizontal channels of communication which address all three levels of concern with respect to the now bankrupt social contract between the people and the regime of that country.

TWO ROADS TO REFORM: PRAGUE AND BUDAPEST

The Prague Spring was both a point of departure and an ideological watershed for those East European intellectuals who sought to subject their respective national realities to critical, or, to use the awkward phrase, "within-system" scrutiny. For the Czechoslovak reformers and their sympathizers everywhere in Eastern Europe, the Prague Spring was an exhilarating and profoundly satisfying experience which demonstrated, *in vivo,* for a period of four to five months, the extent to which a moribund, economically and politically bankrupt state socialist system could be revitalized, democratized and, indeed, humanized.

The crushing of the Czechoslovak experiment has, apart from the obvious geopolitical conclusions, also prompted a new round of soul-searching by both the former participants and their would-be imitators elsewhere in Eastern Europe. The process of reexamination of the Prague Spring, though aided by the appearance of several Western scholarly works as well as by the political memoirs of the former protagonists, is still in progress.[9] However, the question of the delayed impact of Czechoslovak experience on the thinking and critical posture of other East European, particularly of the Hungarian, intellectuals, has only begun.

The influence of the political and philosophical legacy of the Prague Spring on Polish, Hungarian, Yugoslav and East German socialist intellectuals has been limited by several country-specific factors which shaped the perceptions and prejudged the responses of the beholders to the Czechoslovak road to reform. The most obvious of these has been the non-transferability of the ethos of Czechoslovakia's liberal democratic traditions to modify the contemporary political cultures of the other socialist states of Eastern Europe. The kind of political culture among the older and educated generation which could be taken for granted by the Prague reformers did not exist elsewhere in Eastern Europe.[10] Nor was there anywhere else, as in Czechoslovakia, a widely shared and, on the whole, positive attitude among the people, especially the intellectuals, toward the idea of socialism, however defined. And the kind of latent pro-Russian sentiments among Czechs, though considerably less so among Slovaks, that had lingered on, despite the February coup and the Stalinist purges, since the last war simply did not exist in Hungary, Poland and East Germany. Intellectuals of these nations, unlike their colleagues in Prague, did not have to be told, to paraphrase the protest slogan of the post-invasion days, that Brezhnev "had gone mad," therefore Lenin should "wake up," because they had no illusions whatever about Lenin, and considered Brezhnev to be a perfectly sane Leninist.

That the only sign of Hungarian intellectual protest at the Soviet occupation of Czechoslovakia came from five Marxist philosophers of the Lukács School was not surprising, but it did not mean that the rest of the reform-oriented leftist critics of the Kádár regime had not been touched by the spirit of the interrupted Czechoslovak experiment.[11] They had been, but, with the exception of a few Lukács disciples, who had not yet severed the emotional umbilical cords that tied them to their mentor's semi-reformed Marxist orthodoxy, the thinking and behavior of the rest of the leftist intellectual camp was motivated by concerns which had little to do with what had transpired in Prague.

The "country-specific" circumstances which limited or entirely precluded the transferability of the Prague Spring alternative to other East European countries, though axiomatic, require additional explanation in this context. One of the respondents (a linguist) of a recent samizdat opinion survey pointed out that educated East Europeans had been out of touch with one another since the breakup of the Habsburg Monarchy in 1918.[12] First came the intolerant political isolationism and linguistic chauvinism of the interwar years, then the cataclysmic war which destroyed, *inter alia,* the majority of the East European Jewish middle class, which was the international, multilingual and multicultural segment best able to facilitate cultural and intellectual contacts throughout the area. Then came the years of Stalinism and the political isolation and cultural fragmentation of individual East European states and their national intelligentsia. The reintegration of these disparate segments into a culturally coherent and possibly politically interactive whole might come in the late 1980s unless a new cold war or the worsening of the energy crisis puts an end to the large-scale human traffic of East European tourists intent on discovering the cultural treasures (and the second economies) of their little-known neighbors.

Ignorance of each other's languages, recent history and modern cultural traditions has, therefore, compelled those with genuine interest in the existential problems of fellow intellectuals in the next East European country to follow events there through French and German literary weeklies, or, even less directly, from the reading of critical comments and rebuttals of unorthodox works by other East European authors in censored regime publications.

Unfamiliarity with the protagonists and the issues of intellectual

developments in Prague, Warsaw, Berlin, Belgrade and Buchares
has helped reinforce the Hungarian intellectuals' natural inclinatior
to search for the national past for methods and precedents to aid the
critical reassessment of their present condition. For the critical left ii
Hungary the task of "going native" and returning to the past fo
"progressive," hence politically safe, traditions for attacking curren
problems was a realistic strategy. Barely a decade after a defeatec
revolution in 1956, for the intellectuals of Hungary the example o
1848/49, the Austro-Hungarian Compromise of 1867 and the prece
dent of the Age of Dualism (1867–1918) implied proven methods fo
internal rejuvenation and growth under foreign domination. These
were eminently plausible aspirations. They joined with the intellec
tuals' desire to survive as a coherent group to explain their apparen
lack of concern about the Soviet suppression of the Czechosloval
reform movement in August 1968.

To have influence over their political environment it was necessary
for the Hungarian intellectuals to take part in the reenactment of one
or both historically proven methods of cooperation with the power:
that be. The first of these was the adaption to the ethos of wha
George Schöpflin called a "k. und k." mentality and pragmatic
cooperation with the political incumbents of the day (a pattern wel
established in pre-1914 Austria–Hungary).[13] The other was the devel
opment of a more practical alliance (based on the precedent of ar
informal partnership between a right-wing government and the re
form intelligentsia of 1931–6) which assigns to the humanistic intel
lectuals and their technocratic counterparts positive roles in the
formulation of national priorities. Given the Hungarian Communis
Party's need to create a broad pragmatic alliance of all elites fo
political stability and economic development, both kinds of prece
dents had features of a *modus vivendi* that was acceptable to the
regime and to all but the Lukács-inspired intellectuals. The practica
implementation of what became known as the "Kádár Compro
mise," best summarized by the slogan "he who is not against us i
with us," is well described in William Robinson's study on the origins
and the early phases of the New Economic Mechanism (NEM) o
1968.[14] As he explains it, the eventual success of NEM hinged upor
the large-scale cooptation of economists, sociologists and writers intc
the fringes of the policy-making process.

Another rather special facet of the regime-intelligentsia nexus o
the last 15 years has been the atmosphere, to use Edward Banfield's
terminology, of "amoral familism" which surrounded the informa

dissident–police investigator, writer–editor/censor, reformist–conformist intellectual dialogues over issues of political taboos, creative freedoms and acceptable ways of advocating unorthodox ideas. These dialogues and relationships rested on mutually shared and accepted limitations on the exercise of individual rights that Western theory considers inalienable and essential to the exercise of first-class citizenship in a modern state. However, East European realities dictate prudence and the settling for a reduced scope of intellectual self-determination. Regime commitment to resisting attempts of re-Stalinization, the implementation of a clearly specified structure of rewards for conformist behavior and the guarantee to *all* intellectuals of a modicum of personal autonomy (amounting to a promise of virtual immunity from arrest for ideological kinds of political offenses), provided a relatively tension-free framework for the coexistence and extensive collaboration of the intellectuals and the "powers." On the other hand, what the regime obviously did not reckon with was that such policies and tacit understandings, though they helped defuse the dissident potential of most of the intelligentsia, also brought in the contraband of non-Marxist, technocratic and other politically destabilizing ideas and a new assertiveness as to the kinds of roles intellectuals were to play in the policy-making process.

The surfacing in Hungary of the scientific, administrative and cultural elites in the late 1960s as putative partners in the national enterprise of laying the groundwork for the building of an "advanced socialist society" and the launching of a major economic reform program (New Economic Mechanism–NEM) in 1968 also coincided with the coming of age of the first post-war generation of university-trained young professionals. For most of these young people the 1956 Revolution had been a traumatic, but somewhat hazy memory and the "real socialism" of 1965–70 was a flawed, but still promising reality. Those with genuine talent and academic promise were quickly drafted into one of the several Academy of Science or ministry-level research institutes, in the editorial offices of publishing houses and the communications media. Many of the high achievers were sent abroad for advanced training in Western Europe, the US and the Soviet Union. There were several economists, sociologists and physical scientists who went both to the US and the USSR for post-graduate work. Although only a handful of these foreign-trained specialists became active dissidents, they nevertheless amounted to a critical mass of reasonably well-informed, well-paid, yet intellectually still open-minded people who provided a potential constituency for those who sought to probe more deeply into the subsurface dimensions of Hungarian society and economics.[15]

INTELLECTUALS AND CLASS POWER

One of the unintended consequences of the "Kádár Compromise" and the politically more relaxed atmosphere of the early years of NEM was the emergence of a body of critical literature on Hungarian society and social problems. This included works by András Hegedüs, Ágnes Heller, Ferenc Fehér, Mária and György Márkus, Mihály Vajda, the authors of the "Discovery of Hungary" investigative sociology series and an unpublished manuscript *Az értelmiség útja az osztályhatalomhoz* (Intellectuals on the Road to Class Power) by the novelist György Konrád and the sociologist Iván Szelényi.[16] For reasons that will be apparent below, the work could not be published and its authors, following a brief spell in jail, were encouraged to leave the country. This Szelényi did in 1975 while Konrád chose to remain in Hungary.

The Konrád-Szelényi study is of considerable interest for several reasons. This work is the first attempt to analyze the evolution of the structure, political behavior and contemporary existential dilemmas of East European intellectuals from the viewpoint and with the methodologies of modern sociology. The authors' approach to the sociology of the modern intellectuals takes its departure from the "first" Budapest School of critical sociology (1900–18), and specifically from the writings of Karl Polányi, Karl Mannheim, Oscar Jászi and, in a roundabout fashion, from those of the young György Lukács. What Konrád and Szelényi are proposing to do is to offer what their great Hungarian predecessors and, in a more theoretical vein, their German colleagues, Max Weber and Georg Simmel, had attempted sixty years ago: a clinical reconstruction of the economic and political forces which had shaped Eastern Europe's modern intelligentsia.

The work begins with a critical examination of the writings of Marx, Durkheim, Mannheim, Weber and Western New Left theorists on the origins, social position, traditional mission, self-perceived role and economic functions of the early, modern and contemporary intelligentsia. What Konrád and Szelényi intend to show is that in Eastern Europe, perhaps more so than anywhere else, there had been, from the very beginning, a symbiotic relationship between the intellectuals and the wielders of economic and political power. They argue that the historic intimacy among all educated elements of East European societies helped forge a sense of kinship and aspirations for a shared mastery of political power. Indeed, one must agree with Michael Walzer's commentary which calls Konrád's and Szelényi's account of that history (of the East European intellectual's unique relationship vis-à-vis the state) "probably the most brilliant part of their book, a sustained and powerful analysis of the East European social structure since the Middle Ages."[17] Konrád and Szelényi submit that, in functional terms, it had been the intellectuals who had provided the real impetus to the modernization and social transformation of this part of Europe rather than the bourgeoisie, whose appearance was delayed.

In Eastern Europe, therefore, the multiple roles of political counterelite, of an established ruling class, and also that of the bearers of ideologies of modernization were all played by individuals belonging to one and the same class: that of the culturally homogeneous educated elite. In any and all of these roles the intellectuals have parlayed their academic, scientific, administrative, technical, communication and other cultural skills into a powerful currency of functional indispensability and political influence. As the result, the modernizing intellectuals have become indispensable to the modern East European state as key participants of what Szelényi and Konrád call the process of "redistribution" of the chronically inadequate resources that the state controlled. Given the post-war need for rapid recovery via the concentration of all societal and economic resources and its coincidence with the Communist parties' own development strategies, the intellectuals have again become indispensable to the new rulers of the state.

The above summary of Konrád's and Szelényi's extremely closely argued case cannot account for many subtle aspects of their analysis. However, what matters in this context is that they developed a historically accurate framework of analysis which enables us to define the Hungarian and, to a lesser extent, the East European intellectuals' position *not* as an adversary but as a natural partner of the post-totalitarian Communist party. The validity of the argument rests on the proposition that the Communist parties are, for obvious historic and ideological reasons, committed to spearheading a program of accelerated modernization, social transformation and political change. The realization of these objectives requires the mobilization of all available societal resources, as well as the rational and cost-effective management and redistribution of the fruits of the system's creative efforts.[18]

However, the intellectuals' post-war honeymoon with the party elite did not last long. In the age of Stalinism there was no room for idealists and unreliable bourgeois experts in the state apparat. Those who escaped the "higher party academy" of Eastern Europe's gulags found themselves relegated to menial positions and very far from political power. The shared experience of humiliation and powerlessness imparted one important unintended benefit, especially to the humanistic intelligentsia. They were forced to rediscover their primary mission: that of excelling in their craft as artists, writers and poets, philosophers and historians. They also came to realize that without the technocrats who had generally fared much better in the Stalinist period, they were at the mercy of the party bureaucracy.

Recovery from the social devastation of Stalinism was a protracted process, but it was accelerated by mutual concessions by the party elite and the intellectuals. As Konrád and Szelényi explain it, the new "era of compromise" between the wielders of the state's political–economic and scientific–humanistic resources was founded on a clear-cut division of labor between the two. The party elite was to continue to provide ideological and policy guidance but the *implementation* of policies was to be informed by the new legitimating principle of "rational distribution" as defined by non-ideological technocrats and popularized by their humanistic fellow intellectuals. Konrád and Szelényi call this a "historic compromise" with which "the ruling elite in fact assured itself of a new and stabilized supremacy, for thereby it rid itself of the conflict between the elite as a whole and the party elite within the elite . . . and it converted the conflict into a regulated and rationally controlled system of conflicts between the intellectual class and the ruling elite."[19]

However, the "era of compromise" did not last long and, beginning with the Prague Spring, the East European party elites have again felt themselves threatened by displays of autonomous tendencies by the technocrats and especially by the humanistic intellectuals. In the meantime, however, the technocratic elites became entirely indispensable to the regime as providers of essential managerial and scientific skills. Without them the party's consumerist policies would have foundered – as they did in Czechoslovakia in 1964–7 and in Poland at the end of the 1960s, in the mid-1970s and, to an unprecedented degree, in 1980–1. On the other hand, the party did not feel constrained from exercising its coercive powers over the ideologically alert and increasingly assertive philosophers, sociologists and publicists. Selective repression of the literati was both a useful object lesson for the technocrats (the number of economists and engineers who are political prisoners in Eastern Europe outside Czechoslovakia in the 1970s probably could be counted on one hand) and a sufficient deterrent for those who threatened the party's ideological pretensions.

The continued importance of ideological legitimacy for the Communist party is well summarized by Konrád and Szelényi:

> Where Stalinism was a simplistic distillate of a few works by Marx, post-Stalin Eastern European Marxism offers a sophisticated interpretation of Marx's entire oeuvre, and strives to incorporate the achievements of such non-Soviet Marxist thinkers as Lukács, Gramsci, and Althusser as well. From there, however, it is an easy and alluring, but dangerous, step to go on and try to integrate portions of the work of less-orthodox Western Marxists – Bloch and Korsch, Adorno and Habermas, Marcuse and Bettelheim; for broadening the legitimate basis of Marxism in that way leads inevitably to a critical threshold where one must affirm that different, equally legitimate schools of thought are possible within the basic value-range and methodology of Marxism, and that the same question can have several different Marxist answers, among which only scholarly debate can decide (if anything can), not the dictates of higher authority. The leaders of the Communist Parties have recognized, however, that this notion, so modest from the standpoint of scientific method and so banal for the reader unaccustomed to communism's inner debates, represents a mortal danger to the ideological leading role of the party, and for that reason they have cracked down on exponents of a plurality of Marxisms just as heavily as on empirical social scientists whose findings call into question the party's basic social and economic policies.[20]

The present-day socio-political structure of Eastern Europe, as Konrád and Szelényi see it, is made up of a polarized intellectual elite and clusters of economically and politically underprivileged working masses.[21] The intellectual elite has two main components: the party elite (who, by the mid-1970s, are virtually all university graduates and coopted members of the national intelligentsia), and the technocrats and their ideological auxiliaries, the humanistic intellectuals.

Because of their strategic position in the socialist state, the two ruling intelligentsia groups are destined to become players in a conflict-prone drama for political supremacy. The argument, advanced mainly by American behavioral analysts of communist politics, that shared educational backgrounds and astute cooptation by the party of talented but potentially troublesome technocrats into the apparat will somehow alleviate tensions between the two, is implicitly rejected by Konrád and Szelényi. Their case rests on the irreconcilability of differences between the principles of each group's self-legitimation as "expert" and "red" builders of an advanced socialist state.[22] The experts' claim for power is derived from the ethos of scientific training and possession of skills to implement policies of rational redistribution. The "reds," on the other hand, take their departure from the (to them axiomatic) superiority of *telos,* or ideology, over *techné,* or the spirit of scientific rationality. Because the "reds' " power position is upheld by the state's coercive resources and, in the final analysis, by Soviet guns, the experts' only realistic hope for an even contest lies in becoming allied with the humanistic intelligentsia to compete on ideological grounds with the party elite. Competition between the two elites need not be incessant, nor invariably bruising. In periods of political stability, economic growth and steadily improving living standards, which usually coincide with the first, still hopeful, phases of East European economic reform programs, intra-elite differences are usually shelved until the next political and economic crisis comes along.

In the above context, many humanistic intellectuals prefer "voluntary marginality," or self-imposed political powerlessness, to becoming embroiled in the contestation for policy-making authority between the technocrats and the party apparatchiki. The marginal intellectuals – and most East European dissidents seem to belong to this category – have two choices open to them. They can either work within the system or seek out their natural allies, the industrial workers, the young, and the urban poor, and lead them to new confrontations with the party elite.

The foregoing summary sought to outline the essential components of the Konrád-Szelényi case for "class power" versus "marginality" as available options of direct and indirect participation in policy-making processes in post-totalitarian Eastern Europe. Although their study, like all such self-published works from the USSR and Eastern Europe, lacks an empirically verifiable scholarly apparatus, the argument is compelling for its emotional detachment and non-advocacy of instant solutions to Eastern Europe's extremely complex social problems. It is also refreshing as an analysis which, as Michael Walzer pointed out, demonstrates that "socialism with a human face" as an intelligentsia creed ". . . is not human merely, [but] it is the face of men and women, economists, technocrats, managers and professionals," a slogan of a new "technocratic Thermidor," as well as perhaps an inevitable sequel to the Jacobin–Stalinist reign of terror.[23]

The unfolding of events in Poland between late 1975 and the summer of 1980, particularly the development of the industrial worker–marginal intellectual nexus in this period, should serve at least as a partial proof of the validity of the Konrád-Szelényi thesis concerning the marginals' capabilities to help shape the form and content of hitherto poorly articulated working class demands for social justice and political rights. Many important details are still unavailable for an accurate reconstruction of the sequence of events in Poland between the initial debate over the language of Poland's new constitution in December 1975 and the collapse of the regime's political authority in the summer of 1980. However, with the benefit of hindsight it seems clear that the regime, despite the years of spurious economic prosperity since Gomulka's fall in 1971, never recovered from the crisis of public confidence which had been triggered by the bloody suppression of the striking Gdansk and Szczeczyn workers in 1971. The regime's deeply eroded political legitimacy, combined with the resurfacing of its chronic economic troubles in 1976, have contributed to a paralysis of will at the top and helped forge an unprecedented Church–radical intellectual–worker alliance among its opponents. Acts of the intellectuals' solidarity with workers imprisoned or dismissed from work because of their strike actions and other forms of protest laid the foundations of a new working relationship, based on mutual confidence and trust, between the KOR and RPCIO[24] "marginal" intellectuals and the founders of what was to become the Solidarity movement. Although the party leadership had the resources to thwart the emergence of the intellectual–worker alliance and to put an end to the massive proliferation of self-published oppositionist tracts, it chose to temporize, at least until the end of 1981, when martial law was imposed, Solidarity banned, and dissent leaders – both trade unionists and intellectuals – arrested. At any rate, because of regime hesitation prior to December 1981, the initially fragile intellectual–worker nexus was given the time and the opportunity to develop into a sturdy partnership with the capacity, since the summer of 1980, to make a bid for veto power over basic economic and social policies of the state. The resiliency of resistance since December 1981 demonstrates that this alliance has held up even under adverse conditions.

Very little of the Polish scenario, especially that of the worker–marginal intellectual linkup, is applicable to Hungary and the dynamics of dissent in that country in the 1970s. The foregoing discussion about the policy aspects of the Kádár compromise tended to support this assertion. Moreover, the Konrád-Szelényi treatise, much of which was derived from the authors' close empirical study of Hungarian conditions in the late 1960s, also reserves judgment about the likelihood of this kind of alliance coming into being in Hungary. In this connection it should be noted that the Kádár regime has been not only prudent, but lucky as well in its handling of labor relations. In 1972 the Hungarian party's economic reform policies came under attack by the leaders of the government-sponsored trade unions. The issue at hand was the widening of the gap between the incomes of the intellectuals–white collar employees and the industrial workers. Apparently with the benefit of some behind-the-scenes Soviet support, the unions were successful in putting an end (as it turned out, only for about five years) to what they considered as policies of economic discrimination against their constituents. The result was significantly increased regime awareness of working class needs and the effective defusing of the politically explosive potentials of organized workers' opposition to economic reforms, particularly income policies. In view of the results, it seems that Gierek had neither the good luck nor the political foresight of his Hungarian colleagues.

MARGINALITY AND DISCONTENT: "FROM THE OTHER SHORE"

The concluding part of this study provides a partial test of Hungarian intelligentsia attitudes toward politics, society and culture through an analysis of 38 responses to a 1979 opinion survey which was self-managed and self-published by two young Hungarian social scientists. (The text of the questionnaire is shown in Appendix A.) The purpose of the survey was to elicit responses to questions that had been of concern to young and mid-career writers, sociologists, philosophers, historians, teachers, engineers, and other white-collar professionals in Hungary in the late 1970s. The respondents' average age was 37.5 years – not old enough to have experienced the war and the early years of Stalinism, but old enough to remember 1956 and everything that followed it. They graduated from the university when the first slogans of the Kádár Compromise were launched and were probably holding their first professional appointment when the economic reforms were inaugurated. Finally, they were informed and politically conscious witnesses to the Communist party's systemic, albeit non-coercive, suppression of all critical democratic socialist intellectual dissent in the first half of the 1970s. Thus, in a sense, these men and women were survivors of bloodless purges, of subtle manipulation, and of peer pressures to conform to the ethos and life-style of what the Budapest wit calls "the jolliest barrack" in the socialist camp.

What distinguishes the tone and the substance of these respondents' observations about the current Hungarian scene from the similarly self-published views of Polish dissidents of 1976–80 is the Hungarians' fear of the recurrence of political crises, mixed with a sense of self-pity for not having the courage to break away from the regime's policies of "repressive tolerance" of their modest non-conformism. Although the spectrum of Polish intellectual dissent is diverse, in that country there has been, since the mid-1970s, an emerging sense of national unity and intellectual kinship with the aspirations of the average man in the factories, shipyards and mines. The Hungarians' comments seem to be less emotional, more introspective and analytical than those that one reads in most Polish samizdat in recent years. The trauma of 1956 still seems to dim the hopes of the Hungarian dissidents. In Poland armed struggle, military defeat and foreign occupation were avoided in 1956 and at least twenty-five years thereafter. In the absence of recent first-hand experience with bloodshed and direct foreign rule, nationalistic anti-Soviet sentiments in Poland still focus on the Katyn massacre and Stalin's abandonment of the heroic fighters of the Warsaw uprising in August 1944.

A woman lawyer respondent of the "From the Other Shore" micro-survey took a rather grim view of the likelihood and the desirability of drastic political change in Hungary:

Today in Hungary there is a stalemate which I do not want to see come to a resolution because any alternative can only be worse. We are not going to have any say about the world situation. Hungary's fate is in the hands of the Great Powers, and we should be glad because it is so. Look at the history of Hungary. Every upheaval has brought out the worst in people. Just look at this country whose people helped to load its Jews into the cattle cars. . . . I am very skeptical about these things. I do not believe that an upheaval of any kind will help progress. I do not want to see this wretched nation create yet another disturbance, so that people would be killed or carted away. And I cannot honestly say on which side I would find myself should a revolt break out.

A male historian takes the argument a step further and asks:

And today what kinds of programs can we offer? We might articulate pious wishes such as the Russian soldiers should get out of Hungary. But how? Who could make them leave? Shall we throw them out by force? Who should do it? Therefore, there is nothing left but a deep sense of crisis or the escaping into one's dreams. The situation is intolerable but there is nothing that can be done about it. A sane person cannot wish for a war to upset the status quo.

The themes of freedom of the press and freedom of speech have been central to dissident writings in Eastern Europe. Usually these freedoms have been demanded as a quasi-birthright of the intelligentsia, without seeking to extend these to the less well educated segments of the society. Here, again, the Polish situation in 1980–1 was rather unique. In any case, the Hungarian responses imply an altogether different frame of mind.

According to a woman artist:

I was born into this society and I cannot imagine living my life in a different and more honest milieu. If a person is indoctrinated for many years that it is forbidden to wet one's pants, after a point this message becomes so fixed in one's mind that when one is told that it is perfectly all right to wet one's pants, one simply cannot do it.

A woman lawyer is ambivalent about the results of free speech and free communications:

Sometimes I think that [the freedom of press and publication] will have no consequences and sometimes I think that the regime would disintegrate as the result. I do not know whether there are political forces in Hungary, which, upon the attainment of [complete] freedom, would be able to make the existence of this regime doubtful and whether they would actually have the power to do so.

Should such freedoms, adds a male teacher, be achieved,

In my opinion there would be complete chaos [caused by] the currently suppressed passions of the masses who are suffering from the lack of education for democracy. Within minutes we would have a situation which would be intolerable to the country which is closest to us geographically and politically.

It is easy to be misled by the Hungarian dissident intellectuals' gloomy rhetoric and conclude that they have lost sight of the reality of life around them. Perhaps what is most striking about their views is the ease with which they are able to penetrate the facade of regime politics and discuss, with a kind of clinical detachment, some of the basic problems that affect their daily lives as writers, artists, scholars and scientists. The issue of censorship and official interference with creative work seems paramount to all of them. The censor seeks to control both the subject matter and the manner of expression. A historian calls the former "taboos." Of these,

there are four kinds. The first is well known and it concerns links to the Soviets and foreign policy questions in general. Second, it is forbidden to criticize in any way the armed forces, the judiciary and the internal security organs. Third, though it is generally not known by most people, but it is not allowed to criticize anyone by name. Of course, in this case we are talking about people who are alive. The reason must be the need for "cadre stability" so no one need to worry about being attacked from the outside [of the party]. Fourth, certain facts and subjects may not be subjected to sharp criticism. These could be brought out in an anecdotal fashion, in an Aesopian language or by way of a cut-and-dry technical analysis, but not in a radical manner.

On the other hand, the responses of engineers and economists tend to contradict the humanists' experience with censorship. They blame the occasional rejection of their manuscripts and technical papers on inadequate research and other self-inflicted flaws rather than on political bias. However, what is disturbing for humanists and technocrats alike is the absence of clear guidelines between permissible and forbidden subjects, emphasis and medium of publication. This is further compounded by the inconsistent and frequently whimsical application of standards of political acceptability of such intellectual work by editors, publishers and government agencies which commission research projects. The phrase "overtly paternalistic and covertly terroristic" was frequently used by respondents when attempting to explain what appear to them as policies of deliberate ambiguity in the regime's dealings with the intellectuals. The leadership is perceived as a group of frightened men who are still fighting the ghost of the 1956 revolution and see the threat of a "capitalist restoration," or runaway liberalization, behind every intelligentsia proposal seeking to expand the autonomy of the non-party elites.

Unlike the elaborate charade surrounding the issue of censorship, any intelligentsia effort (particularly by sociologists) to investigate the lot of the underprivileged masses, especially the industrial workers, prompts harsh retaliation. This explains why only a handful of dissidents – the best known example is Miklós Haraszti and his samizdat exposé in the early 1970s of working conditions at the Budapest Red Star tractor factory – had the courage to address such politically explosive subjects. Indeed, at least one respondent chose to dispute his fellow intellectuals' condescending opinion concerning the allegedly consumption-oriented, hence apolitical industrial working class:

I know skilled workers who spend their days in a factory which is permeated by politics. Factories and workshops have a power structure and a certain atmosphere. While everybody is diligently saving up for a car, or for some extra food, they are involved in all kinds of conflicts. It is not that they are debating things in their spare time; rather, they constantly find themselves in conflictual situations with their stupid [word in the original] party member bosses and stupid party secretaries. The workers are angry and are full of grievances. For example: "I am making 7,000 forints because I am the best lathe operator in the shop, but that one also makes 7,000 because he is a party member and he gets the best jobs." The party member worker, with few exceptions, will sooner or later become a foreman. Therefore, the class struggle is pretty clear on the shop floor: there is a conflict between the working stiff who is not a party member and those who are less skilled but are members of the party and are running the show. They live through it, they swallow it and have a perfectly clear idea as to where they stand. They do not forget and need not remind themselves of their situation when their shift is over. I do not think that we have to worry about the industrial proletariat losing its correct [political] consciousness. It is fully aware of its situation and does not like it. However, it is not the same as being ready to take positive action about it.

The thirty-eight responses to the survey's seventeen questions are voluminous (about 60,000 words) and diverse. They are helpful for the identification of certain uniquely Hungarian intelligentsia attitudes toward political and existential dilemmas which face all educated middle-class East Europeans. More importantly, however, these responses tend to support the Konrád-Szelényi theses concerning the beliefs of the "marginal" intellectuals in the post-totalitarian period. We might assume that the total number of Hungarian critical intellectuals who can be mobilized on behalf of a relatively low-risk political cause, such as the petition in support of the Prague Ten in the fall of 1979, is approximately the same as the number of those who did sign that petition. If this is the case, then what is one to conclude by looking at the other 98 per cent of the intelligentsia who failed to express their solidarity with the activist minority? Their non-participation in open debates and failure to contribute to unauthorized publications can be regarded as signs of the continued viability of the political modus vivendi, as defined by the terms of the Kádár Compromise, between the party apparat and the technocrats.

OUTLOOK FOR THE 1980s

While the balance of power and the division of policy making and policy implementation prerogatives seem quite stable as the Hungarian elites enter the 1980s, there are several potentially destabilizing factors which could upset the present equilibrium and foster the birth of a technocrat–marginal intellectual alliance. As in all one-party states, in Hungary there are no institutional guarantees that the leader's policy priorities, governing methods, and personal values will be continued unchanged upon his retirement, loss of position, or death. Hungarian politics in the last quarter century have been inextricably tied to the person of János Kádár. His genuine popularity and the kind of low key charisma with which many Hungarians have endowed him cannot be transferred to any of his current heirs apparent in the Hungarian party. Even in the best case, no successor could hope to enjoy the same degree of Moscow's confidence as Kádár has throughout his reign.

Next to political succession the country's economic prospects for the 1980s represent the greatest threat to its political stability, particularly to the technocrats' quest for supremacy over the party bureaucracy. As a sociologist respondent speculated:

> I have the feeling that we can expect a massive deterioration of economic conditions. More and more people will be angry and more and more of them will think that something must be done here. And in the background there will no longer be the seekers of good life and the contented millions, but impatient and seething masses. . . . The events will shake up people very rapidly. People who seem to be completely dumb and incapable of grasping [the meaning of] democracy today will behave responsibly and intelligently if the situation requires it. Therefore, a radical change of the regime is not to be excluded.

The traditional (pre-Communist and Communist) regime strategy to defuse political tensions of all kinds by appealing to lower and middle class nationalistic sentiments has again surfaced in the late 1970s. One might wonder about the coincidence of stagnating living standards (and even zero economic growth as in 1979) and the regime's sudden interest in the welfare of the Hungarian-speaking national minorities in Romania and Czechoslovakia. Official nationalism can be useful for short term tactical purposes, but in the longer run it can become a two-edged sword and bring to the forefront the ultimate issue on the national agenda – that of Hungary's and the Hungarian party's dependence on the Soviet Union. When and if this happens, Hungary and the regime's opponents still will not be in a position similar to Poland on the eve of the strikes of 1980. The Catholic Church has not the following and the influence that the Polish Church has enjoyed since 1957 and, barring the wholesale seizure of Hungary's agricultural output by a very desperate Soviet Union, the country will always be able to feed itself far above the level of any other East European state, especially Poland. Therefore, in the final analysis, the likelihood of a technocrat–marginal humanistic intellectual alliance – let alone the linkage between the latter and the industrial working class – might materialize only under extremely stressful crisis conditions such as the coincidence of a politically debilitating succession struggle within the party with a crop failure *and* East–West tensions over a European issue of "Polish" or "Yugoslav" magnitude. For these reasons, an anonymous Hungarian sociologist's sober assessment of the prospects of change in Hungary might serve as a fitting conclusion for this study:

Many believe that democracy (and a democratic way of life) has been a kind of fleeting interlude in the midst of the growing flood of old and new dictatorships. This is how it was in the 1930s and during the war when democracy was confined to a few neutral and Anglo-Saxon countries. Since then, however, democracy has become stronger, more widespread and better established . . . especially in the minds of the people. In the meantime the disenchantment with dictatorships has assumed massive proportions. Today there are probably more people who are democratic in their beliefs and fearless [to express them] than ever before. I think this is also true for Hungary today. From the absence of institutional forms [of democracy] it does not follow that its substance and the appropriate sentiments are not there. Instead of becoming reconciled to the present situation, we must provide knowledge and information in support of [democratic sentiments] and thus begin the organization of a new democratic world in Hungary. We are at the very beginning, therefore our work must not be theorizing but . . . patient individual spadework.

NOTES AND REFERENCES

1. Cf. Leopold Labedz (ed.), *Revisionism* (London: Allen and Unwin, 1962) especially pp. 215–98; Leszek Kolakowski, *Toward Marxist Humanism* (New York: Grove Press, 1968); Irving Fetscher, "New Tendencies in Marxist Philosophy," *East Europe* 16(5), 1967, pp. 9–14; and Joseph Gabel, "Hungarian Marxism," *Telos*, no. 25 (1975) pp. 185–91.
2. Cf. Bart Grahl and Paul Piccone (eds), *Towards a New Marxism* (St. Louis: Telos Press, 1973); Mihailo Markovič, *From Affluence to Praxis* (Ann Arbor: University of Michigan Press, 1974); Svetozar Stojanović, *Between Ideals and Reality* (New York: Oxford University Press, 1973); Ivan Svitak, *Man and His World* (New York: Dell, 1970)

and Wolfgang Leonhard, *Three Faces of Marxism* (New York: Holt, 1974).

3. Frantisek Silnitsky *et al.* (eds), *Communism and Eastern Europe* (New York: Karz, 1970); András Hegedüs, Ágnes Heller, Mária Márkus and Mihály Vajda, *The Humanisation of Socialism* (London: Allison and Busby, 1976); András Hegedüs, *Socialism and Bureaucracy* (London: Allison and Busby, 1979); Rudolf Bahro, *The Alternative in Eastern Europe* (London: New Left Books, 1978); Ulf Wolter, *Rudolf Bahro. Critical Responses* (White Plains, N.Y.: M. E. Sharpe, 1980); Hans-Peter Riese (ed.), *Since the Prague Spring: Charter 77 and the Struggle for Human Rights in Czechoslovakia* (New York: Random House, 1979) and Rudolf L. Tőkés, "Eastern Europe in the 1970s: Detente, Dissent and Eurocommunism," in R. L. Tőkés (ed.), *Eurocommunism and Detente* (New York University Press, 1978).

4. Rudolf L. Tőkés, "Dissent: Politics for Change in the USSR," in Henry W. Morton and R. L. Tőkés (eds), *Soviet Society and Politics in the 1970s* (New York: Free Press, 1974) pp. 3–59.

5. Chalmers Johnson (ed.), *Change in Communist Systems* (Stanford University Press, 1970); Mark G. Field (ed.), *Social Consequences of Modernization in Communist Societies* (Baltimore: Johns Hopkins University Press, 1976).

6. The term "social contract" has been used by students of the East European dissident scene, though my conceptualization is rather different from theirs. See A. J. Liehm, "Intellectuals on the New Social Contract," *Telos,* no. 23 (1975) pp. 156–64, and Alex Pravda, "Industrial Workers: Patterns of Dissent, Opposition and Accommodation," in R. L. Tőkés (ed.), *Opposition in Eastern Europe, 1968–1978* (Baltimore: Johns Hopkins University Press, 1979) pp. 209–63.

7. One of the more comprehensive listings of such grievances is given in "Declaration of the Founding Committee of the Free Trade Unions of the Baltic Seaboard" (29 April 1978) *Survey* 24, no. 4 (109) pp. 93–102. See also, Peter Raina, *Political Opposition in Poland: 1954–1977* (London: Poets and Printers Press, 1978) and A. Ostoje Ostaszewski, *Dissent in Poland: Reports and Documents in Translation – December 1975–July 1977* (London: Association of Polish Students and Graduates in Exile, 1977).

8. Cf. *August 1980. The Strikes in Poland* (Munich: RFE, 1980) especially pp. 343–447. The grievances of the politically powerless low status social groups are also discussed in my "Human Rights in Eastern Europe: An Overview, 1977–1980," in *Basket III: Implementation of the Helsinki Accords* (Hearing before the Commission on Security and Cooperation in Europe. 96th Congress, 2nd session, March 25, 1980) (Washington: GPO, 1980) pp. 11–29.

9. H. Gordon Skilling, *Czechoslovakia's Interrupted Revolution* (Princeton University Press, 1976); Vladimir V. Kusin, *From Dubcek to Charter 77* (New York: St. Martin's Press, 1978); Zdenek Mlynar, *Nightfrost in Prague* (New York: Karz, 1980); Jiri Pelikan, *Socialist Opposition in Eastern Europe* (London: Allison and Busby, 1976).

10. Cf. Archie Brown and Jack Gray (eds), *Political Culture and Political Change in Communist States* (London: Macmillan, 1977).

11. Rudolf L. Tőkés, "The Czechoslovak invasion and the Hungarian intellectuals," in E. Czerwinski and J. Piekalkiewicz (eds), *The Soviet Invasion of Czechoslovakia: Its Effects on Eastern Europe* (New York: Praeger, 1972) pp. 139–58.

12. Péter Farkas (comp.), *Túlpartról* (From the Other Shore) (Budapest: self-published, 1979).

13. George Schöpflin, "Opposition and Para-Opposition: Critical Currents in Hungary, 1968–78," in Tőkés, *Opposition* . . . , pp. 142–86. The term *"kaiserlich und königlich"* implied deference to "imperial and royal" authority in the Austro-Hungarian empire.

14. William F. Robinson, *The Pattern of Reform in Hungary* (New York: Praeger, 1973).

15. Perhaps the most representative examples of Hungarian dissident writings in the 1970s are András Kovács (comp.), *Marx a negyedik évtizedben* (*Marx in the Fourth Decade*) written by 21 authors (Budapest: self-published, 1977–78) and János Kenedi (comp.), *Profil* (*Profile*) written by 34 authors (Budapest: self-published, 1977–78). See also, Marc Rakowski, *Towards an East European Marxism* (New York: St. Martin's Press, 1978).

16. György Konrád and Iván Szelényi, *Intellectuals on the Road to Class Power*, Trans. by Andrew Arato and Richard E. Allen (New York: Harcourt Brace Jovanovich, 1979).

17. Michael Walzer, "The New Masters," *New York Review of Books*, XXVI, no. 4 (20 March 1980) p. 37.

18. Konrád and Szelényi, *Intellectuals on the Road to Class Power*, pp. 204–5.

19. Ibid., p. 207.

20. Ibid., p. 199.

21. The standard work on this subject is Walter D. Connor, *Socialism, Politics and Equality: Hierarchy and Change in Eastern Europe and the USSR* (New York: Columbia University Press, 1979).

22. The interplay between the "reds" and the "experts" is brilliantly analyzed by Richard Lowenthal in his "Development vs. Utopia in Communist Policy," in Chalmers Johnson (ed.), *Change in Communist Systems*, pp. 33–116.

23. Walzer, "New Masters."

24. KOR (the Committee for the Defense of the Workers) was formed in Poland in 1976. RPCIO (the Movement for the Defense of Human and Civil Rights) was formed in 1978.

APPENDIX A

Péter Farkas and Gábor Németh

"FROM THE OTHER SHORE"

Hungarian self-published survey of opinions of 38 respondents. Dated 1979.

The respondents

Sex   Men, 31; women, 7; average age, 37.5 years

Occupation

writer or poet	8
sociologist	7
philosopher	4
historian	4
high school teacher	4
artist	2
economist	2
engineer	2
lawyer	1
linguist	1
cinema director	1
no data	2

Non–respondents: "approximately 70" (received questionnaire but refused to respond in writing or to be quoted in the self-published version of survey).

The questions

1. What do they [the authorities] have the writer keep in his desk drawer?
2. Are there taboos or restricted subjects in the dissemination of current facts and realities?
3. Have they ever rejected any of your writings on non-artistic/literary grounds?
4. ". . . each citizen . . . has the full and unquestionable right to establish a printing press wherever he wishes and whenever it pleases him without any petition, permission or supervision by a censor." Sándor Bölöni Farkas (1795–1842) (philosopher,

traveler, diarist, author of *Utazás Északamerikában*/Journey in North America, 1834). [Agree or disagree?]

5. What do you think of self-censorship?

6. ". . . we ought to be able to show exactly where this nation is today and where it is going . . ." (Gyula Illyés).
   Do those to whom the "we" refers "show" these exactly?

7. Ten years after it was completed, the movie "Tanú" (Witness) was shown recently in Budapest in a very small cinema. It was shown for only two weeks even though everyone wanted to see it.
   How do you explain this peculiar event? In other words, if the movie was good and truthful art, they should not have withdrawn it in panic, and if it was bad and inaccurate why did they show it in the first place?

8. Following each show by (the popular stand-up comedian) Géza Hofi the opinion is always unanimous: "he really told them off" and it seems that with this pleasant, tingling sensation most people are content until the next show comes around. Don't you think that this so-called "telling them off" is heavily manipulated and, beyond entertainment, also serves the function of a safety valve?

9. a. Do you think it is right that certain views which run counter to the official point of view are being criticized without the contents of those views being made public? (For example, Charter 77).
   b. Could it be the explanation is that people living in a "developed socialist state" lack mature judgment to tell apart, unaided, obvious slander and similar trash from the truth?
   c. Wouldn't it make more sense to deny these [critical allegations] through open discussion and analysis?

10. In your opinion to what extent are the people's needs to know and to be informed being satisfied today and to what extent do people perceive the realization of these needs in practice?

11. Our country is a democratic state. If we can indeed talk about democracy, it should be extended to all spheres of life including the [right] to know and to be informed. If this is the case, then how can you reconcile the theory of democracy with the practice of "confidential circulars" and with the great number of journals and publications which are marked "Z.A." (zárolt anyag – restricted material) in the catalogs of our libraries?

12. In your opinion, do open and factual discussions actually take place about certain extremely negative social phenomena such as alcoholism, drug addiction, the high number of suicides, etc.?

13. "When shall we be united?" – asked [Endre] Ady.

The only basis for cultural and material unity [of the socialist states of Eastern Europe] is the knowledge of one another. To what extent is this being realized in our country? Recently a good friend of mine complained that to him the Soviet Union is as unknown as China.

14. Are you satisfied with the availability of cultural products of other socialist states in our country?

15. In your opinion is it possible to put "lie" and "silence" in one and the same category?

16. Most people reach the point when they say: "there are serious problems in this country" but, instead of doing something about it they choose to reconcile themselves to the "given" conditions. What is your judgment about this kind of posture?

APPENDIX B

"We are protesting the trial and sentences of the representatives of Charter 77. We demand their release."

Petition to the Presidential Council of the Hungarian People's Republic. Dated October 29, 1979.

"Open Letter" to János Kádár, First Secretary, Hungarian Socialist Workers' Party and member, Presidential Council. Dated October 25, 1979.

Sex of signatories   Men 177; women 67

Occupational distribution of signatories

sociologist	24
economist	23
teacher/university lecturer	19
writer	17
philosopher	13
director (theater/cinema)	12
critic/aesthete	10
engineer/technician	10
poet	10
art/literary historian	7

historian	7
psychologist/psychiatrist	7
translator	7
artist/musician/composer	6
editor	6
librarian	6
mathematician	6
designer/sculptor/painter	5
physician	5
journalist	4
architect	3
clergyman	3
philologist/linguist	3
archivist/museum researcher	2
housewife	2
lawyer	2
retired	2
actress	1
director of college	1
private farmer	1
researcher	1
social worker	1
typographer	1
philosopher and gasoline pump operator	1
no data	16

Part III

Eastern Europe and the World

8 Comecon: the Recent Past and Perspectives for the 1980s

STANISLAW WASOWSKI

COOPERATION AND TRADE DURING COMECON'S FIRST TWENTY YEARS

The early post-Second World War period of economic history in the Soviet-dominated sphere was characterized by the need to spend considerable amounts on rebuilding the largely destroyed economic structures of Eastern Europe. This was accomplished without foreign aid and with little foreign trade. Self-imposed separation from the West cut the area off from the Marshall Plan and other forms of cooperation and aid, while the dearth of exportable goods impeded trade with foreign countries.

During the same period the nations of Eastern Europe underwent violent social change and serious upheaval in their economic structures. The new political rulers of these countries, taking their cue from Moscow, undertook a massive agrarian reform and introduced Soviet-type planning procedures. They imposed a brisk rate of growth as well as autarkic tendencies on the economies of the area.

The autarkic tendencies stemmed from several sources. Of these, the most important was perhaps the simple belief that industrial structures in each country on the path to communism, whatever its natural endowments, should have as their starting point such essentials as energy (above all coal and electricity generation), machine building and heavy industry. There was a definite emphasis on the need of each country to have a vast array of industries. Instead of an invitation to specialize, there was a stress on the development of similar industries throughout the area. Not only were the industrial structures in each country to be almost identical, but their products, often developed from Soviet blueprints, would testify to their similarity. There was little complementarity among the industries in the Comecon area and, therefore, relatively little trade among them. Short production runs in many categories of products consequently resulted in high unit costs. This type of system tended to discourage exports unless they were undertaken in a framework of barter, where only relative prices are important.

There was even less incentive for the states of the region to trade with the West than with each other. East European and Soviet goods were of low quality, as can be expected when products are distributed in a seller's market. Their delivered price in foreign currencies was not low, for high nominal domestic costs were not balanced by realistically low rates of exchange for the East European currencies or the ruble. The communist countries' distrust of the free markets of the West provided one more reason for low levels of trade.

TABLE 8.1 *Soviet and East European Trade with the West*

	Foreign trade turnover (imports plus exports) of socialist countries as %age of world trade	East–West trade as %age of world trade	Trade with the Soviet bloc as %age of total trade of Western countries with world
1938	8.6	6.4	9.5
1948	6.3	2.6	4.1
1953	9.3	1.3	2.1
1958	9.9	2.1	3.2

SOURCE: Jozef Wilczynski, *The Economics and Politics of East–West Trade* (New York: Praeger, 1969) pp. 45, 52, 54.

The data in Table 8.1 provide a numerical illustration of the low levels of trade with the West. It is useful to remember that the year 1938, which serves as the basis for the comparisons, was not known for high levels of trade between the East European area and the rest of the world.

Trade that continued to move across the dividing line between East and West owed its existence to Eastern Europe's need for both raw materials unavailable in the Soviet-dominated area and for some items of industrial equipment crucial to industrial development in the East and yet unavailable there. Purchases from the West were made in response to the needs of industrial development and not to competitive prices.

In short, the non-competitive, output-maximizing economies of Eastern Europe were averse to trade with the West in this formative period, and to the development of criteria and mechanisms that would have made profitable trade possible.

Ten years after the conclusion of the war, industrial development was well under way and the planning system well established. The time now came to take a hard look at the efficiency of the system. The slowdown of growth, the lack of modernization, and the insufficiency and maldistribution of raw materials became the most important concerns of economic decision-makers during the second decade of socialism.

The slowdown of growth in the Soviet-type economies that now ensued was caused by several factors such as declining annual additions to manpower, falling productivity of capital, and the emphasis on the extensive type of growth. Low annual growth rates could not be accepted with equanimity. Fast growing defense expenditures were becoming an ever larger burden. Moreover, it was recognized that a slowdown in living standards could lead to political difficulties. An ever more taut economy was furthermore losing prestige among developing countries and other potential sympathizers.

Intensive growth, it was felt, could provide the solution for many of these economic ills. Better technology, and the more efficient use of resources which it implies, could have coped with declining manpower, while increasing the productivity of capital and providing elements of much-desired modernization. But the clue to that type of growth lay in the combination of new technology, better organization of production and management, and large inputs of capital. The first and the last of these things could be obtained, in a pinch, from the West, but reforms of management and economic institutions implied the need for far-reaching, perhaps too far-reaching, changes in the style of the command economy and the command society.

The achievement of lower costs would have required a reliable method for selecting efficient production establishments, more rational combinations of the factors of production, effective production techniques, and the adoption of a large scale of production. Such changes require an introduction of economic criteria into the decision-making process. A comparison of representative costs and realistic pricing, for example, would be necessary to make almost all of these improvements. One way of getting around these problems was by adopting economies of scale. Since large-scale production establishments can, at least within certain limits, reduce costs, economies of scale were embraced with alacrity and ideas leading to bulk production were welcomed. However, it was also recognized that more intensive international trade and greater specialization of production were also among the best means of improving the performance of Soviet-type economies without having to go through the treacherous sands of economic reform, with everything that this implies.

As far as raw materials were concerned, there were two separate issues at hand: uneven distribution of raw material endowment throughout the Comecon area and low world prices for raw materials. The first meant that the commodity and energy-rich Soviet Union was supposed to supply the relatively barren states of Eastern Europe with energy resources. Because the exploitation of energy commodities requires that a large amount of initial capital be sunk in mines, railroads, and the like, the Soviet Union had good reason to feel cheated by having to make large capital outlays in order to export capital intensive goods to its allies. Moreover, in the 1950s (after the Korean war) and the 1960s, world prices for raw materials were rather low, a fact which tended to reduce the Soviets' terms of trade. Soviet leaders felt exploited in much the same way as many less developed countries during the same period. It was therefore hoped in Moscow that integration schemes in Comecon might alleviate this situation and lead to more favorable compensation for Soviet exports.

To sum up, an expansion of economic relations with the industrialized West and economic integration in Comecon came to be viewed as measures which might contribute to the solution of the problems nagging the economies of Eastern Europe. Meanwhile, economic reforms, with their political dangers and economic complexities, could be brushed aside.[1]

There still remained questions about the two remaining economic strategies, namely, expanded relations with the West and closer cooperation within Comecon. For instance, should integration aim at import substitution? Should borrowing from outside Comecon be left to individual governments, or undertaken by Comecon itself in an integrated fashion? Should enterprises built and exploited jointly aim at Western markets, or should they instead concentrate on satisfying the internal needs of the Comecon states? The position taken by this author is that the extent of economic relations with the West is dictated by the general economic strategy, that is, by the planned rate of growth of the economies concerned and by the composition of the desired products. Moreover, whatever the specific form of exchanges with the West, the control of their impact on the most important sectors of the East European economies are greatly affected by the progress of Comecon integration.

While economic strategies for the era of modernization were being set in place during this period, the external economic relations of the Comecon states underwent important changes. The volume of trade with the West increased in absolute and relative terms. In the 1960s, the total volume of trade of the Comecon members grew to about 11 per cent of total world trade, and has more or less maintained itself at this level ever since. Trade with the industrialized countries of the West (that is, roughly speaking, with the members of the Organization of Economic Cooperation and Development, the OECD) increased from $3.719 billion (current) in 1958 to $6.127 billion in 1963 and $14.436 billion in 1970. Even if allowances are made for inflation, this is a hefty increase. In spite of the strenuous efforts to increase exports of high value-added products, Comecon exports were concentrated predominantly in two categories: (1) fuels and non-food materials, and (2) foodstuffs and raw materials for foodstuff. Manufactures were important only as imports from the OECD area. In the late 1960s and early 1970s, machinery and equipment constituted about 7–8 per cent of all Comecon exports to the OECD nations, and industrial consumer goods around 12 per cent. Machinery and equipment amounted to approximately 33 per cent of Comecon imports from the OECD nations, and industrial consumer goods to about 6–7 per cent.[2]

In their trade with the developing countries in this earlier period, the members of Comecon often exchanged manufactures for raw materials, frequently in the framework of operations akin to barter (for instance, locomotives for coffee). While trade with the industrial countries was conducted predominantly in hard currencies, some exchanges with developing countries belonged to the category of switch trade, that is, bilateral (or, more often, trilateral) barter. Purchases from developing countries were sometimes paid in soft East European currencies, good only for purchases in the country of issue. The foreign indebtedness of the Comecon countries at that time was minimal.

PROBLEMS OF COMECON COORDINATION IN THE 1970s

Economic integration as it was formally outlined in the 1971 "Comprehensive Program"[3] evolved from earlier forms of economic cooperation among the members of Comecon. Initially, cooperation was limited to binding one-year (later five-year) trade agreements. It then led to the funding of jointly run enterprises, schemes to coordinate production through international economic organizations and plan coordination, and attempts at supranational planning. It is not within the purview of the present chapter to offer a history of this evolving cooperation, but it is worthwhile to compare the ideas underlying economic coordination with those assumed in joint planning. This should throw some light on the present phase of cooperation within Comecon.

Economic coordination started from the assumption that national economic plans were a given. The sharing of information about projections of economic growth and offers of exchanges between countries ultimately led to the conclusion of binding exchange agreements, and even to some modifications of the plans in order to accommodate the proposed exchanges, but the only formal instrument of cooperation was that of a binding bilateral exchange agreement. The aim of such cooperation was to achieve a rational use of raw materials, the acceleration of economic growth through avoidance of parallel production of identical products, and some degree of equalization in the levels of economic development in member countries. New patterns of production were expected to emerge in response to trade coordination.[4]

The plan coordination that developed as a result of the arrangements just described operated during the years 1966–75, but in the end it failed to meet its framers' expectations. This happened for several reasons. Some of the economic difficulties that were encountered arose from the fact that the actual coordinating agreements were bilateral rather than multilateral. New investments undertaken in each member country also continued to give precedence to the satisfaction of domestic needs over the demands of export trade. Production undertaken in response to existing or perceived comparative advantage did not become equal in significance to production for domestic needs. In addition, there proved to be a lack of satisfactory international measures of costs which could point to the advantage of trade-related activities. The search for economic opportunities through exchange encountered a stumbling block in the form of ingrained attitudes based on the use of quantity targets in production and the rejection of value comparisons as the deciding factor in exchange. Finally, the five-year span for exchange agreements provided too short a horizon for investment activities which matured over much longer periods of time.

In view of these difficulties, the Comprehensive Program suggested, though furtively, that economic criteria should be applied in the search for an optimum level of international cooperation beneficial to the Comecon community as a whole.[5] Moreover, international economic relations were expected to affect national plans. Money-commodity criteria, that is, market forces and prices, were to be used to facilitate coordination in various forms. A reader perusing the Comprehensive Program could not escape the impression that optimization of production and investment in Comecon would be undertaken according to some criteria of joint benefit and would employ indicators having a significant economic content, as opposed to quantity targets.

There were several ways of putting such ideas into practice. One could stretch the methods of national planning to fit the international scale of operation, for example. There was also the possibility of introducing the commodity–money relations which were mentioned prominently in the Comprehensive Program (sections 6 and 7), or of international planning limited to some sectors of the member economies. Khrushchev had suggested supranational planning in 1962, but this idea was soon relegated to cold storage in view of the unwillingness of East Europeans to accept it.[6] While only Romania openly opposed it, the Romanian position was quietly seconded by several other Comecon members. Looking at the incident with the benefit of hindsight, one may suspect that Khrushchev's initiative had little economic content. More than ten years after the event one could still find in leading Soviet publications statements expressing the view that the problem of allocating resources and manpower on a supranational basis within Comecon had not been solved up to that time.[7] There are other indications that this is still the fact now. Supranational planning for the entire Comecon area is still not a feasible proposition.

The alternative, namely, the use of market forces to bring about the economic benefits of integration, was outlined with some care in the Comprehensive Program, but its implementation was neglected. In spite of the support the market alternative obtained from many East European economists, mostly Hungarian and Polish, section 7 of the Comprehensive Program became a dead letter without any explanation. It provided for the introduction of a collective currency, introduction of a single rate of exchange for each country's currency, and the convertibility of all Comecon currencies, with exact dates when these goals were to have been achieved. The reasons for the neglect of these decisions are many. Above all, a recourse to the forces of supply and demand, however muted and circumscribed, would have obliged the planned economies of the Comecon states to adjust their output so as to provide for more complicated trade arrangements than those traditionally associated with bilateral contacts, and this was totally unacceptable.

Joint sectoral planning remained the only alternative that would combine specialization and cost-cutting in production while avoiding the two traps of centralized Comecon-wide planning and an unleashing of the forces of supply and demand. The long-term programs of cooperation (also known as "target programs") first appeared in 1969 at the 23rd session of the Comecon Council and were formally introduced at the 29th session in 1975. These programs were to provide for close cooperation and eventually joint, Comecon-wide planning in five major sectors: fuel, energy and raw materials; machine-building; agriculture and food production; light industry; and transportation. Interest in these various sectors proved to be uneven. The first of them was given precedence, however, and in 1976, at its 30th session, the Comecon Council agreed to spend the sum of 9–10 billion transferable rubles (TR) on joint energy projects under its aegis. This decision did not involve the allocation of any new money, but rather the assignment of existing or expanded investment projects to the newly created institution of target programs. Expenditures for machine building, agriculture and food were also approved at the 30th session, but action on the remaining two programs was postponed until 1979.

TARGET PROGRAMS: PROBLEMS AND IMPLICATIONS

The priority granted to the first target program was connected with the urgency with which the raw material issue is currently viewed in Comecon. First of all, the Soviet Union wishes to see more fuel efficiency in Eastern Europe. The Soviets would also like to limit their exports of fuels to Eastern Europe because of the slow growth of their own production and expanding domestic needs. East European countries find it important to limit imports of fuels and other raw materials because the deterioration of their terms of trade has led to a decrease of the national product available for distribution by approximately 2 to 3 per cent.

Target programs have not appeared on the scene without any antecedents. They have been built upon the existing foundations of multilateral development projects as well as international economic associations and organizations. The best-known example of a multilateral development project is the Orenburg gas pipeline.[8] Other such projects include the Ust–Ilimsky cellulose project, the Kyembaev asbestos plant, the Kursk iron ore open mine and metallurgical complex, the Norilsk copper and nickel project, a nickel ore extraction plant in Cuba, and a high tension power line between Vinnitsa (the Ukraine) and Albertirsa (Hungary). The USSR covers about half the cost of these projects; the rest amounts to a major capital loan from Eastern Europe to the Soviet Union.[9] The first target program took these projects under its umbrella. They have been integrated into a wider framework of institutional arrangements involving joint planning of the respective sectors of member states' economies and the coordination of national five-year plans. As for the international economic organizations which are intergovernmental and not Comecon bodies, it is not yet clear how they will fit into the target programs, but it is difficult to think of them as being completely independent of them, given the considerable overlap between the activities of the two types of institutions.[10]

The target programs are to perform several functions, including: (1) maximizing the economic benefits derived from the division of labor and specialization among Comecon countries; (2) coordinating long-term national perspective plans (10–20 years) of member countries through coordination of production within the sectors involved; (3) assuring an adequate level of cooperation by Eastern Europe in exploiting natural resources in the Soviet Union; (4) providing a training ground for eventual comprehensive supranational planning without the use of market price; and (5) providing opportunities for an overview of economic and technical cooperation between Comecon industries and the industries of the West through the centralized supervision of advanced sectors of the economy. These functions require that the relevant administrators undertake several tasks, such as forecasting all Comecon needs for specified groups of products; coordinating, sponsoring and conducting research; and investing in the industrial capacity required to fulfill the program of specialization. The administrators are also responsible for drawing up sectoral plans for the designated economic sectors of Comecon, monitoring external trade, and making certain that joint sectoral plans are incorporated into the national plans of member states.[11]

This last function raises the issue of balancing resources, inputs and outputs on a Comecon-wide scale and in each national plan. Sectoral planning aims at matching expected supplies with Comecon's predicted needs. However, the balancing of the plans, in the sense of finding the resources required for the achievement of desired production levels, is to be left to the national plans rather than to supranational agencies.[12] This is not an uncontroversial matter. Several East European officials have stressed the importance, even precedence, of national plans as opposed to Comecon-wide plans.[13]

On the implementation side, one notes that the texts describing the other activities of target program administrators (prognostication, nudging trade in the right direction, etc.) seldom differ from earlier examples that may be drawn from the history of coordination of economic activity in Comecon during the last twenty-five years or so. One has to wait for detailed descriptions of new methodology, rules, and so on, to evaluate the differences between the old forms of coordination and the new sectoral planning. While the dearth of published material leaves us in some uncertainty as to the exact meaning and impact of the target programs, one can obtain some indication of the difficulties they involve by looking at discussions, however veiled, of the issues that have arisen so far in connection with the target programs.

Target programs suffer from many ills and problems not necessarily of their own making. Since they represent an exercise in ever closer coordination among the Comecon economies, the inadequacy of a proper framework for socialist international cooperation and integration manifests itself in stark colors. Inadequate measures and means of international optimization, insufficient criteria for the comparative evaluation of national and Comecon-wide concerns and needs, and a lack of criteria for ascertaining the efficiency of production are among the most obvious difficulties.

The necessary framework for joint economic activity still did not exist as late as 1977, according to Rezső Nyers, director of the Institute for Economic Science in the Hungarian Academy of Sciences and one of the fathers of the New Economic Mechanism in Hungary.[14] There are no indications that much has changed since then. Two years after the publication of Nyers's article, a Soviet economist listed a host of unresolved questions in connection with intra-Comecon cooperation and, in particular, the target programs. These included such basic elements as the method for evaluating estimated expenditures and revenue (that is, in actual prices or accounting prices) and the effectiveness of various production alternatives.[15] In short, the economic criteria for decisions were still lacking.

Another problem is that one finds at the center of discussion about sectoral production planning such old Comecon war horses as the "optimum scale of production" and "specialization" as the means for bringing about high efficiency of production. As in past years, these concepts spark sharp controversies over the question of whether greater efficiency would result if each country were to specialize completely in the production of individual products, to the exclusion of other Comecon countries. A positive answer to this question would require that most products necessitating a very large scale of production would have to be produced in very few Comecon countries, most likely the Soviet Union.[16] This is a prospect to which many East Europeans would object. Moreover, there is no clear indication as to how to determine the optimum level of production of any product.

The goals set by the planners and the means employed to achieve them are also considered unsatisfactory by many Comecon economists. They remind their readers that national needs are different from Comecon-wide needs, that there is no methodology appropriate to the task of integrating individual economies or parts thereof, and that optimality problems have not been solved.[17]

Pessimism within Comecon about the adequacy of planning is also based on a critical analysis of some of the basic assumptions of a planned economy. The method of material balances, the backbone of Soviet-type planning, amounts to a mere collection of information on sources and uses of products. It indicates shortages and surpluses but does not provide for the means to bring about an equilibrium.[18] In a national economy the collective judgment of the highest organs of the party and the state provides the formulation of national interests that can be translated into specific commands aiming at an equilibrium. Whatever the objections that may be lodged against the optimality and efficiency of such a procedure, some specific body must formulate the social welfare function of a given society and apply it to specific situations. Comecon has no comparable organization. Thus it cannot formulate a social welfare function for the area as a whole and it cannot provide criteria for the resolution of disequilibria.[19]

Relations between the enterprises and the state in a Soviet-type economy complicate matters even further. The enterprises are seen as having functions quite distinct from those of the state. Briefly, one may say that the enterprise has microeconomic goals while the state's concerns are macroeconomic (using these terms rather loosely). When the state authorities find that the legitimate strivings of individual enterprises result in undesirable developments, they may intervene by changing the parameters of the enterprises' action. (For example, the state can alter the level of prices, wages, subsidies or taxes, order a change in the level of planned output, cancel or limit deliveries to productive consumers and users, and allow or forbid certain activities.)[20] This division of functions between the enterprise and the state, which is different from that prevailing in free market economies, does not deserve high marks for the pursuit of efficiency. Nevertheless it exists, and it provides a more or less well defined framework for the direction of Soviet-type economies. However, when and if the bilateral relationship between the state and the national enterprise is replaced by a trilateral one, by adding multinational enterprises with some supranational characteristics, then the distribution of various functions among the three decision-makers will be lacking in theory or precedent.

Assertions concerning the role of integration, especially sectoral integration, in assuring optimum efficiency in the national economies have also encountered problems. Supporters of sectoral integration are convinced that both better performance and the equalization of development levels will follow in the footsteps of integration.[21] A closer look at the many problems involved, however, leads to a different conclusion. Ceteris paribus, the growth of integrated investment projects slows down the rate of growth of domestic economies, because funds must be taken out of domestic investments in order to finance joint Comecon investments. As a result, either national income must be redistributed and the share of consumption diminished at home in order to provide for both the national and the international investments, or the share of nationally planned investments in the unchanged pool of investment funds must decrease.[22] In addition, Comecon investments take more time to implement than national ones. This is due to the complexities resulting from the cooperation of several tightly knit bureaucracies and their time-consuming, frequently roundabout, negotiations.[23]

In the long run, the integration of production should bring benefits to the national economies, if only because some resources currently underused by a national economy could be mobilized by Comecon-wide production needs. One finds here an interesting echo of the theory of distribution under the influence of foreign trade: that is, exchange with foreign countries increases the productivity of, and the demand for, resources that are relatively plentiful in a given country. However, there is no clear answer to the question of whether sectoral integration would bestow benefits higher than those that would result without integration. At each stage one has to check how Comecon-wide projects compare with national investment schemes. Criteria would have to be formulated to determine whether the effectiveness of a joint venture would be higher than that which could be achieved through separate national activity.[24] One would also have to make constant comparisons with the cost of imports purchased with hard currencies.[25]

The rate of return on international investments is not the only concern shared by the partners of the Soviet Union. They also sense that the arrival of new widely-based schemes would result in a high level of demand for productive resources. One objection already mentioned concerns the limited amount of resources available for Comecon investment; but there is another, more microeconomic, aspect of the same problem. Brisk investment activity soon encounters bottlenecks. The rates of accumulation must not therefore be so high as to make economic planning even more taut than it has been.[26] This warning should be read in connection with the previous discussion concerning the impact of international investments on total accumulation in the Comecon area. If the global investment in each Comecon member country were to be limited to a reasonable level so as to avoid bottlenecks, that is, the level that, at the most, equals the present rate of accumulation, then international investments can occur only by squeezing out some of the national investments. The growth of GNP would slow down at least until more roundabout international investments start showing respectable returns on the resources invested. But national growth would probably not slow down uniformly, due to such factors as different degrees of tautness in the various national economies. Thus, instead of the projected equalization in the levels of development, one can visualize new reasons for disparities in the rates of growth of the individual Comecon countries.[27]

Critics of sectoral planning also take seriously the shift of emphasis from extensive to intensive growth that has marked Comecon development since the late 1960s. They recognize the importance of education, skills and technology as factors of production and give full support to the policies that accept the implications of this fact. One argument in favor of relying more on skills leads to the requirement that industries ought to be developed where such skilled manpower already exists, and where there is a pattern of cooperation between the educational system and the production establishment.[28] This may apply more in some Comecon countries than in others. Another argument based on the acceptance of intensive growth insists that investment funds must be directed not only to heavy industries but also to knowledge industries, to education itself, and to so-called "induced investment." An induced investment is one that responds to new needs and is required by the level of economic development and by the consequences of the growth of heavy industry. In a word, it refers to modern industries and light service industries. The argument boils down, in the words of one Hungarian writer, to correcting a tendency to overdevelop heavy industries.[29]

This change of emphasis from extensive to intensive growth has far-reaching consequences for the structure of the Comecon economies and the location of industry. The new industries based on induced investment would have to be distributed throughout the entire area of Comecon instead of in the Soviet Union, where most of the integrated industries are currently concentrated owing to the ready availability of raw materials there. Moreover, the performance of these industries does not lend itself to simple or modified quantity planning and would not respond to cruder forms of incentives. Problems arising from these complications must therefore be resolved if sectoral planning is to succeed.

Finally, some Comecon economists warn that integration schemes aiming at higher efficiency should heed the cost indicators; lower costs are the ultimate proof of, and reward for, rational decisions undertaken within an integrationist framework. In their view, it is imperative to develop a common set of efficient indicators for the factors of production as well as for the final products.[30] At present, however, the existing international cost indicators do not lend themselves to international, or even national, cost comparisons. They bear the mark of having been set to the advantage of the suppliers, a phenomenon which, in the non-market conditions typical of Soviet-type economies, is equivalent to a seller's market. These problems stem from the combination of tautly planned economies and the excessive power given to all bureaucracies, especially the industrial bureaucracy. By concentrating on the cost side of production and paying insufficient attention to the revenue side, the system has managed to end up with product prices more irrational than those of the factors of production. Ultimately, the domination of the economy by the suppliers will acquire an international dimension as advances in the integration or production result in serious international price distortions.[31] A related problem is that cost indicators and prices are affected by the tendency, quite common in economies where there is no distinction between private cost and social cost, to include the social cost in the price of the product. While this is not by itself a wrong practice in a command economy, the margins are arbitrary and differ from country to country, creating difficulties that would have to be ironed out to facilitate integration.[32] In any event, some reform of cost indicators and prices would probably have a positive effect on both investment and distribution within a more integrated Comecon structure.[33]

Reflecting on the latest stage of economic integration in Comecon, one cannot but perceive the contrast between the growth of administrative and managerial structure on one side, and the inability to use the opportunity presented by the growth of international cooperation to enhance efficiency on the other. One observes the drive towards more interdependence in Comecon as well as official expectations of a revival in the sluggish rate of growth, and the resolve to limit the degree of dependence on the outside world.[34] Yet there is a lack of decisive steps – intellectual, managerial and political – to use resources in optimal, or even near-optimal, fashion.

IMPACT ON EAST–WEST RELATIONS

From the integration dilemma in Comecon there follows a somewhat ambivalent attitude towards economic relations with the West. Imports of Western equipment are crucial for the modernization of Comecon economies, as is borrowing from the West to make up for the insufficiency of domestic savings and the lack of success with exporting to hard-currency markets. Joint ventures and long-term contracts between Western and Eastern enterprises are entered into because it is essential for the states of Eastern Europe to participate in Western progress and to develop access to Western markets. At the same time, the growing hard-currency debt is worrisome, and the increased dependence on the West is unacceptable to many Comecon officials. Thus, while closer economic relations with the West are helpful in promoting economic integration in Comecon,[35] since they provide resources and ideas for future development, they are also perceived as objectionable. This is due to the fact that trade with the West may interfere with the region's self-centered, centrally directed integration patterns, which have been undertaken precisely in order to promote self-sufficiency. Indeed, the target programs themselves are designed to play an important role in the achievement of these somewhat autarkic goals.

OUTLOOK FOR THE 1980s

My conclusion is not an exercise in predicting events. It merely aims to indicate some underlying issues that are not likely to disappear from the scene or change substantially over the next several years. These issues can be listed under three categories: basic economic problems; measures designed to resolve them; and the interplay between conflicting interests and tendencies.

All Comecon countries share a concern with insufficient modernization and inefficiency in their economies, flagging growth rates, and a squeeze on raw materials. Modernization is needed to resume growth at an acceptable rate and to open doors to competitive free markets. The extensive nature of growth is viewed by many as the culprit responsible for the near stagnation of the social product, with all its dangerous political and social implications. Modernization, in turn, requires imports of advanced equipment. However, expanding or even maintaining exports to the hard-currency area is not a realistic proposition without modernization unless the Comecon countries decide to pay their way in the world by marketing products with a low value-added content. In addition, the Soviet Union is likely to stress the need for modernization in order to prop up the development of advanced and competitive armed forces. Finally, the raw material squeeze requires from all Comecon members greater efficiency in the extraction, processing, transportation and use of minerals and agricultural products. A positive solution to these problems would give Comecon both the security of badly needed supplies and an assurance of efficient economic performance.

Similarity of interests does not extend to all the economic issues that face Comecon. In addition to the requirements of efficiency and economy, which is common to all Comecon members, there is a serious difference between the net exporters of raw materials (that is, the Soviet Union) and the net importers (that is, the East European members of Comecon). The Soviet Union wishes to be adequately compensated for its raw materials by being paid high prices for energy supplies or by receiving large capital loans. Eastern Europe secures raw materials by paying for them with its own exports; in addition, it has to increase its growth rate to counteract the decline caused by a sharp fall in the terms of trade following recent increases in the price of raw materials, especially energy.

The East Europeans' need for sustained economic relations with the West is different from that experienced by the Soviet Union. East Europeans have to sell in the West the products of their wits, while for the Soviet Union it is a matter of extracting and exporting to the West coveted raw materials. One will therefore not be surprised if these two parts of Comecon entertain different ideas about the meaning of, and the need for, more self-sufficiency for Comecon. In Soviet eyes, a significant degree of insulation from the West helps maintain the bloc's cohesion and removes the sense of uncertainty arising from excessive dependence on non-planned economies given to unpredictable changes. For the East Europeans, the last argument may make sense to some extent, but the call to cohesion is of little interest and dependence on imports from the West is a necessity. Centrifugal forces are stronger on the East European periphery of Comecon than in Moscow.

Issues call for solutions. Of the five adopted and implemented thus far, two have not had a significant impact: systemic reforms centering on a half-hearted attempt to introduce market forces and prices have been stashed away in a dusty corner reserved for unfeasible and suspect intellectual foibles, while the reform of management, despite some success in achieving some measure of decentralization and a certain streamlining of the command structure, has yet to make more than a limited impact. The other three solutions (namely, the use of modern technology, the promotion of economies of scale, and the securing of assured supplies of important factors of production) are the tools of policy in which the greatest hopes of Comecon planners are currently being placed. All three are closely related to the target programs. To a large extent, their successful implementation depends, in fact, on the target programs. Until and unless some new economic concept is designed to replace them, the target programs will remain firmly entrenched in the center of the economic policies pursued by the Comecon states.

Although they are thus critical to the economic effort of the socialist camp, the application of the target programs is not likely to be free of contradictions. One results from the incompatibility between institutional arrangements and efficiency, the other from the conflict between centralizing tendencies and the drive to expand cooperation with non-Comecon markets. The implementation of target programs is likely to excel in forming administrative structures, institutions for joint decision-making and coordination, and networks of contractual commitments. But there is thus far no formula for assuring efficiency or an optimum allocation of resources. Among the relevant economic and political decision-makers, some will stress the value of organizational achievements while others will underline the need to improve economic performance. After achieving some advances in restructuring the common apparatus, these policy-makers will next have to turn their attention to the problem of low efficiency. Somewhat similar differences are likely to emerge between the tendency to make Comecon-wide interdependence more permanent, detailed and compulsory, and the urge to maintain and develop links with non-Comecon sources of raw materials and technology. The latter need will require that at least some sectors of the Comecon economies show a measure of competitive spirit, flexibility, initiative and inventiveness, virtues not at a premium in an ever more tightly knit web of intra-Comecon bureaucracies.

Integration and the target programs intended to promote it ideally aim at removing these contradictions and conflicts. They are designed to combine a dovetailing of the Comecon economies with greater efficiency, and to diminish dependence on the West through self-sufficiency. However, the tools, the attitudes, and, by implication, the personnel and the political assumptions needed to accomplish this feat are simply not in evidence, and they are not about to emerge in time to have their impact felt in the 1980s.

NOTES AND REFERENCES

1. For a comprehensive discussion of the reform movement in Comecon and of the retreat from it, see Michael Gamarnikow, "Balance Sheet on Economic Reforms," in Joint Economic Committee, US Congress, *Reorientation and Commercial Relations of the Economies of Eastern Europe* (Washington: US Government Printing Office, 1974) pp. 164–213, and Morris Bornstein, "Economic Reform in Eastern Europe," in Joint Economic Committee, US Congress, *East European*

Economies Post-Helsinki (Washington: US Government Printing Office, 1977) pp. 102–34.

2. Benedykt Askanas, et al., East–West Trade and CMEA Indebtedness in the Seventies and Eighties (Vienna: Zentralsparkasse und Commerzbank, 1979) pp. 8, 13. See also Committee for Economic Development, East–West Trade, A Common Policy for the West (New York, 1965) pp. 48, 49.

3. CMEA Secretariat, Comprehensive Programme for Further Extension and Improvement of Cooperation and the Development of Socialist Economic Integration by the CMEA Member-Countries (Moscow, 1971).

4. J. Kleer, Integracja gospodarcza w RWPG (Warsaw: PWN, 1978) pp. 86, 95.

5. CMEA Secretariat, Comprehensive Programme, pp. 29, 33.

6. N. Khrushchev, "Current Problems of the Development of the World Socialist System," Problemy Pokosu i Sotsializmu, September 1962.

7. Z. Knyziak, "Elementy mezhdunarodnogo planirovania v natsionalnykh planakh khoziaistviennogo razvitia," Planovoe khoziaistvo, no. 8, 1975, pp. 27–9.

8. Development projects are ventures set up to extract raw materials and fuels. Although multilateral in nature, they are implemented through a series of bilateral agreements. The East Europeans usually contribute skilled manpower and equipment for the extraction, refinement and transportation of Soviet-based resources, while the Soviets in return promise stipulated amounts of raw materials. See Arthur J. Smith, "The Council of Mutual Economic Assistance in 1977: New Economic Power, New Political Perspectives and Some Old and New Problems," in East European Economies Post-Helsinki.

9. N. W. Faddiejew, "Uzgodniony plan wielostronnych przedsiebiorstw integracyjnych," Gospodarka Planowa (May 1977) p. 219.

10. Harry Trend, International Economic Associations – a New Form of Comecon Economic Integration, Radio Free Europe, EE/14, 4 September 1972.

11. Faddiejew, "Uzgodniony plan."

12. A. Kosygin, "K novym uspekham stran sotsialisticheskovo sodruzhestva," Planovoe khoziaistvo, no. 9, 1975, pp. 3–8; Knyziak, "Elementy mezhdunarodnogo planirovania"; Heinz Lathe, Handelsblatt (Hamburg), 6 October 1975.

13. For a discussion, see Heinrich Machowski, "Die sozialistischen multinationalen Unternehmungen der Comecon-Länder," Neue Zürcher Zeitung, 25 November 1977.

14. Rezső Nyers, "The Effects of Comecon Integration Measures on the Hungarian National Economy in the Years 1976–1980," Gazdasági Szemle (April 1977) as translated and summarized in Radio Free Europe Research, Hungarian Situation Report, 26 April 1977.

15. O. Rybakov, "Effektivnost' uchastiia SSSR v sotsialisticheskoi ekonomicheskoi integratsii," Planovoe khoziaistvo, no. 1, 1979, pp. 17–25.

16. K. Morgenstern, "The International Specialization of Production and its Concentration in CMEA," Voprosy ekonomiki, no. 2, 1978, translated

in *Soviet and East European Foreign Trade*, vol. xv, no. 1 (Spring 1979) p. 55.

17. Knyziak, "Elementy mezhdunarodnogo planirovania"; Tadeusz Juja, "Rozwoj Polski warunkach integraciji socjalistycznej" (The Development of Poland's Economy under Conditions of Socialist Integration), *Zycie Gospodarcze*, 23 April 1978, p. 4.

18. Tibor Kiss, "International Cooperation in Planning within Comecon," *Közgazdasági Szemle*, no. 6, 1975, translated in *East European Economics*, vol. xiv, no. 4 (1976).

19. János Szita, "On the Road to Socialist Economic Integration," ibid., no. 9, 1976.

20. Katalin Botos, "Coordination of Investment Policies in the CMEA," *Közgazdasági Szemle*, no. 3, 1978, translated in *Soviet and East European Foreign Trade*, vol. xv, no. 2 (Summer 1979).

21. See the review of Jurij Shiriaiev, *Miedzynarodowy socjalistyczny podzial pracy* (Warsaw: PWE, 1979), in *Zycie Gospodarcze*, 23 March 1980, p. 12.

22. J. Kleer, "Wzrost i integracja w gospodarce socjalistycznej" (Growth and Integration in Socialist Economics), *Gospodarka Planowa*, no. 2, 1978, pp. 78–82.

23. Ibid.

24. Knyziak, "Elementy mezhdunarodnogo planirovania."

25. Piotr Glinski, review of *Planowanie i rachunek ekonomiczny w handlu zagranicznym*, in *Zycie Gospodarcze*, 6 August 1978, p. 4.

26. Botos, "Coordination of Investment Policies."

27. Kleer, "Wzrost i integracja."

28. Katarzyna Zukrowska, "RWPG, deficyt pracy a integracja" (Comecon, Lack of Manpower and Integration), *Zycie Gospodarcze*, 8 April 1979, pp. 13 ff.

29. Botos, "Coordination of Investment Policies."

30. See, for instance, the complaints of the Czechoslovak Prime Minister Strougal and his Hungarian colleague, Lázár, at the 1977 session of the Comecon Council, reported by Harry Trend, "Initial Evaluation of the Comecon Meeting," *Radio Free Europe Research*, 24 June 1977.

31. Adam Lipowski, "Efektywność a racjonalizacja cen" (Effectiveness and Rational Prices), *Zycie Gospodarcze*, 22 January 1978, p. 11.

32. Ibid.

33. Glinski, "Review."

34. See, for example, Jurij Shiriaev's discussion of the monopoly of eternal economic relations, in *Miedzynarodowy socjalistyczny podzial pracy.*

35. For details, see Edwin M. Snell, "East European Economies between the Soviets and the Capitalists," in *East European Economies Post-Helsinki*, as well as current releases of the US Department of State on trade with communist countries.

9 The Warsaw Pact

THOMAS CASON

The Warsaw Treaty Organization (WTO), or the Warsaw Pact, as it is more commonly known, is at once both the strength and the potential weakness of the Soviet-dominated socialist system in Eastern Europe. Whether one is to be awed by the quantitative and qualitative dimensions of this uncommon military alliance or be somehow comforted by its problems depends in part on what one wants to see. Both views are possible because the realities are both present – great strengths and great problems. In this chapter an attempt will be made to examine the Warsaw Pact in its own context and to assess its impact on Eastern Europe and the outside world. As with most assessments of the problems and prospects of this region, there will probably be more questions raised than answered and perhaps all that can be hoped for is a more sharpened focus on the context in which these questions – and answers – exist. The Warsaw Treaty Organization is not an alliance system in the sense of NATO or any other present or historical Western alliance system.[1] It is from this premise that the Warsaw Pact will be examined here.

PATTERNS OF INTERACTION WITH THE OUTSIDE WORLD

ORIGINS AND PURPOSES OF THE WARSAW PACT

The WTO was created by a treaty signed by the USSR, Albania, Czechoslovakia, Hungary, Bulgaria, Romania, and Poland on 14 May 1955. (East Germany joined in 1956, and Albania withdrew in 1961.) However, the military experiences and arrangements that had existed in Eastern Europe from at least 1949 had a direct influence on the actual treaty that was signed in 1955. The facts are that the Soviet Union had concluded bilateral treaties with each of the East European

213

nations.[2] In addition, Soviet troops had been stationed in Poland, Romania, Hungary, and East Germany since 1944–5. Each of the national armies of the East European nations had Soviet advisors assigned down to and including the regimental level.[3] In addition, the area of Eastern Europe was integrated into an expanded air defense network controlled directly from the Soviet Union. There is little evidence that much regard was given to the national borders or national concerns of the individual nations in the structure or operation of this network. Hence, one must conclude that the Soviet Union exercised direct control of the East European national armies through the tightly controlled communist regimes (at least during Stalin's lifetime) and through the placement of key Soviet military officers throughout the national armies. In terms of a military organization in Eastern Europe, one can conclude that a functioning alliance, in spite of the lack of formal institutional arrangements, already existed at the time the formal Warsaw Pact Treaty was signed in May 1955.

The Warsaw Pact was created six years after the establishment of NATO in 1949. In many ways the Warsaw Treaty of Friendship, Cooperation, and Mutual Assistance is very similar to the treaty that established NATO.[4] The principal provisions of the treaty are contained in articles creating the Political Consultative Committee and the Joint Command of the armed forces.[5] The signing of the treaty did usher in a potential new actor on the European scene. The significance of the organization, as a military alliance or as a political alliance, depends in part on what one perceives to have been the purposes for its establishment. In order to comprehend the functioning of the Warsaw Pact in today's world, it is essential to understand the original purposes of the organization. Only by examining these initial aims can we better understand the fundamental changes of purpose and role that have taken place in the WTO over the past twenty-seven years.[6]

Although it is not difficult to cite general agreement on the reasons why the WTO was created, it is important to note that there was a vast difference of emphasis and priority in the reasons set forth by the treaty's signatories. Not only did these differences occur along political/military lines, but they also occurred separately within the military and political spheres as such. This was particularly true of the political sphere, since there were a number of political explanations as to why the Warsaw Pact was created.

The principal military reason for creating the Warsaw Pact clearly appears to have been to establish a formal collective security system. The terms of the treaty itself address the need for such a system.[7] From the perspective of the Soviet Union, the advantages of a collective security system were recognized in 1955 in the sense that the Soviet troops stationed in East Germany, Poland, Hungary, and Romania were already providing the geo-strategic advantages of a collective security arrangement. If the purpose of the alliance was to provide for Soviet security by formalizing the military arrangements in effect at the time, then the 1955 agreement can be rationalized militarily.[8] A related military reason cited for the creation of the Warsaw Pact was as a response to the decision by NATO to rearm West Germany and to accept it as a member of the North Atlantic Alliance.[9] Given the very strong anti-German sentiments in the Soviet Union and in Eastern Europe which were outgrowths of the Second World War, it is quite plausible that the Warsaw Pact was created as a counter to German rearmament. The major limitation of this argument, however, is that the military threat that a rearmed West Germany could have posed to the Soviet Union or Eastern Europe was limited, despite Soviet fears of possible resurgent German militarism.

The political reasons for the establishment of the Warsaw Pact were more numerous and, in many ways, more sophisticated because they ascribed to the Soviet Union more complex and subtle motives for its actions. One of these reasons was that the Soviet leaders "needed a political organization through which they could continue to transmit directives to their East European allies and organize East European support for Soviet policies."[10] It has also been argued that the Warsaw Treaty Organization was created by the Soviet Union as a negotiation partner that would be equal to NATO in future European talks.[11] With the landmark Geneva talks scheduled to begin in July of 1955, this rationale seems credible. A related explanation of the creation of the WTO is that it was designed as a negotiating pawn (or in the modern vernacular, a "bargaining chip") for the Soviets to use in dealing with the West.[12] The creation of the Warsaw Pact has also been explained politically as an "institutionalized substitute for the personalized Stalinist system of Soviet hegemony in Eastern Europe."[13] Thus, the WTO provided a multilateral political organization which, along with Comecon, replaced the Stalinist system which was neither wanted nor viable after Stalin's death. A final political argument for the creation of the Warsaw Pact centers around the premise that the Soviet Union needed a means of justifying its placement of troops in Hungary and Romania once the Austrian State Treaty became effective on 15 May 1955, one day after the Warsaw Treaty was signed. The signing of the Warsaw Treaty is seen as providing the Soviet Union with the rationalization and legitimacy for maintaining its troops in these countries.[14] It is not clear that this argument can stand alone, however, given the network of bilateral treaties already in existence.[15]

In this rather limited treatment, an effort has been made to survey the various military and political explanations of why the Soviet Union created the Warsaw Pact when it did. Although we cannot know precisely the Soviet rationale for creating the Warsaw Pact, it is likely that it was a complex mixture of all of these military and political explanations. The purposes or roles of the Warsaw Pact have changed since its inception in 1955, however, and its organizational structures as well as its operational dimensions reflect these changes.

ORGANIZATIONAL STRUCTURES OF THE WTO

The focal point of the political–military organization of the Warsaw Pact, at least from the perspective of the treaty provisions, is the Political Consultative Committee. Comprised of the top party and government officials of the member states, the Committee was empowered by the treaty to create other organizational elements as deemed appropriate.[16] At the first meeting of the Political Consultative Committee in January 1956, it approved the creation of a Unified Command with Marshal Koniev as the Commander-in-Chief of the Unified Forces. A Standing Commission and a Joint Secretariat headed by the Chief of Staff of the Joint Command, a Soviet general officer, were also created. The Political Consultative Committee also approved the acceptance of the newly created army of the German Democratic Republic (GDR) into the Unified Armed Forces under the Joint Command.[17] It is interesting to note that the Political Consultative Committee has not really operated in the manner prescribed by the treaty or by the terms laid down in its first meeting. It met only seven times between 1955 and 1965, and there is little evidence that this body has served as a policy-making body for the WTO. When the Political Consultative Committee did meet during this ten-year period, the communiques and subsequent actions did not suggest that serious military policy deliberations took place. Critical military decisions for the WTO ought to have taken place outside the Political Consultative Committee if a functional military alliance were to have existed. Here one must look at the military organizational structure.

Article 5 of the WTO Treaty called for the establishment of a single military structure: the Joint Command. An agreement establishing the Joint Command was signed on the same day the treaty was signed. This agreement, officially approved in January 1956, called for the selection of Marshal Koniev as Commander-in-Chief of the Joint Armed Forces, provided for the ministers of defense of the other signatory states to serve as Deputy Commanders-in-Chief of the Joint Armed Forces, and created a staff of the Joint Armed Forces under the Commander-in-Chief, to be located in Moscow and composed of permanent representatives of the general staffs of the member nations. The Chief of Staff of the Joint Command heads the joint staff; he has always been a Soviet general. (The same has been true for the First Deputy Chief of Staff.) From the beginning, the Joint Command has been structurally dominated by the Soviet Union. This is evidenced by the fact that all of the top military positions in the Warsaw Pact have been held by Soviet officers.

At the meeting of the Political Consultative Committee in March 1969, held after the intervention of August 1968 in Czechoslovakia, several organizational changes were introduced. One of the changes, and the only one that affected the Political Consultative Committee directly, was the removal of the ministers of defense from the Political Consultative Committee and the formation of a separate Council of Defense Ministers. The ministers of defense also ceased to be Deputy Commanders-in-Chief of the Joint Command (a position which had formerly made each minister of defense subordinate to the Commander-in-Chief of the Joint Command, who held the rank of First Deputy Minister of Defense of the Soviet Union). Deputy ministers of defense of the East European states now became the deputy commanders-in-chief of the Joint Command (see Figure 9.1). This change corrected the problem of prestige that had arisen from the earlier structure, with its subordination of the East European defense ministers to Soviet military authorities, and potentially increased the stature of the national governments vis-à-vis the Joint Command by adding one additional bureaucratic layer between the Joint Command and the national government.[18] A second change made at the 1969 Budapest meeting was the creation of the Military Council which appears to "run under the guidance of the Commander-in-Chief and includes the Chief-of-Staff."[19] The membership of the Military Council includes the deputy ministers of defense. The principal role of the council seems to be an advisory one.[20] A third change made by the Political Consultative Committee in Budapest was the establishment of a permanent Joint Staff consisting of the Chief-of-Staff of the Joint Command, the First Deputy Chief-of-Staff (a Soviet general), two Soviet Deputy Chiefs-of-Staff, and one Deputy Chief-of-Staff from each of the East European countries. All of the Deputy Chiefs-of-Staff have the rank of major general or its equivalent.[21]

EVOLUTION OF THE WARSAW PACT

Whatever the specific reasons for the creation of the Warsaw Pact in 1955, it is very clear that the alliance's capabilities, both military and political, have changed in the past twenty-seven years. During the early years of the alliance, it was apparent that the East European military forces had only marginal military utility. Nor did the alliance appear to have had a particularly important political role from either the Soviet or East European perspective at this time. It was evident that from the outset the organizational structures of the Warsaw Pact were designed to support a peace-time military organization with administrative, training, and equipping functions. These structures were also clearly not designed to formulate or execute joint military operations (offensive or defensive) in wartime conditions. Leadership in wartime passes from the Warsaw Pact to the Soviet Supreme High Command of the Soviet General Staff.[22] In the intervention in Czechoslovakia in 1968 – the only case to date of a joint military operation involving Soviet and East European forces – the operation was conducted by the Soviet General Staff.[23]

The significance of this wartime command structure is that it clearly excludes the Warsaw Pact command apparatus once fighting begins. In addition, the WTO Headquarters in Moscow has no operations directorate, no intelligence directorate, and no separate rear services organization.[24] Hence the organizational structure of the Warsaw Pact must be viewed not as an operational command but rather as one that performs significant military support functions both in peacetime and wartime.[25] In spite of this lack of combat command functions, the organizational structure of the Warsaw Pact can be particularly useful in the areas of conflict preparation, logistics preparation, and a variety of maintenance and equipment related tasks. Malcolm Mackintosh has described the Warsaw Pact as an "organization which enables the Soviet exploitation of the military

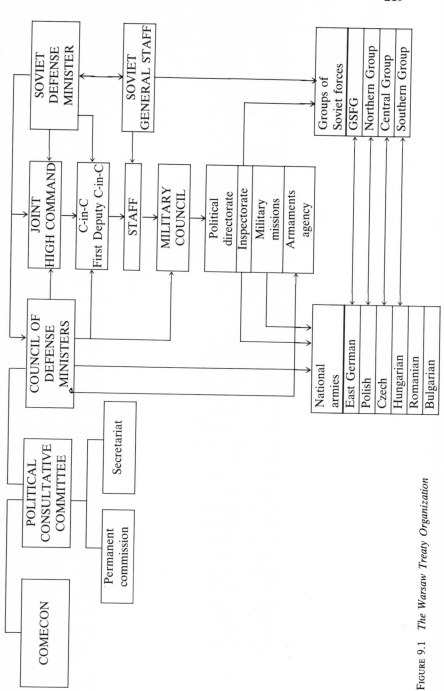

FIGURE 9.1 *The Warsaw Treaty Organization*

manpower of Eastern Europe."[26] Thus one must not at the outset miscast the Warsaw Treaty Organization into a military role that it was not designed, nor has the capability, to play.

From the Soviet perspective, the East European military forces present a dilemma: how to use the military forces in defensive, interventionist, or offensive operations which may become necessary. Because the control of the national armies in Eastern Europe (with the exception of East Germany) rests with the national governments (that is, the communist party leadership in each state), the Soviet Union will likely have to convince the leaders of the governments to support their military actions. Since the commitment for such support will probably have to be ascertained prior to the initiation of the military operations in order to have East European military forces participate at the start of the operation, the Soviet leaders will have to inform the East European leaders of the intended action and thus risk the loss of surprise in a military operation. However, tactical and strategic surprise are critical elements of Soviet military doctrine, particularly if the operations are against NATO forces.

In retrospect, the Czechoslovak intervention in 1968 provides some clues as to the process of ascertaining such commitment. In the process of securing a commitment from its East European allies – Poland, Hungary, Bulgaria, GDR, but *not* Romania – to participate in the intervention, the Soviet Union had to overcome the reluctance of at least one member (Hungary), and even then received only a half-hearted commitment from it.[27] Given that the intervention in Czechoslovakia was not a situation in which any of the East European nations were really risking their own security, or one in which there was much chance of military resistance or retaliation, and in view of the fact that the Soviets still had difficulties securing the necessary commitments from its East European allies, it is very difficult to posit a situation in which the Soviet Union could secure a quick commitment of the East European military forces against NATO. This would be particularly difficult in the case of a surprise attack by the Soviet alliance against the West since the security risks to Eastern Europe would be very high and the likelihood of stiff NATO military resistance and immediate retaliation very high. The only exception to this rule would most likely involve a strictly defensive effort following a bona fide NATO attack. Otherwise it would be very difficult for the Soviet Union, particularly in a crisis situation, to conceal its surprise attack plans while trying to secure the required commitments from the East European leaderships. In addition, the East European military forces have a number of mobilization problems which further limit their utility in combat.

The Warsaw Treaty Organization thus does not function principally as a vehicle to deal with threats external to the Soviet Union and Eastern Europe. Rather, it functions as a conduit between the Soviet Union and the Soviet military and the East European countries and their respective military establishments. In this respect the Warsaw Pact can be viewed primarily as an institutional means for conducting intra-bloc relations, relations whose dimensions and intensity are determined to a great extent by the Soviet Union.

COORDINATION OR FRAGMENTATION?

The evolution of the Warsaw Treaty Organization over the past twenty-seven years has been characterized by ever-increasing cooperation and coordination between the Soviet Union's military establishment and the military forces of the East European states. (Since the mid-1960s Romania has remained a prominent exception to this trend.) Joint field exercises and large scale command and control exercises have apparently produced a high degree of effectiveness in inter-military operability, at least in peacetime. Perhaps more important, at least from the Soviet perspective, has been the continuous interaction between the Soviet and East European military elites over the past three decades. Although it cannot be measured with precision and most assuredly varies from one East European state to another, this interaction among the leading military officers from the WTO nations in the joint exercises, in WTO-sponsored activities, and in the senior military service schools in the Soviet Union (which almost all of the top officers in the East European military establishments attend) has to be viewed by the Soviet Union as a positive factor and one that gives the Soviet military leaders a higher degree of confidence in their East European counterparts. It is interesting to note that in the Czechoslovak crisis in 1968, the *senior* military leaders in Czechoslovakia (with a few notable exceptions) were among the most outspoken critics of Dubcek after he was ousted from leadership, and many of the officers remained in their positions when the new government took over.[28]

Again in the Polish crisis of 1980–1 there was a good deal of speculation about the likely response of the Polish military to a

Soviet-Warsaw Pact intervention in Poland. At least until the appointment of General Jaruzelski as head of the Polish United Workers' Party in October 1981, there was some uncertainty as to whom the senior military leaders would obey in a crisis: the Polish government or the Soviet military. Many Western analysts argued at the time that nationalism would lead the Polish military hierarchy to side with the national government in a confrontation with the Soviets. Others, however, suggested that, like their Czech and Slovak counterparts in 1968, the Polish leaders would for the most part side with the Soviets.[29]

General Jaruzelski's accession to the top party post, however, and his imposition of a martial law regime on Poland on 13 December 1981, have at least for the time being reduced the margin of potential conflict between the Polish high command and the Soviet leadership over the issue of Soviet intervention in Polish affairs. Although the choice of Jaruzelski for the foremost political position in Poland was surely made at Moscow's behest, and the Kremlin no doubt encouraged the measures of 13 December, the Soviet military has not as yet intervened directly in Poland as it did in Czechoslovakia. As long as local authority in Poland continues to be exercised by Poles, the question of a clash of interests between the Polish military leadership and the Soviet Union becomes moot. Both sides have an interest in restoring political order in Poland and in maintaining close cooperative ties. Indeed the selection of a military figure to preside over the party and over a martial law regime in Poland was a masterful stroke from the Soviet point of view, as it achieved Moscow's principal aim of repressing the Polish free trade union movement while maintaining the framework of a native leadership draped in the colors of Polish nationalism.

Meanwhile, the administration of martial law itself has resulted in a vast increase in the domestic activities of the Polish military, reaching levels unprecedented in post-war Eastern Europe. In many instances the army has come to replace the party as the dominant administrative institution, even at local levels. This preoccupation with the minutiae of governing may very well leave the Polish military with less time for fulfilling its normal functions within the Warsaw Pact, and it is therefore quite possible that Poland's role within the Pact may be declining at the very moment when its internal responsibilities are expanding.

Although the martial law strategy has been relatively successful for the Soviet Union as of the start of 1983, the prospects for continuing coordination between the Polish military government and the USSR are by no means certain. Mass dissatisfaction with the martial law administration may erode the Polish military's traditional prestige among the Polish populace, leading some military officers to waver in their support for the current regime. (Although no general purge of the officer corps has yet taken place, support for martial law is probably at low ebb among the rank and file of the Polish troops.) Moreover, the possibility of an outright Soviet invasion cannot be entirely discounted as yet. If the discontent with the Jaruzelski regime that was manifested in the streets of Gdansk, Warsaw and other Polish cities at various times in 1982 should erupt into new outbursts of protest which the local authorities cannot control, the Soviets may yet feel compelled to step in with their own forces. Should this happen, the questions raised prior to Jaruzelski's appointment about what the Polish military would do if confronted with a Soviet invasion would rise to the surface once again, with similarly uncertain results.

Whatever the outcome of such a hypothetical occurrence, one must conclude for the present that the Soviets have in fact effected a considerable degree of coordination with the structures of the Warsaw Pact in recent years. For example since 1969, when two new organs were added to the WTO structure, the meetings of the Council of Defense Ministers and, more particularly, the meetings of the Military Council, have added new opportunities for the WTO to function as a positive agent of military coordination within the bloc.

One of the prime motivators of cooperative action among the East European members of the WTO is their dependence on the Soviet Union for new military hardware, spare parts, ammunition, logistic support, and critical fuels. Uncooperative WTO members – such as Romania – can find themselves in a very disadvantageous position in terms of relative military strength when compared with the more cooperative members. In the recent Polish crisis, the Soviet Union has held a death grip on the Polish military in terms of critical shipments of military fuels, ammunition, spare parts, and so on. The overall potential effectiveness of the Polish military in resisting a potential Soviet-led Warsaw Pact intervention was considerably reduced prior to December 1981 when the Soviets withheld critical items from the military pipeline for only a few months. All East European members of the WTO are similarly vulnerable to actions by the Soviet Union in any future crisis. The most rudimentary function of the East European military forces – the defense of the state – is thus, in part, contingent upon the actions of the Soviet Union. Cooperation and coordination with the Soviet Union in military matters result in newer and more impressive military equipment as well as a free flowing pipeline of critical military supplies.

One would be incorrect in assuming that the Warsaw Treaty has produced only coordinated military policies and harmonious actions among the East European member states and the Soviet Union. Tensions and open disagreements, as well as more subtle forms of fragmentation, have indeed been evident in the WTO, particularly in recent years. As noted above, Romania has simply not been a loyal member of the WTO in many respects; it has had to pay the price for its actions in a number of ways. Militarily, Romania has the least modern military establishment in the WTO; it has difficulty in maintaining some equipment due to shortages in spare parts. Romanian leaders have responded by orienting their military policy to a defensive one along the lines of the Yugoslav military. Romanian military forces are thus prepared to carry out only one major combat mission: defense of the Romanian state against any invading forces. The training and arming of the Patriotic Guard, which apparently has over 700,000 members, for partisan warfare is seen in the West (and perhaps in the Soviet Union and WTO) as an effort by the Romanian leadership to deter any potential intervention in Romania. Romania has turned to Yugoslavia and indirectly to the West to help offset the effects of its adverse relationship with the Soviet Union.[30] When the Soviet Union at the 1979–80 Warsaw Pact Meetings urged its East European allies to increase their defense budgets, this effort was successfully resisted by Hungary and Poland and openly defied by Romania, which actually announced a defense budget reduction. The collective nature of the WTO meetings probably facilitated the effective resistance. It is likely that such resistance would have been much more difficult in direct, bilateral negotiations between the individual East European countries and the Soviet Union.

Another area where there is some evidence of fragmentation within the WTO is that of East European support for Soviet foreign policy. Manifestations of outright resistance to Soviet initiatives on the part of at least some of Moscow's allies have frequently surfaced on occasions when the Soviets have sought explicit WTO endorsement of their foreign policy decisions. Some of the more prominent examples of this phenomenon have centered on such issues as the condemnation of Israel in the Middle East wars of 1967 and 1973,[31] the condemnation of the People's Republic of China in the border disputes of 1969,[32] the decision to intervene in Czechoslovakia in 1968,[33] and, more recently, the problem of potential WTO intervention in Poland.[34] Romania openly defied the Soviet Union in 1967 by refusing to brand Israel as the aggressor in the 1967 war and by not severing relations with Israel when all other WTO members followed the Soviet lead. Moreover, it was clear that both Poland and Hungary did not follow Moscow as closely as Czechoslovakia, Bulgaria or the GDR, as the Poles and Hungarians modified their condemnation statements and delayed severing relations with Israel. Similar differences can be found in the responses to the 1973 Arab-Israeli War. Romania continued to pursue a foreign policy quite different from that of the Soviet Union and the other Warsaw Pact nations. In another foreign policy incident in 1976, János Kádár of Hungary took a very different view from that of the Soviet Union and the hardline East European nations over the pronouncements of the Spanish Communist Party leader, Santiago Carillo, who in 1977 asserted that the Soviet Union was not a socialist country.[35] Thus the Warsaw Treaty Organization has not provided a forum for getting the East European members of the bloc to support the Soviet Union unequivocally on either internal bloc matters or on foreign policy issues.

IMPACT ON EAST-WEST RELATIONS

The creation of the Warsaw Treaty Organization in 1955 did not produce an initial response by the West that could be described as particularly positive or negative. It has been argued that the creation of the WTO exacted little response from the West and NATO because the organization was seen merely as a formal extension of the Soviet Union's dominance of Eastern Europe and not as an organization with any particular role or power apart from that of the Soviet Union itself.[36] Because of this perception, which was reinforced by the fact that the Soviet Union reacted to the Hungarian and Polish crises of 1956 without any joint WTO action or consensus, there was little reason for NATO to have regarded the WTO as its political counterpart in any sense of the word. The limited number of meetings of the Political Consultative Committee during the first ten years (only seven in all) lent little support to the political credibility of the WTO as a bona fide international or regional actor. One could argue that the Warsaw Pact's influence on East-West relations was minimal during the first decade. After 1965, the emergence of Romania as a maverick in the Warsaw alliance and the WTO's intervention in Czechoslovakia in 1968, however small the East European contributions may have been,[37] raised the political credibility of the WTO in the eyes of the West. The articulation of the Brezhnev Doctrine and the Budapest Meeting of the Political Consultative Committee in March of 1969 ushered in a new era for the WTO as a regional political actor and a budding counterpart to NATO. The ouster of such leaders as Gomulka in Poland and Ulbricht in the GDR, and their replacement with Gierek and Honecker respectively, together with the success of West Germany's "Ostpolitik" since 1969 gave a new impetus to relations between Eastern and Western Europe. These developments have increased the potential political utility of the WTO for both the East European members and the Soviet Union by raising the level of interaction between the two groups of states. The new political relations between Eastern Europe and the West and the ensuing expansion of economic relations have finally dispelled the monolithic model of Eastern Europe and have thus elevated the status of the WTO to that of an "almost" bona fide alliance and an "almost" equal counterpart to NATO.[38] Although the failure to negotiate any kind of Mutual Balanced Force Reduction (MBFR) agreements has had a negative impact on the credibility of the WTO as an alliance actor, MBFR is not necessarily a clear-cut WTO activity. Finally, the success of the Helsinki Conference on Security and Cooperation in Europe in settling some of the outstanding border issues in Central Europe has also paved the way for improved relations among European nations on the basis of acceptance of the political and territorial status quo. The evolution of the political role of the WTO has thus resulted in an East–West environment where it is possible for the two European alliances – NATO and the WTO – to address key political and military issues that affect both alliances.

It would be premature to argue that the WTO has become a paramount political actor in Europe, especially if one did not first properly assess the military role of the WTO as perceived by the West. Certainly there is likely to be a correlation between the build-up of the WTO's military capabilities and its newly found political importance. During the first five or six years of the WTO's existence, one can argue that the WTO's political inactivity was paralleled by its military ineptitude and the lack of a concerted effort by either the Soviet Union or the East European countries to develop credible national military forces in Eastern Europe. Little or no pressure was apparently exerted by the Commander-in-Chief of the Joint High Command of the WTO, Marshal Koniev, to modernize the East European forces or to integrate these forces with the Soviet military forces stationed in Europe. An analysis of the East European military forces in 1960 reveals that many of these countries were still using Second World War and early post-war equipment while the Soviet forces were outfitted with the latest Soviet equipment.

When Marshal Grechko became the Commander-in-Chief of the Joint High Command in 1960, he instituted a number of very significant changes in the WTO military force posture. First, he took the initial step in modernizing the East European forces; that trend has continued to the present day. Second, Grechko organized and executed joint operations aimed at improving the overall military performance of the East European and Soviet forces in the WTO and at establishing patterns of integration and cooperation among the various East European military forces and with Soviet military forces. By 1967 the national armies of Eastern Europe, including the small one in East Germany, had become considerably more credible than in 1960. When Grechko became the new Soviet Minister of Defense, he was replaced by Marshal Yakubovskii, who continued to stress the developments that Grechko had started.

During the early 1960s NATO officially took notice of the military developments in Eastern Europe and began to increase its assessment of the WTO's military strength, specifically attributing large manpower and equipment capabilities to the East European national armies. Once the recognition of military capability took place – even if it was strongly based on quantitative and not qualitative assessments – the military dimension of the WTO assumed a growing importance for the United States and its allies. Since then Western estimates of the military balance have included comparisons of the WTO and NATO.[39] There is, however, an apparent contradiction between the military cohesiveness attributed to the Warsaw Pact on the one hand and the political diversity attributed to the East European WTO members on the other. It is the military strength of the WTO and the continuous build-up of that strength that tends to alarm the NATO members, and particularly the United States.[40] However, the political diversity among the East European members of the WTO provides the NATO countries, particularly West Germany, with the opportunity to make serious economic (and political) inroads into Eastern Europe, a fact which may help counterbalance the effects of the Warsaw Pact's military superiority in Europe.

The Warsaw Treaty Organization's impact on East–West relations therefore must be viewed from at least two perspectives, one military and the other political. Militarily the WTO, due particularly to the recent build-up of its military equipment, has had and continues to have a disruptive effect on East–West relations. The current debate on nuclear missiles in Europe exemplifies the negative impact of WTO (and NATO) military activities on East–West relations. Politically the WTO has had a mixed impact on relations with the West. The political diversity of certain WTO members – Romania, Poland, and Hungary – has facilitated much more cordial relations between these WTO members and the West. On the other hand, the political (and military) pressures put on Poland in the current crisis by the Soviet Union and the other WTO members, with the exception of Romania, have produced a very tense political atmosphere in Europe. Despite differences between the US and certain of its key West European allies on the proper response to be taken to the martial law regime (with West Germany, for example, preferring a more cautious approach to economic sanctions on the USSR and Poland than the United States), the NATO states have severely condemned the repression of Solidarity and the jailing of its leaders. Unless the Jaruzelski regime takes measures to ease the internal repression and initiate effective economic reforms (and assuming that there is no direct Soviet military intervention), ongoing political and economic activities between the West and Eastern Europe may be disrupted even further.

OUTLOOK FOR THE 1980s

The Warsaw Treaty Organization celebrated its 25th anniversary in May of 1980. The prospects for the organization in the 1980s do not seem particularly bright, even with the achievements in overall armaments levels and general military capabilities of the Soviet and East European military forces. At the outset of the 1980s, it appears that the US and its NATO allies are prepared to take measures to offset the WTO military gains. If conventional conflict were to erupt between the WTO and NATO, numerous military and political military uncertainties would face both alliances and it is not clear that either side would have a clear-cut advantage. The political diversity already in evidence in the WTO has created unique national interests among the East European members of the WTO which would be ill-served by a WTO–NATO military conflict. (The same unique national interests exist among NATO members, notably West Germany, and those interested would be equally ill-served by a conflict between the Warsaw Pact and NATO.) A popular theme of many Western analysts, including this author, over the past few years has been the uncertainty of East European political–military reliability in case of a WTO–NATO war.[41] This political–military reliability is seen as a particularly significant question from the Soviet perspective. It is not the purpose of this chapter to weigh the merits of the various arguments about this issue, but it is important to note the fundamental and lingering historical bases on which many of the arguments about political–military reliability are based. The Soviet Union has as its WTO allies a group of nations, which, for a variety of political, economic, religious and other reasons, have historically not only *not* been Russian or Soviet allies but have been enemies of the Russian or Soviet state. The crux of the question of the political–military reliability of the East European members of WTO to the Soviet Union is not the reliability of the governments and communist parties (with the possible exception of Romania). The real question is grounded in the populations of the East European states. In spite of Soviet domination of Eastern Europe since the Second World War and the preeminence of the communist parties in the East European states over most of the post-war period, the loyalty of the East European people to their own communist regimes, much less to the Soviet Union, apparently has not been secured. The Polish crisis of 1980–1, as well as the Czechoslovak crisis in 1968 and even the Hungarian crisis of 1956, are examples of attempts to alter the existing communist system either through the communist party apparatus or outside of it. In the cases of the Hungarian and Czechoslovak crises, once the Soviet Union intervened in the crisis and replaced the top leadership of the communist party, that party itself regained its position of preeminence in the political sphere with only minimal changes in its total membership. Soviet military forces were permanently stationed in both Hungary and Czechoslovakia to ensure that there were no future popular uprisings from inside or outside of the party. Thus it seems that in spite of the "communization" of the political systems over the past 35 years, there is still within the East European countries – admittedly to various degrees – a popular potential for anti-Soviet and anti-communist turmoil. Perhaps the recent labor union movement in Poland is the most subtle and most sophisticated of these popular challenges to Soviet and communist dominance in Eastern Europe. Since the military forces of these East European states are manned by officers and conscripts drawn from the societies as a whole, it is difficult to separate the problems of the two. In Poland, soldiers and workers are both drawn from a society that has challenged the Polish communist party.

When the political–military reliability of Eastern Europe is viewed in this context, it becomes both a lesser and a greater problem for the Soviet Union and both a greater and lesser advantage for the West. For the Soviet Union, the military reliability of the East European national armies in a defensive, interventionist or even offensive military operation may not be as serious a concern as some Western analysts claim. The effects of joint exercises conducted over the past twenty years, the integration of the East European military forces with the Soviet forces, the "earmarking" of key East European military units to perform specific operations and missions,[42] and the overall Soviet military dominance in Eastern Europe, particularly in the Northern Tier, all combine to minimize the potential effects of any East European military unreliability, particularly in a conflict where the Soviet-led military forces are apt to have initial military successes. Reliability of the East European military forces becomes an issue of concern for the Soviet Union in the long-term political and political–military spheres. It is here that the Soviet Union seems to be unable to effect a change which can produce an alliance whose members are held together by factors other than Soviet military power. The political reliability of the East European military establishments to the Soviet Union seems anything but certain. Thus the Soviet Union faces another decade in the 1980s in which its alliance system in Eastern Europe seems destined to be strained by even more political diversity than in the past. Military intervention by the Soviet Union in Poland, Romania, or *any* of the other WTO East European member states to restore Soviet political, political–military, or even military dominance cannot be ruled out in spite of the heavy price the Soviet Union would pay. In the long run, this inherent potential political instability may eventually spell the end of the Warsaw Treaty Organization as an effective military alliance system.

From the perspective of NATO and the West, the potential political–military unreliability of the East European members of the Warsaw Pact does not translate into an immediate advantage. Militarily, the West will likely be sorely mistaken if it believes that the East European military forces represent a military liability to the Soviet Union; they most assuredly do not. The ability of the Soviet Union to orchestrate a military conflict with the West to optimize the contribution of selected East European military units should not be underestimated or discounted. The East European national armies have undergone a decade of modernization and represent – admittedly in widely varying degrees – a formidable military force. NATO and the West must prepare to deal with a realistic Soviet–East European military threat throughout the 1980s. On the other hand NATO, and particularly the US, should be ready to exploit further the potential political diversity in Eastern Europe through all political, economic, and cultural means available. Herein lies the opportunity for the West to act in a manner supportive of the fundamental forces for change already at work in Eastern Europe. Political diversity in Eastern Europe means increased ties with the West and with the Third World; Soviet dominance of Eastern Europe cannot help but become more tenuous and more difficult to sustain. The Warsaw Treaty Organization, although it may be able to sustain its military superstructure, will be difficult to maintain substantively if its political and economic substructures are undermined.

NOTES AND REFERENCES

1. Ole R. Holsti, P. Terrence Hopmann, and John D. Sullivan, *Unity and Disintegration in International Alliances* (New York: John Wiley, 1973).
2. Bilateral Treaties: USSR with Bulgaria (3/18/48), Czechoslovakia (12/12/43), Hungary (2/18/48), Poland (4/21/48) and Romania (2/4/48); Bulgaria with Czechoslovakia (4/23/48), Hungary (6/16/48), Poland (5/29/48), and Romania (1/16/48); Czechoslovakia with Hungary (4/16/49), Poland (3/10/47) and Romania (4/28/48); Hungary with Poland (6/18/48) and Romania (1/24/48); and Poland with Romania (1/26/48).
3. Andrzej Korbonski, "The Warsaw Pact," *International Conciliation* (May 1969) pp. 9–10.
4. For a comparison of the two treaties, see Roman Kolkowicz (ed.), *The Warsaw Pact: Report on a Conference on the Warsaw Treaty Organization* (Arlington, Virginia: Institute for Defense Analysis, 1969) Appendix D.
5. "The Warsaw Treaty of Friendship, Co-operation and Mutual Assistance" cited in Robin A. Remington, *The Warsaw Pact: Case Studies in Communist Conflict Resolution* (Cambridge: MIT Press, 1971) Document 1, pp. 201–5.

6. Malcolm Mackintosh, "The Evolution of the Warsaw Pact," *Adelphi Papers* (No. 58, June 1969). Mackintosh believes that the Warsaw Pact became a more serious military organization after 1961. Also, see Thomas W. Wolfe, *Role of the Warsaw Pact in Soviet Policy* (Santa Monica, California: Rand Corporation, March 1973). Wolfe examines the roles of the Warsaw Pact in 1955 and compares those to the roles as he sees them in 1973.
7. See the Preamble, Article 3, and Article 4 of the Treaty, in Remington, *The Warsaw Pact,* pp. 201–6.
8. Wolfe, *Role of the Warsaw Pact in Soviet Policy,* p. 5.
9. Korbonski, "The Warsaw Pact," pp. 8–9.
10. Mackintosh, *The Evolution of the Warsaw Pact,* p. 1.
11. Korbonski, "The Warsaw Pact," p. 12.
12. Ibid.
13. A. Ross Johnson, *Soviet–East European Military Relations: An Overview* (Santa Monica, California: Rand Corporation, January, 1975) p. 2.
14. Richard F. Starr, *The Communist Regimes of Eastern Europe: An Introduction* (Menlo Park, California: Hoover Institution on War, Revolution, and Peace, 1967) pp. 215–6.
15. Remington, *The Warsaw Pact,* p. 19.
16. Mackintosh, "The Evolution of the Warsaw Pact," p. 21.
17. "Communique on the Session of the Political Consultative Committee of the Warsaw Treaty Powers, 28 January 1956," cited in J. P. Jain, *Documentary Study of the Warsaw Pact* (London: Asia Publishing House, 1973) pp. 149–50.
18. Lawrence T. Caldwell, "The Warsaw Pact: Directions of Change," *Problems of Communism* (September–October 1975) pp. 3–4.
19. John Erickson, *Soviet–Warsaw Pact Force Levels* (Washington: United States Strategic Institute, 1976) p. 65.
20. Johnson, *Soviet–East European Military Relations,* pp. 15–16.
21. Ibid.
22. V. D. Sokolovskiy, *Military Strategy* (3rd edition) (Menlo Park, California: Stanford Research Institute, 1971) pp. 409–10. Translation, analysis and commentary by Harriet Fast Scott.
23. Raymond L. Garthoff, "The Military Establishment," *East Europe* (September 1965) pp. 14–15.
24. Malcolm Mackintosh in an interview with the author in London on 21 January 1977.
25. Erickson, *Soviet–Warsaw Pact Force Levels,* p. 76.
26. Malcolm Mackintosh interview, op. cit.
27. Foreign Broadcast Information Service (FBIS), *Eastern Europe, Daily Report,* 10 September 1968, pp. F1–F2. Also see Richard Lowenthal, "The Sparrow in the Cage," *Problems of Communism* (November–December 1968) p. 21.
28. H. Gordon Skilling, *Czechoslovakia's Interrupted Revolution* (Princeton University Press, 1976) p. 720.
29. John Erickson, "The Warsaw Pact: Past, Present, Future." Unpublished paper, 1980.
30. The Romanians and Yugoslavs have engaged in the joint development of

a ground attack fighter. Romania and Yugoslavia apparently have an integrated air defense system.

31. *FBIS Daily Report: Eastern Europe* and *FBIS Daily Report: Soviet Union* were used to research and detail the responses for each country during these crises.

32. Ibid.

33. Ibid.

34. Kevin Klose, *The Washington Post*, 7 April 1981, p. 1. Klose relates the speech made by Czechoslovak party leader Gustav Husak in which he stated the WTO would defend its interests in Poland.

35. Edward Crankshaw, "Europe's Reds: Trouble for Moscow," *The New York Times Magazine*, 30 November 1975, p. 18.

36. Lawrence S. Kaplan, "NATO and the Warsaw Pact: 1955 and 1980," in Robert W. Clawsen and Lawrence S. Kaplan (eds), *The Warsaw Pact: Political Purpose and Military Means* (Wilmington: Scholarly Resources, 1982), pp. 67–91.

37. Skilling, *Czechoslovakia's Interrupted Revolution*, pp. 720–7.

38. See *The Military Balance, 1980–1981* (London: International Institute for Strategic Studies, 1980) pp. 110–15. Comparisons between WTO and NATO are given in terms of ground forces, battle tanks, and tactical aircraft.

39. For example, see the annual issues of *The Military Balance* produced by the International Institute for Strategic Studies in London.

40. The addition of the MIG–23 (Flogger), the T–62 and T–72 battle tanks, and the BMP armored vehicles to the East European military arsenals are examples of the military build-up. For a summary of each of the East European military arsenals, see *The Military Balance, 1980–1981*, pp. 14–18.

41. See Dale R. Herspring and Ivan Volgyes, "Political Reliability in the Eastern European Warsaw Pact Armies," *Armed Forces and Society*, vol. 6, no. 2 (Winter 1980) pp. 272–96.

42. This point has been made by John Erickson for a number of years. See his *Soviet–Warsaw Pact Force Levels*, p. 67.

10 Eastern Europe and the Third World: The Expanding Relationship

ROGER E. KANET

The countries of communist Eastern Europe have entered the decade of the 1980s with far less optimism than they had a decade ago. Their position in both the international political and economic systems is currently in a state of significant change. The first half of the past decade witnessed a substantial increase in political and economic relations with the industrialized countries of the West as part of the growing detente in East–West relations. This growth in contacts with the West represented an integral part of policies aimed at expanding the economic capabilities of the European communist states by means of increasing imports of high-level technology from the West. However, a number of serious economic problems, compounded by the deterioration in Soviet–American relations, have required the leaders of these countries to reconsider at least some aspects of their relationships with the outside world. Their inability to expand exports to match imports, with the result of serious balance of payments problems; their heavy and growing dependence on raw materials imports, and the recent staggering rise in the price of some of those materials, in particular petroleum; and the failure of past technology imports to affect significantly the level of labor productivity in most of the East European countries have all required East European governments to reduce their optimistic predictions for future economic growth and to reassess their economic relations with various groups of countries. For example, the inability to expand significantly its markets for manufactured goods in the West has already resulted in Romania's decision to emphasize the expansion of trade relations with the developing countries. Trade with the Third World has grown from five per cent of total Romanian trade in 1970 to sixteen per cent in 1975 and to more than twenty per cent in 1978. Although this is by far the most significant shift in the trade patterns of the six East European members of the Council for Mutual Economic Assistance (CMEA), it is representative of a visible increase in East European economic interest in the Third World. Between 1970 and 1978 the combined trade of the six countries with the developing world rose from slightly less than six per cent of total trade to more than eight per cent. (See Table 10.1.)

It is very likely that the less-developed countries of the southern hemisphere will become far more important for Eastern Europe in the future than they have been in the past because of the need for stable sources of raw materials and for expanding markets for their own industrial production. For at least several of the East European states, support for "socialist" revolution in the Third World is likely to become less important than it has been, except in so far as support for revolutionary movements is viewed as an important means of assuring future access to raw materials and to markets. At least for the foreseeable future most of the East European states are likely to be so involved in dealing with their own political and economic problems that they will find expensive, politically motivated involvements abroad far less inviting.

The purpose of the present examination is to trace the evolution of relations between the smaller communist states of Eastern Europe[1] with the Third World and to assess the likely development of those relations in the coming decade. In spite of the increasing importance of political and economic relations between Eastern Europe and the developing countries of Asia, Africa, and Latin America, relatively few American scholars have devoted attention to this subject.[2] An additional purpose of the present study will be to determine the degree to which the policies of individual East European states toward developing countries coincide with or diverge from the policies of other East European countries and those of the Soviet Union.

THE EVOLUTION OF EAST EUROPEAN RELATIONS WITH THE THIRD WORLD

To a very substantial degree the policies of the East European countries – with the partial exception of those of Romania – have followed closely the policies of the Soviet Union throughout the

TABLE 10.1 Trade of East European states with the non-communist developing countries
(millions of current US dollars)

	1960		1965		1970		1975		1976		1977		1978	
	Exports	Imports	Exports	Imports	Exports	Imports	Exports	Imports	Exports	Imports	Exports	Imports	Exports	Imports
Bulgaria														
Total trade	571	625	1,176	1,178	1,831	2,004	4,810	5,531	5,320	6,198	6,342	6,300	7,534	7,366
with LDCs	18	13	52	37	81	125	463	209	430	238	286	657	264	822
Czechoslovakia														
Total trade	1,929	1,816	2,688	2,673	3,695	3,792	8,158	8,874	8,745	9,410	10,745	9,902	12,253	11,468
with LDCs	200	161	255	197	214	331	706	501	658	498	703	808	595	962
German Dem. Rep.														
Total trade	2,207	2,194	3,085	2,823	4,923	4,647	10,680	11,947	11,645	13,514	13,445	12,186	15,637	14,236
with LDCs	89	90	131	120	182	183	431	483	473	605	727	824	733	583
Hungary														
Total trade	874	976	1,510	1,520	2,505	3,317	5,694	6,758	6,643	7,252	10,207	9,282	12,813	10,444
with LDCs	58	58	107	113	177	137	364	498	392	524	1,020	832	1,125	975
Poland														
Total trade	1,326	1,495	2,228	2,340	3,608	3,548	10,510	12,752	10,969	13,823	14,859	12,468	16,504	15,738
with LDCs	93	99	172	210	196	258	845	597	878	577	711	1,058	881	1,099
Romania														
Total trade	717	648	1,102	1,077	1,960	1,851	5,420	5,418	6,175	6,062	7,111	7,116	8,628	7,959
with LDCs	40	20	68	55	117	153	985	732	1,089	1,087	1,230	1,578	1,639	1,751
Total Eastern Europe														
Total trade	7,624	7,754	11,789	11,618	18,522	18,159	45,272	51,280	49,497	55,626	62,709	57,254	73,099	67,211
with LDCs	498	441	785	732	967	1,187	3,794	3,020	3,920	3,522	4,683	5,516	5,241	6,433
% with LDCs	6.5	5.7	6.7	6.3	5.2	6.5	8.4	5.9	7.9	6.3	7.5	9.6	7.2	9.5

Source: Central Intelligence Agency, National Foreign Assessment Center, *Handbook of Economic Statistics 1978: A Research Aid*, ER 78-10365, October 1978, pp. 67-8. Data for 1977 and 1978 calculated from Sovet Ekonomicheskoi Vzaimopomoshchi, *Statisticheskii Ezhegodnik Stran-Chlenov Soveta Vzaimopomoshchi 1978*. (Moscow: Statistika, 1978, pp. 323-5 and *Ibid*., 1979. (Moscow: 1979), pp. 371-3. Romanian trade with developing countries for 1977 and 1978 was calculated by using the percentage of trade with those states that appears in International Monetary Fund, *Direction of Trade Yearbook 1980*, p. 322. (The substantial increase in trade between 1976 and 1977 for Czechoslovakia, Hungary and Romania is, in part, the result of differing information included in the two sources.)

Third World ever since the 1950s. The political leaders of the CMEA countries share a common view with the Soviets concerning the significance of the developing world in the historic struggle with the capitalist West. This aspect of East European interest can probably best be seen in the upsurge of contacts with and support for revolutionary movements and regimes in Sub-Saharan Africa during the 1970s. Along with the Soviet Union and Cuba, several of the East European countries have played an important role in providing military and economic support to Angola, Mozambique and Ethiopia, among others.[3] In the Middle East, with the visible and notable exception of Romania, the East Europeans have followed the lead of the Soviet Union in providing support of various types to the more "radical" of the Arab governments in their struggle with Israel. In recent years, for example, periodic East European propaganda campaigns against the Egyptian–Israeli negotiations and treaty have been modeled almost precisely on Soviet statements.

In addition to the fact that the East European political elites share a common worldview with the Soviets,[4] there has been the added factor of Soviet efforts to ensure that the members of the CMEA coordinate their foreign policies vis–à–vis the outside world, including the developing countries. The reports published at the conclusion of meetings among high-level Soviet and East European government and party officials in recent years virtually always indicate that issues related to the Third World have been among the topics of common concern. In the words of a Soviet editorial on the significance of the series of summer meetings in the Crimea between General Secretary Brezhnev and the leaders of the East European communist parties, "Co-ordinated action heightens the effectiveness also of socialist foreign policy."[5]

In the standard view of the European communist states, support for national liberation movements in the Third World is an integral element of the historical struggle with capitalism. In the first stage of the revolutionary process, local nationalists, even bourgeois nationalists, who are committed to the establishment of politically independent states throughout the developing world are viewed as a progressive force and, therefore, worthy of support from the communist states.[6]

The second stage of the struggle for liberation, which focuses on the attempt to gain economic independence, requires active participation of the most progressive forces – that is, those committed to scientific socialism.[7] The only means by which the developing countries can successfully achieve full economic development is by emulating the experience of the communist states, according to the standard view of the East European states. As a result, the CMEA states have emphasized support for the expansion of those areas of the economy in Third World states that strengthen the "non-capitalist" aspects of the economy – that is, nationalization of industry, investment in the state-controlled sectors of the economy, and so on.

In recent years there has been increasing evidence that factors other than ideologically-based interest or Soviet political concerns have stimulated East European involvement in the developing world. During the late 1970s, in particular, Eastern Europe turned to the Third World as both a market for industrial goods not easily sold on the world market and as a source of industrial raw materials, including energy.[8] Since the oil crisis of 1973–4 and the growing evidence that the Soviet Union is neither willing nor able to meet the expanding East European demands for petroleum imports, the East European states have been searching for new supplies of oil from various Third World OPEC countries. However, while coordination has been an important element of recent East European–Soviet political relations with the developing countries, no comparable cooperation is yet visible in the economic sphere.[9]

In addition to the general political interests of the CMEA countries in the developing world, there are more specific political concerns that have motivated several of them. Both Romania and the German Democratic Republic have sought to bolster their international political position by expanding relations with Third World countries. Romania has been interested primarily in strengthening its autonomy vis-à-vis the Soviet Union by emphasizing its position as a developing country and by expanding its ties with other developing countries – much in the way in which Yugoslavia established its international position as a non-aligned state in the 1950s and 1960s.[10]

The GDR, on the other hand, has been especially interested in establishing its position as a recognized sovereign state independent of the Federal Republic. While this motive clearly played a much more important role prior to East German recognition by the West in the early 1970s, it continues to influence GDR policies in the Third World.[11]

In the following pages I shall discuss briefly the evolution of both political–military and economic relations between the CMEA countries and the developing world. Although I shall deal with these relations at a relatively high level of generality, I shall also attempt to point out those areas in which individual East European countries have tended to deviate from a common pattern in their politics.

THE IMPORTANCE OF SOVIET–EAST EUROPEAN COORDINATION IN POLITICAL RELATIONS WITH THE THIRD WORLD

Although economic issues have become increasingly important in the relations of the East European states with the developing countries during the past decade, political factors continue to play a significant role in the expansion of those relations. Throughout the past thirty years the European members of the Council of Mutual Economic Assistance, with the important exception of Romania, have adopted a position on virtually every major and minor event or political development in the Third World that parallels almost exactly that of the Soviet Union.[12] On issues such as the Arab–Israeli conflict, Indian–Pakistani relations, the national liberation struggle in southern Africa, and the need to eliminate the influence of the capitalist West from the developing world, the East Europeans have followed faithfully the political line adopted by the Soviets. The one important exception has been Romania, which has developed its own policies ever since the mid-1960s – policies that are often clearly distinguishable from those of the USSR and the other communist states. The most important issues relevant to the Third World on which the Romanians have refused to follow the Soviet lead have been the Arab–Israeli conflict, the role of China in the Third World, and the creation of a new international economic order. Not only has Romania been the only member of the CMEA that has maintained diplomatic relations with Israel since the 1967 war, but it has been the only European communist state that has not condemned the Egyptian–Israeli peace agreements of 1979. In fact Ceauşescu reportedly played an important part in bringing Sadat and Begin together in the fall of 1977.[13] As I have already noted, this aspect of Romanian foreign policy is a part of the Romanian effort to establish autonomy in relationship to the Soviet Union.

The area in which the coincidence of Soviet and East European policies has been most evident in recent years has been in their relations with national liberation movements and revolutionary governments in Sub-Saharan Africa. As they did in the early 1960s in Ghana, Guinea, and Mali, East European governments have coordinated their political support and military assistance programs in a number of countries with those of the Soviet Union. In Mozambique, for example, Hungary has been supplying military assistance and training officers of the Mozambique military, while Romania has reportedly agreed to assist in the training of Mozambique's military forces in the use of Soviet weapons.[14] This form of military cooperation between an East European country and the USSR is not new. As early as 1947–8, at the time of the creation of the state of Israel, Czechoslovakia, with the support and encouragement of the Soviet Union, provided military equipment and training in the use of that equipment to the Israelis, in order to support what the Soviets then viewed as the major challenge to Western influence in the Middle East.[15] Again in 1955, after Soviet policy on the Middle Eastern question had shifted, Czechoslovakia functioned as a Soviet surrogate when it acted as the intermediary for the initial major shipment of Soviet military equipment to a developing country – this time to Egypt.[16]

More recently the most active of the East European states in the military field has been the GDR. In early 1979 it was estimated that between three thousand and four thousand five hundred East German instructors in police and security operations were working in various countries in Africa and the Middle East.[17] In all of the cases of East European military involvement in the developing world, there is a clear indication of cooperation with one another and with the Soviet Union. For the most part, recipients of military deliveries from Eastern Europe – in particular from Czechoslovakia, the GDR, and Poland – have been the very same countries that have received Soviet military exports.

However, while military assistance and sales have comprised an increasingly important part of Soviet relations with the developing countries, they have remained relatively less important for Eastern Europe. Soviet arms commitments to developing countries have increased from an average of slightly more than $390 million per year in the period 1955–68 to an annual average of more than $5,200 million after 1972. In the same period new commitments of economic assistance have risen from an earlier average of $400 to $1,375 per year. The figures for Eastern Europe indicate that economic assistance continues to hold a much more important place, relative to military aid, in the policies of the East European countries as a group, than it does for the USSR. Commitments of new military aid have risen from $58 million per year in 1955–68 to $430 million annually for 1973–9, while those of economic assistance have risen from about $150 million to more than $775 million per year (See

Tables 10.2 and 10.3). A portion of that military assistance has been provided as training for the military forces of individual Third World countries. During the period 1955 to 1979, for example, more than six thousand military personnel from the developing countries received training in Eastern Europe – compared with more than 45,000 in the Soviet Union.[18]

Soviet military assistance and arms trade have been associated with attempts to gain a presence in various Third World regions – in particular in such strategically important areas as the Eastern Mediterranean, the Horn of Africa, and southern Africa. While East European military assistance has been largely ancillary to and coordinated with that of the Soviet Union, it has also been motivated increasingly by financial considerations – as has that of the USSR itself – since military equipment supplied to some Third World countries is paid for in hard currency. In addition, countries such as the GDR and Romania have used the expansion of military ties of various sorts in the attempt to strengthen their international position.

TABLE 10.2 *Arms sales and deliveries of USSR and Eastern Europe
to non-communist developing countries*
(millions of current US dollars)

	Agreements		Deliveries	
	USSR	*Eastern Europe*	*USSR*	*Eastern Europe*
Total	47,340	4,285	35,340	3,405
1955–69	5,875	935	5,060	840
1970	1,150	50	995	75
1971	1,590	120	865	125
1972	1,690	155	1,215	75
1973	2,890	130	3,135	130
1974	5,735	635	2,225	210
1975	3,325	835	2,040	285
1976	5,550	345	3,085	330
1977	8,715	475	4,705	345
1978	2,465	555	5,400	470
1979	8,365	250	6,615	525

Note Components may not add to totals because of rounding to nearest five.

SOURCE: Central Intelligence Agency, National Foreign Assessment Center, *Communist Aid Activities in Non-Communist Less Developed Countries 1979 and 1954–79: A Research Paper*, ER 80-10318U (October 1980), p. 13.

TABLE 10.3   *Soviet and East European economic assistance
to non-communist developing countries*
(millions of current US dollars)

	Agreements		Deliveries	
	USSR	Eastern Europe	USSR	Eastern Europe
Total	18,190	9,830	8,170	3,590
1954–69	6,565	2,790	3,225	910
1970	200	195	390	145
1971	1,125	485	420	190
1972	655	920	430	170
1973	715	605	500	220
1974	815	820	705	230
1975	1,935	510	500	250
1976	980	800	465	375
1977	425	405	545	470
1978	3,060	1,575	485	380
1979	1,720	730	500	255

Note   Components may not add to totals because of rounding to nearest five.

SOURCE: Central Intelligence Agency, National Foreign Assessment Center, *Communist Aid Activities in Non-Communist Less Developed Countries 1979 and 1954–79: A Research Paper,* ER 80-10318U (October 1980), p. 17.

Overall the political and military relations of the East European countries with the Third World have grown immensely over the course of the past two decades. East European states now maintain diplomatic relations with the vast majority of the countries of the developing world. To a very substantial degree, however, these relations are closely coordinated with those of the Soviet Union and represent more an extension of Soviet policy than they do any form of independent East European policy.[19] Only the Romanians have deviated in their policy from that of the USSR and even they have coordinated certain of their activities with their Soviet allies – for example, the military training in Mozambique. At the political level the policy goals in the Third World for most of the East European states remain the establishment of a European communist presence, the development of influence relationships, and, ultimately, the creation of Marxist–Leninist regimes that are dependent on the Soviets and their East European allies for their very existence.

Developments in Angola, Ethiopia, and Afghanistan in recent years provide the most telling examples of the continued – even heightened – role of these goals in Soviet and East European policy.

FRAGMENTATION IN SOVIET–EAST EUROPEAN ECONOMIC RELATIONS WITH THE THIRD WORLD

The effort of the East European states to expand economic relations with the developing world became an increasingly important element in their overall policy during the 1970s. It is in this area, as we have already noted, that policy coordination among the CMEA members has yet to be developed effectively. Trade between the European communist states and the developing countries has expanded by more than twelve times during the course of the past two decades. Between 1960 and 1978 total trade turnover between the two groups of countries rose from $939 million to more than $11,600 million, in current prices. However, as a percentage of the trade of the European communist states, trade with the developing world remained relatively stable until quite recently. While trade with developing countries comprised 6.1 per cent of total East European trade in 1960, by 1970 it had fallen to 5.9 per cent. In recent years it has risen to 7.1, 7.7 and 8.3 per cent in 1976, 1977 and 1978 respectively (See Table 10.1).

The growth of commercial relations between European communist states and the developing world is directly related to developments in the domestic economies of the European states themselves and in their relations with other major trading partners. The fact that virtually all of the East European countries are heavily dependent on imports of raw materials – in particular of energy – has meant that they have been interested in establishing stable, long-term agreements with the developing countries for the supply of petroleum and other raw materials. For example, prior to 1978, Poland's trade with Iraq consisted almost entirely of exports, and Polish exports to Iran greatly exceeded imports. In 1978, however, Polish imports from both of these countries greatly surpassed exports. In 1979 imports – almost entirely petroleum products – exceeded exports by almost three to one.[20] Before the overthrow of the Shah in Iran most of the East European countries had signed agreements with Iran calling for expanded gas and oil imports. Kuwait, Libya, Mexico, and even Saudi Arabia have become the suppliers of increasing amounts of energy imports for the East European countries.[21] This search for new supplies of petroleum and natural gas is the result of a two-fold development during the past decade. First of all, the modernization drive in the domestic economies of all of the communist states has resulted in a rapidly growing demand for new supplies of energy, especially for their expanding petro-chemical industries. At the same time the Soviets have indicated that they cannot continue to meet these increasing energy demands of their East European "partners," in particular if they are going to continue to export considerable amounts of oil and gas to Western Europe in order to cover the costs of imports of Western industrial goods and technology.

Given the chronic lack of convertible currency in the communist states,[22] the primary method that has been employed to cover imports of petroleum and other industrial raw materials has been through semi-barter agreements. Poland, for example, is currently building twenty major industrial projects in Iraq on which approximately 2,500 workers and specialists are engaged. In return, Iraq will make payment in oil exports in the coming years.[23] This represents a pattern that has become quite common in the trade between the European communist states and many of the developing countries. Overall, economic and technical assistance programs of the East European countries have become more closely tied to the economic concerns of the donor country than has generally been true for Soviet economic assistance, even though the Soviets have, in recent years, begun to relate their project assistance to the needs of the Soviet economy.[24] Not only has East European assistance been motivated by the desire to ensure future oil supplies, it has also been closely coordinated with efforts to build up markets for East European industrial and agricultural equipment in the Third World. This aspect of East European economic assistance has been especially visible in Latin America where more than nineteen per cent of total East European credits has been committed (See Table 10.4). Virtually all of these credits have been supplied to cover exports of various types of East European industrial products to Latin America.

Another example of the growing importance of this type of assistance can be seen in Romania's economic activities, especially in Africa. Romania, which by the mid-1970s had replaced Czechoslovakia as the primary East European source of developmental assistance for Third World countries,[25] has become deeply involved in the creation of joint ventures in Sub-Saharan Africa. In these ventures the Romanians provide capital, equipment and technical expertise,

TABLE 10.4 *Soviet and East European credits and grants extended to non-communist developing countries* (millions of current US dollars)

	1954–79				1978*				1979			
	USSR	%	Eastern Europe	%	USSR	%	Eastern Europe	%	USSR	%	Eastern Europe	%
Total	18,190		9,830		3,707		1,502		1,720		730	
Africa	4,115	22.6	2,425	24.7	2,010	54.2	627	41.7	95	5.5	135	18.5
N. Africa	2,920	16.1	980	9.9	2,000		110	7.3	–	–	45	6.2
Algeria	715		525		–		–		–		–	
Mauritania	10		10		–		–		–		–	
Morocco	2,100		170		2,000		89		–		–	
Tunisia	95		230		–		–		–		–	
Other	–		45		–		20		–		45	
Sub-Saharan Africa	1,200	6.6	1,445	14.7	11	0.3	517	34.4	95	5.5	90	12.3
Angola	15		100		1		76		–		–	
Benin	5		na		–		–		–		–	
Cameroon	10		–		–		–		–		–	
Cape Verde	5		negl		3		–		–		–	
Central African Empire	5		–		–		–		–		–	
Chad	5		–		–		–		–		–	
Congo	30		60		–		–		–		–	
Equatorial Guinea	negl		–		–		–		–		–	
Ethiopia	225		95		negl		45		95		negl	
Gabon	–		negl		–		–		–		–	
Ghana	95		145		–		–		–		–	
Guinea	210		110		–		–		–		–	
Guinea–Bissau	10		na		–		–		–		–	
Kenya	45		–		–		–		–		–	
Madagascar	20		negl		6		negl		–		–	
Mali	90		25		1		–		–		–	
Mauritius	5		–		–		–		–		–	
Mozambique	5		15		–		2		–		–	
Niger	negl		–		–		–		–		–	
Nigeria	5		80		–		na		–		75	
Rwanda	negl		–		–		–		–		–	

continued

	USSR	%	Eastern Europe	%	USSR	%	Eastern Europe	%	USSR	%	Eastern Europe
Senegal	10		35		–		–		–		–
Sierre Leone	30		–		–		–		–		–
Somalia	165		10		–		–		–		–
Sudan	65		240		–		24		–		–
Tanzania	40		50		–		3		–		–
Uganda	15		–		–		–		–		–
Upper Volta	5		–		negl		–		–		–
Zambia	15		60		–		12		–		–
Other	70		420		–		352		–		15
East Asia	260	1.4	550	5.6	–	–	170	11.3	–	–	–
Burma	15		175		–		140		–		–
Indonesia	215		290		–		–		–		–
Kampuchea	25		15		–		–		–		–
Laos	5		5		–		–		–		–
Philippines	–		65		–		30		–		–
Latin America	965	5.3	1,870	19.0	15	0.4	244	16.2	–	1.1	285	3(
Argentina	220		295		–		–		–		–
Bolivia	70		50		–		–		–		–
Brazil	90		620		–		200		–		–
Chile	240		145		–		–		–		–
Colombia	210		80		–		10		–		–
Costa Rica	15		10		–		–		–		–
Ecuador	negl		20		–		–		–		–
Guyana	na		30		–		–		–		–
Jamaica	30		285		–		28		–		250
Mexico	na		35		–		–		–		–
Nicaragua	–		10		–		–		–		–
Peru	25		215		–		–		–		–
Uruguay	50		30		–		–		–		–
Venezuela	na		10		–		–		–		–
Other	15		35		15		6		–		15
Middle East	7,870	43.3	3,735	37.9	1,399	37.7	441	29.4	1,600	93.0	28	3
Cyprus	–		5		–		–		–		–
Egypt	1,440		890		–		–		–		–
Greece	10		na		–		–		–		–
Iran	1,165		685		–		–		–		–
Iraq	705		495		–		–		–		–

continued

	USSR	%	Eastern Europe	%	USSR	%	Eastern Europe	%	USSR	%	Eastern Europe	%
Jordan	25		na		–		–		–		–	
Lebanon	–		10		–		–		–		–	
North Yemen	145		40		38		–		–		25	
South Yemen	205		65		90		6		–		–	
Syria	770		955		–		150		–		–	
Turkey	3,330		395		1,200		85		1,600		–	
Other	75		195		71		200		–		–	
South Asia	4,980	27.4	1,245	12.7	283	7.6	20	1.3	25	1.5	305	4.2
Afghanistan	1,290		135		–		–		25		25	
Bangladesh	305		210		–		–		–		50	
India	2,280		455		–		–		–		–	
Nepal	30		–		–		–		–		–	
Pakistan	920		215		225		–		–		90	
Sri Lanka	160		95		60		20		–		–	
Other	–		140		–		–		–		140	

Note Components may not add to totals because of rounding to nearest five.

* Totals of aid for 1978 are taken from the 1978 CIA research paper and differ somewhat from the 1979 revisions of these data.

negl = negligible
na = not available

SOURCE: Central Intelligence Agency, National Foreign Assessment Center, *Communist Aid Activities in Non-Communist Less Developed Countries 1979 and 1954–79: A Research Paper*, ER SO-10318U (October 1980), pp. 18–20.

while the African partner provides labor and raw materials. Such projects provide a number of potential benefits to Romania and the other East European states. In return for their investments the East Europeans are able to acquire raw materials and, in some cases, to gain indirect access to the West European market under the terms of the Lomé Convention.[26]

The distribution of East European economic assistance by region illustrates an important difference in this assistance from that provided by the Soviets. While the USSR has concentrated its aid efforts on a relatively small number of countries in the Middle East, North Africa and South Asia (almost eighty-seven per cent of their assistance from 1954 to 1979), East European aid has been much more evenly distributed by both region and recipient country. During the years 1954–79 the Middle East has received 38 per cent of East European aid commitments, Latin America 19 per cent, Sub-Saharan Africa 15 per cent, South Asia 13 per cent, North Africa 10 per cent, and East Asia 6 per cent.

Most of the East European countries initiated industrial modernization drives in the early 1970s based on the acquisition of credits from the West. It was assumed that, within a relatively short period of time, the new industries would be in operation and that the exports of these new industries to the West would be used to repay the original loans. However, delays in completing the projects, the rising cost of imports resulting from worldwide inflation, recession in the West, and a variety of other factors have all proven this assumption false. The East Europeans have had to search for markets elsewhere – both within the CMEA community and in the developing world. Clearly the developing world represents a potential market for the surplus production of the East European states, and, as the recent trade figures indicate, exports to the developing countries have been rising more rapidly than overall exports.

Another element of commercial relations between the developing countries and Eastern Europe that has been growing in importance has been the technical services program (See Table 10.5). Initially technical services were part of the economic assistance program of the communist states. In recent years, however, a growing percentage of East European technicians has been paid in hard currency for services unrelated to economic assistance projects. Of approximately 48,000 East Europeans abroad in 1979, almost half were in Libya and an additional 1,000 were in Algeria and other Middle Eastern oil-producing countries. At the same time that the number of East Europeans working abroad has risen, the number of technical personnel from the developing world receiving training in Eastern Europe has fallen. By 1979 only 3,000 technicians were resident in the Soviet Union and Eastern Europe – down from 4,390 five years earlier.[27]

An additional important aspect of long-term development assistance provided by both the Soviet Union and the East European countries has been the education of substantial numbers of academic students from the developing countries. The numbers of such students have risen consistently and by 1979 more than 24,000 were studying in Eastern Europe – up from about 9,000 in 1970 (See Table 10.6). An interesting aspect of this program has been the focus on Sub-Saharan Africa. Since the inception of the academic training

TABLE 10.5 *Soviet and East European economic technicians working in non-communist developing countries*

	1970		1975		1977	1978	1979
	USSR	Eastern Europe	USSR	Eastern Europe	USSR and Eastern Europe	USSR and Eastern Europe	USSR and Eastern Europe
Total	10,600	5,300	17,785	13,915	58,755	72,655	80,820
Africa	4,010	3,150	5,930	10,290	34,390	43,805	48,285
N. Africa	—	—	—	—	21,850	36,165	37,845
Sub-Saharan Africa	—	—	—	—	12,540	7,640	10,440
East Asia	100	60	25	30	125	85	90
Latin America	35	140	330	225	830	700	595
Middle East					20,010	23,890	25,905
South Asia	6,455	1,950	8,375	3,370	3,475	4,145	5,945

SOURCES: Central Intelligence Agency, National Foreign Assessment Center, *Communist Aid to Less Developed Countries of the Free World, 1975*, ER 76-10372U (July 1976), p. 8; *Idem*, for 1977, ER 78-10478U (November 1978), p. 9; *Idem, Communist Aid Activities in Non-Communist Less Developed Countries, 1978*, ER 79-10412U, pp. 14–15; *Idem, Communist Aid Activities in Non-Communist Less Developed Countries, 1979 and 1954–79*, ER 80-10318U (October 1980), p. 21.

TABLE 10.6   *Academic students from developing countries being trained in communist countries*

	1970	1975	1977	1978		1979	
	All communist countries*	All communist countries†	All communist countries‡	USSR	Eastern Europe	USSR	Eastern Europe
Total	21,415	27,275	40,345	26,445	18,560	30,970	24,025
Africa	10,990	14,895	20,780	13,635	9,755	14,690	12,400
N. Africa	2,115	2,370	2,965	2,035	1,520	1,825	1,605
Sub-Saharan Africa	8,875	12,525	17,815	11,600	8,235	12,865	10,795
East Asia	650	335	20	25	10	25	10
Latin America	2,425	2,940	4,445	2,760	1,890	2,860	2,150
Middle East	5,770	6,270	11,320	6,615	5,525	6,745	6,405
South Asia	1,580	2,825	3,780	3,400	1,375	6,635	3,050

* Approximately 12,500 of these students were in the Soviet Union and the remainder in Eastern Europe.

† Approximately two-thirds of the students were in the Soviet Union and most of the remainder in Eastern Europe.

‡ More than sixty per cent of the students were in the Soviet Union and most of the remainder in Eastern Europe.

SOURCES: For 1970 data, Bureau of Intelligence and Research, US Department of State, *Communist States and Developing Countries: Aid and Trade in 1970*, p. 13. For the 1975–9 data see the publications of the Central Intelligence Agency listed in Table 10.5.

program in the late 1950s and early 1960s, close to forty per cent of all students in Eastern Europe have come from Black Africa, even though less than fifteen per cent of total economic assistance has been committed to that region.

East European academic and technical training programs for students from the Third World have had two major purposes. First, they help to provide the skilled personnel needed to modernize the economies of countries receiving economic assistance and to staff the projects and programs established with East European aid. In this respect they represent an important component of the overall East European aid programs. In addition, however, the academic training program in particular is geared to prepare a future elite that, at a minimum, is favorably disposed toward the European communist states.

Even though there has been relatively little effort to date to coordinate the economic relations of the individual European CMEA members with the developing world – as has clearly occurred in the military and political spheres – there are recent indications that the European communist states plan to coordinate some of their economic activities in the developing countries in the future. Czechoslovak government officials announced in spring 1979 that the members of the CMEA envisage the joint supplying of complete industrial plants to Third World countries as a "new step" in economic cooperation. The primary purpose of this type of cooperation will be to pay for increased imports of fuel, energy, and raw materials from the developing countries.[28] The success of such a cooperative program will depend not only on the ability of the communist states to compete effectively with Western suppliers of modern industrial equipment, but also on the continued willingness of developing countries to enter into what are still essentially barter arrangements. Unless the East Europeans are able to provide goods and materials competitive with those available from the West, it is likely that they will have to provide more expensive "commercial packages" that cover both exports and the provision of technical assistance.

An additional question concerns the likelihood that East European investments in aid will pay off in future supplies of raw materials. The developing countries that are likely to be the most receptive to barter-type arrangements are the very ones that are the least developed and the least stable politically.[29] It is conceivable that the East Europeans will find it difficult to continue to negotiate such agreements with those countries in the Third World which command the resources that they are seeking.

Finally, the East Europeans, along with the Soviets, are learning that representatives of developing countries are unwilling to differentiate between capitalist and socialist developed countries when making their demands for the establishment of a new world economic order. Although the socialist countries have been willing to support, in principle, many of the demands of the developing countries, they have refused to commit themselves to guaranteed prices for raw materials or to specific amounts of economic assistance.[30] Only the Romanians, who have viewed themselves as part of the developing world, have been willing to support the specifics of the proposed new world economic order.[31]

OUTLOOK FOR THE 1980s

What is clear from this very brief survey of East European relations with the countries of the Third World is that most of the European communist states are increasingly interested in the potential role of the developing countries in helping to stabilize and strengthen the economies of the CMEA members themselves. Their own domestic and international economic situation is of far greater interest to the East Europeans than are most other matters related to the Third World. The significant industrial growth that occurred in most CMEA countries in the 1970s has resulted in a notable increase in both the need for secure sources of raw materials and the availability of industrial exports. The developing countries represent both potential suppliers of industrial raw materials and markets for a portion of the available industrial exports. Stability and economic growth in the Third World is, therefore, likely to become an important interest for countries such as Hungary and Romania – as well as the other CMEA countries – which are basing their own future economic growth on expanding relations with the Third World. In addition, it is very likely that the East Europeans will be forced to coordinate their economic activities more effectively if they are going to compete successfully in developing countries. Most of the smaller European communist states individually have neither the amounts of capital nor the technological expertise required for major developmental projects in the Third World. Unless they coordinate their activities – either among themselves or with Western firms – they are not likely to gain the contracts that they have been seeking and are likely to seek even more in the coming decade.

However, in spite of Eastern Europe's growing economic interest in the Third World and in the political stability that successful economic relations imply, the East Europeans are still heavily involved in supporting revolutionary movements and regimes in concert with the Soviet Union. However, these two sets of apparently dichotomous relationships are not necessarily contradictory, for military–political support for a revolutionary movement may well be viewed as a means to ensure the establishment of favorable future economic relations. Yet, in other cases it is likely that the dual nature of European communist relations with developing countries may well result in serious problems. For example, the Soviet invasion of Afghanistan in December 1979 has resulted in a deterioration in relations with a number of the more radical of the Arab Moslem states, most notably Iraq.

East European relations with the countries of the Third World have expanded markedly over the course of the past two decades. Political relations are now maintained with the majority of the independent states of Asia, Africa, and Latin America. It is most likely that efforts to continue to strengthen such relationships will continue. Not only do the East European states themselves have their own reasons, largely economic, for expanding ties with the Third World, but the dynamics of Soviet global interests are likely to push several of them into greater efforts at involvement in the developing world. Yet, as we have noted above, domestic problems in Eastern Europe may well limit the degree to which countries such as Poland can contribute to Soviet–Warsaw Pact involvement.

The implications of this assessment of East European–Third World relations for the future of East–West relations is quite mixed. If the East European states continue to suffer from the types of domestic economic problems that have become visible in the past few years and do, in fact, become increasingly dependent upon the development of prosperous and stable political–economic systems throughout the Third World, then their interests in the southern hemisphere will coincide much more with those of the West than they have in the past. However, those East European states that have been most active in the Third World in supporting Soviet efforts to expand their influence – the GDR, in particular – are likely to continue these attempts at moving Third World states into close alignment with the Soviet Union–Warsaw Pact. Clearly such a development will have a number of implications detrimental both to East–West relations and to stability within the Third World itself.

The expansion of Soviet military and political power in the Third World during the past decade – much of it in conjunction with its smaller European allies – has significantly strengthened the communist states' ability to impede or undermine Western interests. A continuation of efforts to expand and solidify their position in the Third World is likely to result in further East–West conflict.[32] Challenges from communist-supported Third World states against those favorably inclined toward the West may result in a decision in the West to prove greater military support to Western-oriented regimes. The end result might well be a greater risk of East–West confrontation in the Third World. Moreover, continued communist support for radical regimes and the possible incorporation of those regimes more fully into the Soviet bloc will exacerbate regional tensions throughout the Third World. Examples of this have already been seen in the Horn of Africa where the original arming of Somalia by the communist states provided the preconditions for the Somalian attempt to achieve its primary foreign policy objective of reunifying all the Somali people. More recently it has been Soviet and East European military equipment and training that have enabled Libya to occupy Chad and present a threat to a whole group of Western-oriented states across the breadth of Africa. Such a pattern in the future is likely to result in the further splitting of the non-aligned movement, as states throughout the Third World gravitate to the two major power blocs in search of security.

The determining factors in the future direction followed by the East European states, individually and collectively, in their relations with the Third World will be a combination of domestic economic and political factors, the outlines of Soviet foreign policy, and the reactions of the major Western states. Domestic economic and political turmoil – as in Poland since mid-1980 – will force East European states to deemphasize or even forego political–military activity in the Third World in favor of the development of stable economic relations. A revitalized Western policy of effective support for moderate regimes throughout the Third World and of penalties for those, including the communist states, who attempt to undermine Western interests would also likely lead to a reassessment of Soviet and East European behavior in the Third World.

NOTES AND REFERENCES

1. For the purposes of the present discussion "Eastern Europe" will apply

only to the European members of the Council for Mutual Economic Assistance and the Warsaw Treaty Organization, minus the USSR: Bulgaria, Czechoslovakia, the German Democratic Republic, Hungary, Poland, and Romania.

2. In her excellent bibliography, *The International Relations of Eastern Europe: A Guide to Information Sources* (Detroit: Gale Research, 1978) Robin A. Remington lists only eight entries that treat East European relations with the Third World. Of these, however, only one deals explicitly with East European relations separately from those of the USSR. An important recent contribution to the study of East European involvement in the Third World is the series of six articles on the relations of Eastern Europe with the countries of Sub-Saharan Africa published by Radio Free Europe in early 1979: *Radio Free Europe Research, RAD Background Report* (hereafter *RFER*), nos. 50, 75, 77, 92, 118, and 142. A somewhat more extensive literature on the subject has appeared in West Germany, in particular on East German policy in the Third World. See, for example, Hans Siegfried Lamm and Siegfried Kupper, *DDR und Dritte Welt* (Munich–Vienna: R. Oldenbourg Verlag, 1976) and Part V, "Beziehungen zu anderen Kontinenten und weltweite Aktivität," in Hans-Adolf Jacobsen, Gert Leptin, Ulrich Scheuner, and Eberhard Schulz (eds), *Drei Jahrzehnte Aussenpolitik der DDR* (Munich–Vienna: R. Oldenbourg Verlag, 1979) pp. 641–728. See, also, Roger E. Kanet, "Eastern Europe and Sub-Saharan Africa," in Thomas H. Henriksen (ed.), *The Communist States and Sub-Saharan Africa* (Stanford: Hoover Institution Press, 1981) and Roger E. Kanet, "Patterns of East European Economic Involvement in the Third World," in Michael Radu (ed.), *Eastern Europe and the Third World: East vs. South* (New York: Praeger, 1981).

3. For example, Hungary has developed inter-party relations with a number of Marxist–Leninist parties in Africa and has promised military assistance to Mozambique. The GDR has been especially involved in training security forces in several African countries and a number of East European states participated actively in the 1977–8 transport of more than $1 billion in Soviet military equipment to Ethiopia. See Aurel Bereznai, "Hungary's Presence in Black Africa," *RFER*, no. 75, Hungary, 2 April 1979; Elizabeth Pond, "E. Germany's Quiet African Role," *The Christian Science Monitor,* 22 February 1979, p. 6; Colin Legum and Bill Lee, *The Horn of Africa in Continuing Crisis* (New York–London: Africana Publishing, division of Holmes and Meier Publishers, 1979) pp. 14, 63.

4. For a comparison of Soviet, Polish, and East German perceptions of developments in the Third World, and in particular, for their assessments of the campaign for a new international economic order, see: G. Skorov, "Novyi mezhdunarodnyi ekonomicheskii poriadok: problemy, perspektivy," *Aziia, Afrika segodnia,* no. 2 (1978) pp. 2–5; Marian Paszynski, "Nowy międzynarodowy ład ekonomiczny (Refleksje na tle IV Swiatowej Konferencji Handlu i Rozwoju)," *Ekonomista,* no. 1 (1977) pp. 119–143; Heinz Joswig, "Zur Perspektive der ökonomischen Zusammenarbeit zwischen Ländern des RWG und den

Entwicklungsländern," *Deutsche Aussenpolitik,* xx, no. 3 (1975) pp. 331–9. For a Western survey see Jürgen Nötzold, "Die RGW-Staaten und der Nord-Süd Dialog," *Aussenpolitik,* xxx (1979) pp. 192–209.

5. "Socialist Community Plans for the Future," *New Times,* no. 35 (1979) p. 1.
6. For a more extensive discussion of Soviet views see Roger E. Kanet, "Soviet Attitudes Toward Developing Nations Since Stalin," in Roger E. Kanet (ed.), *The Soviet Union and the Developing Nations* (Baltimore: Johns Hopkins University Press, 1974) pp. 27–50. An excellent discussion of the Soviet views of national liberation and development is contained in Stephen Clarkson, *The Soviet Theory of Development: India and the Third World in Marxist–Leninist Scholarship* (University of Toronto Press, 1978).
7. See, for example, Paszynski, "Nowy miedzynarodowy ład ekonomiczny," pp. 128–32 and Joswig, "Zur Perspektive der ökonomischen Zusammenarbeit," p. 332.
8. See, for example, Joachin Oesterheld, Ursula Padel, and Renate Wünsche, "DDR-Indien: Eine neue Etappe freundschaftlicher Beziehungen," *Deutsche Aussenpolitik,* xxiv, no. 3 (1979) pp. 5–11.
9. At a conference of Africanists from the European communist states held several years ago it was argued that economic relations of the CMEA states with Africa were developing erratically because of a lack of common principles, strategies and programs. See Bereznai, "Hungary's Presence in Black Africa," p. 19.
10. For a recent analysis of Romanian foreign policy see Aurel Braun, *Romanian Foreign Policy Since 1965: The Political and Military Limits of Autonomy* (New York: Praeger Publishers, 1978). For a perceptive treatment of Yugoslav relations with the developing world and the importance of those relations for overall Yugoslav foreign policy, see Alvin Z. Rubinstein, *Yugoslavia and the Nonaligned World* (Princeton University Press, 1970).
11. See Lamm and Kupper, *DDR und Dritte Welt,* especially pp. 203 ff.
12. In a study of East European voting at the United Nations Robert Weiner notes slight variations in voting on several issues related to the developing world. However, only Romania's position has deviated significantly from that of the Soviet Union and of the other East European states as group. Robert Weiner, "The Communist Balkans at the United Nations," in Ronald H. Linden (ed.), *Foreign Policies of East Europe: New Approaches* (New York: Praeger, 1980) pp. 265–84.
13. See *RFER,* Romanian Situation Report, no. 36, 23 December 1977 and *ibid.,* no. 7, 9 April 1979. For a discussion of Romania's position on the new international economic order see Nicolae Călina, "Romania's Relations with the Nonaligned Countries," *Revue roumaine d'études internationales,* xiii, no. 2 (1979) pp. 201–10.
14. Bereznai, "Hungary's Presence in Black Africa," p. 20 and Paul Gafton *et al.,* "Romania's Presence in Black Africa," *RFER,* no. 118, Romania, 23 May 1979, p. 11.
15. See Arnold Krammer, *The Forgotten Friendship: Israel and the Soviet Bloc, 1947–1953* (Urbana: University of Illinois Press, 1974) pp. 54 ff.

16. For a recent discussion of the background of the Soviet–Czechoslovak arms shipment see Mohamed Heikal, *The Sphinx and the Commissar: The Rise and Fall of Soviet Influence in the Middle East* (New York: Harper and Row, 1979) pp. 57–60. At the more general level Gavriel D. Ra'anan examines the military cooperation of the Soviet Union and its allies in *The Evolution of the Soviet Use of Surrogates in Military Relations with the Third World, with Particular Emphasis on Cuban Participation in Africa* (Santa Monica: Rand Corporation, 1979) (P-6420).

17. Pond, "E. Germany's Quiet Africa Role," p. 6. In an earlier article Pond noted that East German military and security training was occurring in Guinea–Bissau, São Tomé, Angola, Mozambique, Ethiopia, and South Yemen, "East Germany's 'Afrika Korps'," *The Christian Science Monitor*, 26 June 1978, p. 14. According to CIA estimates, only 1,300 East European military technicians were in developing countries in 1978, while 10,800 Soviets were working abroad. See Central Intelligence Agency, National Foreign Assessment Center, *Communist Aid Activities in Non-Communist Less Developed Countries 1978: A Research Paper*, ER 79-10412U, (September 1979) pp. 3–4. See, also, Kanet, "Eastern Europe and Sub-Saharan Africa."

18. Central Intelligence Agency, National Foreign Assessment Center, *Communist Aid Activities in Non-Communist Developing Countries 1979 and 1954–1979: A Research Paper*, ER 80-10318U, pp. 5–6.

19. By far the most careful discussion of the Soviet–East European connection in relations with the Third World is Michael Radu's "East vs. South: The Neglected Side of the International System," in Radu (ed.), *Eastern Europe and the Third World*.

20. Głowny Urząd Statystyczny, *Rocznik Statystyczny 1980* (Warsaw: Głowny Urząd Statystyczny, 1980) pp. 313, 315.

21. See *RFER*, Czechoslovakia Situation Report, no. 7, 21 February 1979; *RFER*, Poland Situation Report, no. 4, 27 February 1979; and *RFER*, Romania Situation Report, no. 2, 9 February 1979. For additional information on the energy situation in Eastern Europe see Daniel Park, *Oil and Gas in Comecon Countries* (London: Kogan Page; New York: Nichols Publishing, 1979); Jeremy Russell, *Energy as a Factor in Soviet Foreign Policy* (Westmead, England: Saxon House; Lexington Books, 1976) esp. pp. 89–130; and Jonathan P. Stern, *Soviet Natural Gas Development to 1990: The Implications for the CMEA and the West* (Lexington, MS.: Lexington Books, 1980).

22. For a discussion of the hard currency debt of the East European states see Joan P. Zoeter, "Eastern Europe: The Growing Hard Currency Debt," and Kathryn Melson and Edwin M. Snell, "Estimating East European Indebtedness to the West," in US Congress, Joint Economic Committee, *East European Economies Post-Helsinki* (Washington: US Government Printing Office, 1977) pp. 1350–68 and 1369–95 respectively.

23. *RFER*, Poland Situation Report, no. 4, 27 February 1979.

24. For a discussion of Soviet assistance policy see Roger E. Kanet, "Soviet Policy Toward the Developing World: The Role of Economic Assist-

ance and Trade," in Robert Donaldson (ed.), *The Soviet Union and the Third World: Success and Failure* (Boulder: Westview Press, 1981) pp. 331–57.

25. See United Nations, Department of International Economic and Social Affairs, Statistical Office, *Statistical Yearbook,* New York: United Nations, for the appropriate years.

26. See Michael Radu, "Romania's Relations with Sub-Saharan Africa," in Radu (ed.), *Eastern Europe and the Third World.*

27. See *Communist Aid Activities 1979,* pp. 2–3.

28. Czechoslovak Television, 7 March 1979; cited in H. G. Trend, "COMECON Joint Investments in Third World as Payment for Raw Materials?" *RFER,* Eastern Europe, no. 55, 9 March 1979. For an overview of research on the small amount of East–West cooperation in industrial and raw materials projects in the Third World see Carl H. McMillan, *The Political Economy of Tripartite (East–West–South) Industrial Cooperation* (Ottawa: Institute of Soviet and East European Studies, Carleton University, East–West Commercial Relations Series, Research Report no. 12, 1980).

29. A recent example of the negative impact of political instability on East European economic interests is visible in Iran. Soon after the over-throw of the Shah the new government cancelled a contract with the Soviet Union – and several other East and West European countries – which called for the construction of a second gas pipeline from Iran to the USSR. The Soviets were to receive additional Iranian natural gas and, in turn, were to expand their exports of gas to both Eastern and Western Europe. The more recent war between Iran and Iraq has also had important implications for oil supplies in several of the East European states.

30. See Peter Knirsch, "The CMEA Attitude to a New Economic Order," *Intereconomics,* XIII (1978) pp. 106–7; and Heinrich Machowski, "Development Aid from the CMEA Countries and the People's Republic of China," *Intereconomics,* XIV (1979) p. 209. In an interesting article the Polish economist Stanisław Polaczek has admitted that, although the socialist states are not responsible for the economic backwardness of the developing world, this does not mean that they should not commit themselves to increased assistance. He also discusses at some length the reasons that the proposals of the socialist countries concerning a new world economic system have not always received a positive response in the developing world. See Stanisław Polaczek, "Nowy Międzynarodowy ład ekonomiczny a kraje RWPG," *Sprawy Międzynarodowe,* no. 12 (1978), esp. pp. 68–9. See also Marian Paszyński, "Kraje socjalistyczne w wielostronnej debacie o światowych stosunkach ekonomicznych," *Sprawy Międzynarodowe,* no. 5 (1979) pp. 85–96. For excellent discussions of Soviet views of a new world economic order see Elizabeth K. Valkenier, "The USSR, the Third World, and the Global Economy," *Problems of Communism,* XXVIII, no. 4 (1979) pp. 17–33, and, also, Robert H. Donaldson, "The Second World, the Third World, and the New International Economic Order," in Donaldson (ed.), *The Soviet Union in the Third World,* pp. 358–383.

31. See Călina, "Romania's Relations with the Nonaligned Countries."
32. For an excellent discussion of this point see Radu, "East vs. South."

Index